TALES FROM THE FREUDIAN CRYPT

Tales from the Freudian Crypt

THE DEATH DRIVE IN TEXT AND CONTEXT

Todd Dufresne

STANFORD UNIVERSITY PRESS
Stanford, California 2000

Stanford University Press
Stanford, California
© 2000 by the Board of Trustees
of the Leland Stanford Junior University

Printed in the United States of America
CIP data appear at the end of the book

For Clara, confidante and better half

Contents

	Foreword by Mikkel Borch-Jacobsen	ix
	Preface	xiii
1.	Twilight of the Idols: From Freud to Lacan	1
	The Freudian Currency, 1. Beyond the "French Freud"—in America, 5. A Continental Breakfast at L'Hôtel Abyss, 9.	
2.	The Heterogeneous *Beyond*: An Introduction to the Dead and Dying	13
	In Media Res: Given, Taken, Denied, and Forgotten 'Beyond's, 14. Biographical 'Beyond's, 27. Biological 'Beyond's, 43. Klein and the "Clinical" 'Beyond', 65. Philosophical 'Beyond's, 80. Derrida and the Deconstructive 'Beyond', 129.	
3.	The Other *Beyond*: a.k.a. Group Psychology and the Analysis of the Ego	145
	Becoming Dead, 147. The Hypnotic 'Beyond', 166.	
	Afterword: How to Be a Freudian; or, The Economics of Not Thinking	184
	Notes	187
	Bibliography	207
	Index	223

Foreword

On November 29, 1993, *Time* asked on its cover: "Is Freud Dead?" Sigmund Freud died in 1939, so the question must bear on the "long shadow" this man cast on our century: Is psychoanalysis still viable as a proper applied science and an appropriate clinical practice in the age of biochemistry and psychotropic medications? Or is it, as critics contend, a thing of the past, an outdated nineteenth-century theory with a hopelessly ineffectual therapeutics, which ought to be confined to the dustbin of history (a popular website is entitled *Burying Freud*)? The stakes are high, and the question gets angrily debated. "Freud wars" are waged in the press, Freud exhibits are mounted and protested, anti-Freudian petitions are met by Freudian counter-petitions, thus providing the defenders of psychoanalysis with a foolproof argument: would psychoanalysis elicit such sound and fury if it weren't alive and well?

Todd Dufresne turns this old argument on its head. Far from proving the inherent vitality of psychoanalysis, he claims that attacks against it are precisely what infuse it with life. Here Dufresne invokes Freud's own theory of life and death, as announced in *Beyond the Pleasure Principle*: an organism lives only to the extent that some external excitation threatens its repose, forcing it to defend itself by erecting a "protective shield" (*Reizschutz*)—thus enabling its growth. Life, according to good Freudian doctrine, is but an annoying disturbance, a detour from the pure and simple absence of excitation, nirvana, death. Psychoanalysis, therefore, is not alive *in spite* of its critics, but *because* of their irritating (literally exciting) attacks. Left to itself, psychoanalysis is already dying. Worse, it has always already been dead. When all is said and done, psychoanalysis reveals itself to have been a tale from the crypt.

One might find Dufresne's argument a little too clever, a little too facetious. In turning Freud's own theory against him, doesn't he simply repeat it without taking any critical distance? But that is precisely Dufresne's point: psychoanalysis is nothing but an immense defense, a *Reizschutz* against the so-called "outside." As such, the more we attack it, the more it grows and expands, one protective layer added on to the other—Kleinism, Freudo-Marxism, Lacanianism, the "hermeneutic" Freud, the "deconstructionist" Freud, and the rest. Dufresne surveys this huge and untidy literature, but he knows better than to simply critique it. Rather than adding one more critical life-support system to the ever-proliferating body of psychoanalysis, he advocates its right to die: leave it alone, let it choke to death on its own waste, like the infusorians described by Freud in *Beyond the Pleasure Principle*.

Dufresne reads Freud as no other, understanding full well that psychoanalysis is fundamentally immune to criticism, because it was never concerned with reality. Critics think they inflict deadly wounds upon psychoanalysis by showing that it does not measure up to its scientific claims. But they miss the point. Psychoanalysis was never a psychological science, but rather a metapsychological fantasy, the product of Sigmund Freud's utter indifference to the world and to others. Freud often claimed, in positivistic fashion, that his metapsychological theories were mere "speculative superstructures" (1925a, 32) built on clinical "observations," and that they could "be replaced and discarded without damage" (1914b, 77) if the clinical material required it. But this is a pleasant joke: Freud never took "no" for an answer, whether it came from his patients, from his critics, or from reality itself. Freud would purely and simply dismiss evidence that contradicted his metapsychological constructions, as when Jones pressured him to drop his Lamarkian conclusions in *Moses and Monotheism*: "My position, no doubt, is made more difficult by the present attitude of biological science, which refuses [!] to hear of the inheritance of acquired characteristics by succeeding generations. I must, however, in all modesty confess that nevertheless I cannot do without this factor in biological evolution" (1939: 100).

Such an attitude is not that of a scientist, nor even that of a philosopher. It is that of the narcissistic dreamer, of "His Majesty the Ego." Dufresne puts it well: "At the end of the day, everyone plays a secondary role to the absolute narcissist that Freud imagined in his metapsychology and reserved for himself as the undisputed father of psychoanalysis. Psychoanalysis was his idea, after all, his psychic apparatus projected onto the world of all Others." Here again, one might object that Dufresne uses the very terminology of Freudian metapsychology that he attacks. But such a strategy is unavoidable, since metapsychological speculation is so radically focussed upon itself. From the *Project for a Scientific Psychology* to "On Narcissism: An Introduction," through *Beyond the Pleasure Principle*, Freud's metapsychology describes one and the same thing: the mind's stubborn indifference to reality and to others, the "omnipotence of thoughts" of the "absolute narcissist," his incorporation of all reality, of all "objects" (what I have called elsewhere the "Freudian subject"). What would be the point of arguing with Freud, the egotistical super-baby? Freud couldn't care less. He is beyond our reach, *meta*, in the psychoanalytic yonder where he plays with us, his speculative bobbins: *Fort, da! Fort, da!* Dufresne is right: let's leave him alone.

—Mikkel Borch-Jacobsen

Preface

> In his attempt to describe the role of the death instinct, Freud discovered that hardly an aspect of life was not vulnerable to its destructive force. This disturbing concept, once the source of bitter dispute, is now [ca. 1959] regarded as one of the very foundations of modern psychology and indispensable to the understanding of modern society.
> —Gregory Zilboorg, back-cover recommendation for the Bantam edition of *Beyond the Pleasure Principle*

I have long been grateful for Freud's later work, especially his fifty-eight-page essay of 1920, *Beyond the Pleasure Principle*, wherein sexuality, therapy, and the art of interpretation are irredeemably contaminated by, among other things, death, philosophy, and the science of biology. It is a gratitude born of the illicit pleasure that comes from playing amongst such a great mess, where commentary on the foundational and indispensable nature of Freud's death-drive theory sits side by side with verdicts that are precisely the opposite. Faced with this dilemma, I have been variously tempted to launder this untidy essay, arrange its bits and pieces into order, discard the rotten parts, and add to the whole thing fresh contributions of my own. Of course, there is nothing new in these temptations; the greatest part of the secondary literature on *Beyond the Pleasure Principle* (hereafter *BPP*) takes a page from here, a line from there, and imports a whole lot of other concerns from outside, in what is often a desperate attempt to repair or create anew a more acceptable portrait of life and death in psychoanalysis.

Temptations notwithstanding, my starting point is rather different. I am not interested in purifying Freud by discarding those parts of his theory that are absurd or plainly wrong or by transforming his blatant biologism into a trite but acceptable metaphor about, say, "modern society." These are the modus operandi of those who want to extricate Freud from his own difficulties or, among the more "emancipated" critics, to save psychoanalysis from Freud's mistakes. From the perspective of intellectual history, I am much more interested in following Freud down the different paths of his text, reading *BPP* against his other works and against the social, historical, and intellectual context of his time—just as one would approach any figure in the history of ideas. Similarly, I am interested in the many commentaries on Freud's life and work that, for better and for worse, continue to define and redefine the stakes of the interpretive game. To these ends, I have proceeded by way of spring cleaning: sifting through the material to find what is precious, worthless, interesting, or simply bizarre. I have, in short, tried to catalog the historical and intellectual tangle created by Freud's essay, all the while allowing the different voices to speak for themselves—and also for me—as much as possible. This critical work is, in a rigorous philosophical sense, a necessary first step that clears some much needed space for fresh interpretation of Freud's text, interpretation that I have attempted in what follows, most especially in the last chapter, "The Other *Beyond*." The result is a general introduction, or reintroduction, to the dead and dying along the detour of the relevant primary and secondary texts involved.

It goes without saying (although I am always forced to say it) that I find the literature on *BPP* at once fascinating and disturbing: fascinating because so provocatively heterogeneous, disturbing because so often delirious. Either way, *BPP* is a site overripe for fresh analysis and criticism. It may be worth recalling, however, that a critical introduction is not a substitute for reading the relevant texts involved. This is true even though all of the texts related to *BPP* are derivative, including those primary texts that Freud himself cites or fails to cite—the foundations of which are always elsewhere and multiple. So I recommend that readers consult the relevant primary, secondary, or tertiary literature that digs more deeply into any one spot that I may have explored superficially, too quickly, or not at all. Inevitably I have chosen to discuss certain theorists and ideas at greater length than others and cannot claim to have covered every aspect of the literature.

Even so, I have managed to trace the logic of the death-drive theory through its incarnations in biography, biology, clinical discourse, philosophy, deconstruction, and, finally, in the political maneuvers of a psychoanalysis desperate to steer clear of its great Other, suggestion. To help situate the death-drive theory, I begin with a general introduction to the analytic scene in North America today, after which I quickly outline the social, historical, and intellectual context of Freud's *Beyond the Pleasure Principle*. Psychoanalysis has continued to gather interest over the years, and the present study is offered as bank book, audit, and prospectus for future research in the field.

Critical Freud studies are still the exception, in part because analysts and academic Freudians have done their best to cast such work as mere "Freud bashing," or as a revisionism flawed by naive positivism or worse. The truth is that the history of psychoanalysis is a source of continuous embarrassment, already so thoroughly "revisionist" (invented, fraudulent, mythological) that advocates of psychoanalysis are always bound, knowingly or not, to spin that history, and the critical assessments based upon that history, in false directions.

I could not have liberated myself from these unfounded prejudices if not for the work of a small group of scholars that I was lucky enough to read, and sometimes to meet: Mikkel Borch-Jacobsen, François Roustang, Frederick Crews, Frank Sulloway, Peter Swales, and Paul Roazen. I do not assume, of course, that this diverse group will approve of my efforts, for which I alone am responsible and about which they are mostly unaware. Special thanks goes to Mikkel for his intelligence, good humor, and friendship; and also to the reviewers who provided independent assessments and critiques of the manuscript.

During my years in the Graduate Programme in Social and Political Thought at York University, Toronto, I found additional encouragement, stimulation, and bureaucratic assistance from numerous friends and colleagues: Clara Sacchetti, Kenneth Little, Helmar Drost, Rodolphe Gasché, Raymond Dufresne, Gary Genosko, Andy Beardsal, Paul Antze, David McNally, Hans Mohr, and Julian Patrick. Cheers. I am also pleased to acknowledge, as inspiration, everyone involved in the edited collections I organized and published during my graduate years. Kind regards to my colleagues at the Psychoanalytic Thought Program, Trinity College, University of Toronto, where I found temporary shelter as a Social Science and Humanities Research Council postdoctoral fellow, and as a research associate. My deep gratitude to the SSHRC for continued financial support in 1997–99, in addition to the graduate support I received in 1994–95, and also to the Queen Elizabeth II Ontario Fellowship of 1995–96, which I was honored to hold.

Parts of this book were presented as invited lectures, and I want to thank everyone involved for their interest, including Guy Allen, the Psychoanalytic Thought Program, University of Toronto (February 6, 1997); Thomas

Kemple, Department of Anthropology and Sociology, University of British Columbia (April 9, 1998); Mikkel Borch-Jacobsen, Department of Comparative Literature, University of Washington (April 12, 1998); Frederick Crews and Richard Hutson, Department of English, University of Berkeley (November 6, 1998). A version of Chapter 1 appeared as the editor's introduction to *Returns of the "French Freud": Freud, Lacan, and Beyond* (New York and London: Routledge, 1997); I thank Routledge for permission to reproduce this work. My appreciation to D. Jaro Kotalik, oncologist, and Dr. Joseph Wasielewski, pathologist, for procuring slides of cancer cells for the book cover. Much obliged.

A heartfelt thanks to Helen Tartar and Elizabeth Berg of Stanford University Press, who brought this book into existence with rare sagacity and professionalism.

A queer instinct indeed, directed to the destruction of its own organic home!
—Sigmund Freud, *New Introductory Lectures on Psycho-Analysis* (1933)

This was the shocking thing; that the slime of the pit seemed to utter cries and voices; that the amorphous dust gesticulated and sinned; that what was dead, and had no shape, should usurp the offices of life.
—Robert Louis Stevenson, *The Strange Case of Dr. Jekyll and Mr. Hyde* (1886)

CHAPTER I

Twilight of the Idols

FROM FREUD TO LACAN

The Freudian Currency

> The effect of psychoanalysis has something of an inexorably tightening noose. One cannot engage in it without, as it were, crying for help or at least struggling with it incessantly.
> —Viktor von Weizsaecker[1]

In keeping with an apocalyptic tone appropriate for the fin de siècle, and no doubt exaggerated by the close of the millennium, it has become fashionable in many quarters to announce the failure or bankruptcy of psychoanalysis, if not its immanent death. Whether one takes such dire prophesies seriously or not, it is at least superficially true that the "psychoanalytic century" has finally drawn to a close. Of course, many critics declared the "death" of psychoanalysis well before its founder, Sigmund Freud, died in 1939. For them, psychoanalysis was always something of a con game, a stillborn science, the sublimated gift of Freud's own anality. As one critic put it, psychoanalysts are mere *psychoanalen*.[2]

At the same time, the chorus announcing the death of psychoanalysis has slowly become its own "tradition" within psychoanalysis (Hale 1995: 355). In fact, interminable controversy has had an ironic result: more may have been written about Freud's life and work than almost any other figure in Western history. It is certainly remarkable that the autobiographical "science" of one man has made possible not only a vast body of secondary literature but an enduring institutional body as well. Given this long and divisive history, it is not surprising that our picture of Freud and psychoanalysis has changed dramatically, especially over the last twenty-five years or so of revisionist scholarship. With the gradual release of previously restricted documents from the Library of Congress, coupled with new, complete, and uncensored editions of Freud's private correspondence, our view of psychoanalysis was bound to change. And surely it will continue to change, since, for instance, only about six thousand (filling over a dozen volumes) of the estimated thirty-five thousand letters Freud wrote have appeared in print.

If the accumulation of new primary-source material hasn't been enough to shake the old hagiographic picture of Freud, certainly the revisionist and pathographic research on the history of psychoanalysis has. Clearly the emergence of critical studies on Freud has not enforced our transference onto the man and his theories: for many it has weakened this tie to its breaking point. We live in a time of critical reassessment, when scholars are taking a close second and third look at the legend(s) of Freud, the group psychology of his followers, the foundations of his "science," the therapeutic efficacy of analysis, and so on.

From a medical and therapeutic perspective, these are no longer the glory days that psychoanalysis enjoyed in urban America during the 1950's. But having unearthed, as Frederick Crews (1993) put it, "the unknown Freud," have we finally committed psychoanalysis to the grave? Echoing a 1966 cover story about the "death of God," *Time* recently (1993) captured this sentiment, asking plainly "Is Freud Dead?" This, however, was and remains an altogether audacious and ambivalent question. For when we pose the same question of God and Freud, we already presuppose that Freud's death has or will cast, as Nietzsche put it, a similarly long shadow. In this way, *Time* deferred and sidestepped at least one very important question about our transference onto Freud and his theories: who among us still mistakes Freud for God?

While the Freudian corpus began to decompose in America during the 1970's, it gathered an afterlife of its own in France. As Sherry Turkle (1992) suggests, the psychoanalytic movement became a genuine "culture" there after the May 1968 student uprisings and throughout the 1970's. Disillusioned with the large questions of social reform, young radicals turned their attention to the individual and to psychoanalysis. As French philosopher Mikkel Borch-Jacobsen puts it:

> In the wake of May '68 and its utopian dream, there weren't that many exciting intellectual projects around. May '68 had failed, you couldn't believe in Marxism anymore, and structuralism was hopelessly removed from life. Psychoanalysis, with its transgressive and initiatory aspects, seemed to be the only theory left that could claim to effectively "change life"—*changer la vie*, as the May '68 slogan would have it. Remember, the May '68 movement wanted to revolutionize "everyday life," and, in retrospect, it seems clear to me that my generation's interest in psychoanalysis was a way of pursuing this revolutionary project by other means. We all longed for that "high" that May '68 had provided, and that is how so many of us got hooked on psychoanalysis. Psychoanalysis was a substitute for the impossible revolution. (Borch-Jacobsen 1994)

Like other intellectual trends in France, psychoanalysis thrived as a cult of personality, one centered around the name and legend(s) of Jacques Lacan. "It is to him," writes analyst-historian Octave Mannoni, "that we owe the very faithful and very creative rebirth of Freudianism in France" (1968: 179). Or as Stuart Schneiderman states, echoing Alfred North Whitehead's famous remark about Plato, "Before Lacan, the history of psychoanalysis was a series of footnotes to Freud" (1983: 19). "Lacanism" quickly spread among intellectuals and, through the popular media, to everyone else; French psychoanalysis thus became synonymous with Lacan's name. In turn, psychoanalytic literature, or anything with an opportunistic dash of Freud in its title, became a large, profitable, "infinitely elastic" publishing industry in France (Turkle 1992: 195–96). After decades of apathy toward psychoanalysis, thoughts finally turned to a French standard edition of Freud's work. Unfortunately, as debates still rage over the proper translation of Freud's original German, this publication has yet to appear in its entirety.[3]

In this atmosphere, exciting new ideas emerged about psychoanalysis, arguably for the first time since Freud and some of his more talented followers wrote and published. While the majority of people hardly understood Lacan's baroque writings and free-associational seminars, everyone nonetheless agreed that his work was timely and somehow significant. As Lacan himself put it: "We are confronted by this singular contradiction—I don't know if it should be called dialectical—that the less you understand the better you listen. For I often say very difficult things and see you hanging on my every word, and I learn later that some of you didn't understand. On the other hand, when you're told things that are too simple, almost too familiar, you are less attentive" (1954–55: 141; trans. modified).[4] True to his word, Lacan certainly did his best to say "very difficult things" in his published writings and in his weekly *séminaire de textes*.

With the acrimonious debate over *la passe* (the contentious process whereby analysands became recognized analysts) by the mid 1970's, the dissolution of the École Freudienne de Paris in 1980, and Lacan's death the following year, the once fertile climate for psychoanalysis in France began to change. The same popular media that propelled psychoanalysis into the public eye became the site of bitter and divisive feuds among traditionally silent analysts. If it didn't have this quality before, Lacanian psychoanalysis became strangely surreal. This may not be altogether accidental, since—to Freud's great displeasure—it was the surrealists alone who embraced psychoanalysis in France during the 1920's (see Roudinesco 1990: ch. 1). In this regard it is worth recalling that Lacan, with his eccentric and sometimes outrageous persona, was very much influenced by the early surrealists and contributed to their magazine *Le minotaure*.

The corrosive atmosphere of the late 1970's and early 1980's crystallized around the role that Lacan's son-in-law, philosopher Jacques-Alain Miller, increasingly played in the institutional affairs of psychoanalysis. A nonanalyst married to Lacan's daughter Judith, Miller was the official editor of Lacan's seminars, the main power in the department of psychoanalysis at Vincennes (developed in the wake of May 1968), and designated heir-apparent to Lacan's name and considerable fortune; a fortune that consisted, among other things, of rare books, paintings, and gold bullion. Without delving too deeply into this family (and legal) romance, it is enough for us to note that many of Lacan's older, more established followers could never support Miller's La Cause Freudienne after the controversial dissolution of the École Freudienne. Consequently, although Miller may have successfully advanced one psychoanalytic movement among others in France, he has not managed to preserve the unique psychoanalytic "culture" that thrived under Lacan. To put it more bluntly, Miller has been unable to preserve and enhance Lacan's regal power in his own name. But, to be fair, who could?

While many mistook (and still mistake) Lacan for God, the transference onto his life and work has weakened considerably since his death. Recovering from their Lacanian hangovers, former and sometime analysts like François Roustang now plainly ask, "Why did we follow him for so long?" (1990: ch. 1). In turn, it has become impossible to avoid asking today whether or not Lacan, like Freud in America, has become a "dead" or purloined letter. For, on the one hand, the "French Freud" first associated with his name has begun to disappear as quickly as it appeared in France. On the other hand, this turn of events may not be very important, since the French version of the psychoanalytic plague has already spread well beyond the geographical borders of France to encompass much of the world; it has become what James Clifford (1992), following Edward Said, calls a "travelling culture." Consequently, the spirits of French psychoanalysis have successfully appropriated outside resistance into the Freudian field. This in fact was already an important feature of the Lacanian program, for as Lacan once remarked, "Psychoanalysis currently has nothing better for ensuring its activities than the production of analysts" (in Borch-Jacobsen 1991: 165). Or as Roustang puts it, "If you want analytic knowledge to be generally recognized, it is both necessary and sufficient to produce analysts who will in turn produce others. . . . Once there is no longer anything *outside* psychoanalysis, its teachings will no longer meet with any objections and will be considered valid" (1990: 12). To this overtly proselytizing, politico-religious end (along with, as usual, the financial one), many prominent Lacanians have relocated their practices to more receptive Romance-language countries with a large neurotic middle class, such as Argentina. In fact, with the election of an Argentinean to president of the International Psychoanalytic Association, institutional power has taken a decisive shift away from traditional strongholds in either North America or France.

Beyond the "French Freud"—in America

It is well known that Lacan's "return to Freud" was fueled, at least in part, by his dislike of the more conformist, individualistic, and anti-intellectual aspects of Anglo-American ego psychology. French analysts "behave," according to Mannoni, "as if that area of highest psychoanalytic density"—America—"were a void as far as theoretical developments are concerned" (1968: 181). In the first place, unlike most American analysts, Lacan's interests extended far beyond the traditional domain of medicine to include structural anthropology, linguistics, literature, mathematics, law, and philosophy. As Borch-Jacobsen convincingly argues, Lacan was an "autodidact" who "plagiarized" the works of great thinkers, including G. W. F. Hegel, Ferdinand de Saussure, Martin Heidegger, Claude Lévi-Strauss and, most of all, the Alexandre Kojève of *Introduction to the Reading of Hegel*. "Could it be," Borch-Jacobsen playfully taunts, "that Lacan did his analysis (the *real* one) with Alexandre Kojève?" (1991: 9). Though much less critical of psychoanalysis than Borch-Jacobsen, historian Elisabeth Roudinesco agrees that Lacan followed Kojève in many respects, stating that he "borrowed from the seductive master not only his concepts but a [flamboyant] teaching style. . . . For Kojève was, in his own way, a clinical observer, an artisan of the capital letter, a formalist of discourse, a mesmerizer of students, a legendary commentator on texts" (1990: 135).

Although Lacan was interested in the science of the unconscious, having dabbled with structural and mathematical models or "topologies" (e.g., Borromean knots, Klein's bottle, and so on), he mostly effected ties between psychoanalysis and the less exact "human sciences" (or humanities, taken in the broadest sense)—especially literary studies (see Lacan 1966: 147). Meanwhile, on this side of the Atlantic, analysts like Harry Stack Sullivan had tied psychoanalytic research to the mixed fortunes of the social and behavioral sciences. These interdisciplinary ties have proved crucial for the specific transmission and reception of psychoanalysis in both countries. Among other things, it has meant that French analysts remain less affected by the crisis in America over the uncertain medical, therapeutic, and scientific claims of psychoanalysis. Thus, in what is a typical French response, analyst Serge Leclaire states: "What happened to Freudian psychoanalysis in America is the fault of Americans. They froze things into a doctrine, almost a religion, with its own dogma, instead of changing with the times" (in Gray 1993: 50).

With the exception of France (and perhaps the Netherlands), no nation has embraced psychoanalysis with the enthusiasm of America. But while Freud remains the singular reference point for all psychoanalytic movements, the reception and transmission of his work has always hinged on quite specific cultural conditions—a relativity that would have troubled Freud and some of his adherents. For although psychoanalysis was his own subjective creation, Freud believed that it was, or would become, an objectively true universal science. As a result, he tended to overvalue the membership of gentiles like Carl Jung and Ernest Jones, not only as *Parade-Goy*, but because their inclusion confirmed that psychoanalysis wasn't a product of his own, uniquely Jewish, delusions.

Reflecting upon his visit to Clark University in 1909, Freud wrote: "As I stepped on the platform at Worcester [Massachusetts] to deliver my *Five Lectures on Psychoanalysis* it seemed like the realization of some incredible daydream: psychoanalysis was no longer a product of delusion, it had become a valuable part of reality" (1925a: 52). An event that ended his "splendid isolation," this was only the second time that Freud received official recognition from a university; in 1902, he had been awarded the title of Professor Extraordinarius at the University of Vienna, and at Clark University the 53-year-old Freud received (with Jung) an honorary doctor of law degree. The rank of professor gave Freud the added social standing needed for attracting new followers and, moreover, for increasing his hourly rate.

Yet, despite the importance of such recognition, Freud disliked America and Americans. This is significant for our understanding of psychoanalysis as a specifically European invention. After all, America has long been a convenient scapegoat for Europeans seeking to protect their historical and cultural traditions from what Lacan called the "cultural ahistoricism peculiar to the United States of America" (1966: 115). To some extent, then, one can argue that Freud's negative reaction to America is instructive and puts the spirit of Lacan's own anti-American "return" in an interesting and sometimes overlooked light.

At one point Freud told Ernest Jones that "America is a mistake; a gigantic mistake, it is true, but none the less a mistake" (in Jones 1955: 60). Elsewhere he called America a *Missgeburt*, a miscarriage (in Eastman 1962: 129), and an "Anti-Paradise" (Freud and Zweig 1970: 178). "These sentiments," historian Peter Gay admits, "run through Freud's correspondence like an unpleasant, monotonous theme" (1988: 563). It is also well known that in 1930 Freud began to write, with American diplomat William Bullitt, a biased "psychological study" of President Woodrow Wilson.[5] Freud characteristically didn't keep his dislike of Wilson a secret; as he put it to Max Eastman in 1926, "Your Woodrow Wilson was the silliest fool of the century, if not all centuries" (in Eastman 1962: 127). Neither Bullitt nor Freud liked Wilson, which hardly speaks in favor of their objectivity when preparing a pathography. Needless to say, after the book was released in 1966 the analytic community reacted with a mixture of denial, silence, and horror. It is no accident that this is the only work of Freud's that has been allowed to go out of print.

While Freud had many reasons for railing against America, including the rich food, which, he implausibly claimed, was the cause of his intestinal troubles, he seemed to dislike America for the paradoxical reason that Americans *liked* psychoanalysis. Freud reasoned that anyone who accepted his views about childhood sexuality without the accompanying resistance must have misunderstood the radical intent of psychoanalysis. He felt, in effect, that his findings merited the kind of serious resistance missing in America. Instead he prophesied that the future of psychoanalysis was destined to unfold in the place of greatest resistance: "The ancient centres of culture, where the greatest resistance has been displayed, must be the scene of the decisive struggle over psycho-analysis" (1914a: 32). In retrospect, this center turned out to be France.

Freud viewed America as a land of savagery, a kind of playground that, by its very existence, might invalidate his universal findings. To his patient Smiley Blanton Freud once said: "You Americans are like this: Garlic's good, chocolate's good—let's put a little garlic on chocolate and eat it" (Blanton 1971: 78). Freud despised the kind of vulgar commercialism that would make of his findings a hybrid or "bastard psychoanalysis." About the popularization of psychoanalysis, Gerard Lauzun complains, "The magic words 'Freud' and 'Freudian' were used to open the sluice-gates to floods of print which gave a new impulse to sentimental banalities, to pornography, drawing-room conversation, the cinema and serial fiction" (1963: 81). Certainly the myth of a wild and experimental America didn't sit well with Freud's image of the Victorian bourgeoisie beset by unconscious conflict and neuroses. Like Dostoevsky and Nietzsche before him, Freud rather believed that our capacity for suffering was an ennobling aspect of existence; greatness, in this view, was achieved through resignation to or stoic endurance of hardship. Against the notion of a "psychoanalysis without tears" (Sachs 1945: 127), often associated with Alfred Adler's Individual Psychology, Freud liked to say that "one must learn to bear some portion of uncertainty" (145). Freud's America was far too optimistic, wild, simple, non-European—in a word, *healthy*—to appreciate the virtues of the psychoanalytic sickness. Consequently, when he wasn't too low on filthy American lucre, Freud could afford to dismiss Americans—as when he refused to continue treatment of an American patient, ironically claiming that he had no unconscious.

However, according to Turkle (1992) psychoanalysis thrived in America precisely because it lacked the sort of culture that produced someone like Freud—a *gebildet Mensch*. Unburdened by the weight of history on the one hand, but suffering an uncertain identity on the other, Americans easily turned psychoanalysis into a theology of liberal individualism and self-conquest, that is, into a kind of frontier analysis. Freudian psychoanalysis was received in America as a powerful new *therapy*, not as a grand metapsychological *theory*. Thus the speculative depths of psychoanalysis were dropped for the surface effects of everyday American life. As French sociologist Jean Baudrillard remarks, "Here in America only what is produced or manifest has meaning; for us in Europe only what can be thought or concealed has meaning" (1988: 84).

It is therefore not surprising that the "American" Freud has been distinguished by its optimistic streak. In America there has been little room for Freud's darker, pessimistic theories of human existence—including the dualistic life and death drives posited in *Beyond the Pleasure Principle* (1920). Against what is perceived as the "suicidal therapeutic pessimism" of Freud's late dualism, some American philosophers have instead proposed a more dialectical, implicitly *Christian* psychoanalysis. As Norman O. Brown argues, "Our modification of Freud's [dualistic] ontology restores the possibility of salvation" (1959: 81). Similarly, and whether he knew it or not, Erik Erikson's dialectically prescriptive "eight ages of man" is consistent in many respects with Hegel's *Phenomenology of Spirit* (1950: ch. 7). In these ways Freud's Jewish science slowly became quasi-Christian, while dualism, when considered at all in postwar America, became "onto-theologic."

A Continental Breakfast at L'Hôtel Abyss

In stark contrast, war-torn Europe was more inclined to read Freud's pessimistic theory of the death drive, *Todestrieb*, in light of then current existential theory. Unlike America, which prospered after the war, economically depressed Europe was ripe for Freud's darkest thoughts on death, aggression, war, and (in the spirit of German Romanticism) civilization and its multiple discontents. In a remarkable passage, Freud emphasized the enduring value of war, against which he contrasted American superficiality:

> Life is impoverished, it loses interest, when the highest stake in the game of living, life itself, may not be risked. It becomes as shallow and empty as, let us say, an American flirtation, in which it is understood from the first that nothing is to happen, as contrasted with a Continental love-affair in which both partners must constantly bear its serious consequences in mind. (1915b: 290)

It is in this feisty spirit that Lacan rejected ego psychology, which took its inspiration from Freud's later texts, and emphasized instead the early "id"psychology of Freud's *Interpretation of Dreams* (1900), *The Psychopathology of Everyday Life* (1901b), and *Jokes and Their Relationship to the Unconscious* (1905). In this way Lacan returned psychoanalysis to the origins of a depth psychology proper, one uncontaminated by Freud's late, agency driven, topographical model of superego, ego, and id.

To put it briefly, Lacan preferred the old model of "conscious, preconscious, unconscious," since it downplayed the role of agency and subjectivity. From this orientation Lacan reasoned that American ego psychologists mistook the patient's ego for their therapeutic ally, unaware that "the core of our being does not coincide with the ego" (1954–55: 44).[6] And thus Lacan challenged the received flavor of Freud's 1933 announcement, *Wo Es war, soll Ich werden* (translated by James Strachey as "Where the id was, there ego shall be" [1933a: 80]), which seemed to advocate ego reinforcement, and called instead for the dissolution of the ego in the murky depths of the chaotic id: "There where it was," Lacan retranslated Freud, "it is my duty that I should come into being" [*La où c'était . . . c'est mon devoir que je vienne à être*] (1966: 129; cf. Lacan 1954–55: 246). In turn, Lacan launched a powerful critique of the modernist subject implicit within all metaphysical systems of thought.

"The fundamental fact which analysis reveals to us," Lacan often repeated, "is that the *ego* is an imaginary function" (1953–54: 193). For Lacan, Freud's early (non)concept of the unconscious was best understood as an unknown something, an *x* which abolished the idea of an all-knowing subject (1968: 46). Or again, the unconscious undid the truth of the ego passed down via the rationalism of Cartesian "clear and distinct" ideas, the self-sufficient ground upon which Descartes sought to erect the modern subject, the *res cogitans*. The humanist conception of man, *zoon logon echon*, was thereby deconstructed by Lacan, left hanging over the proverbial abyss, mortally wounded if not dead.

For Lacan the arrogant self-certainty of man and the developmental history of (the philosophy of) consciousness that sustained that conception, was decentered—that is, erased by the unconscious. Freud's "Copernican revolution" thus suggested that "the very centre of the human being was no longer to be found in that place assigned to it by a whole humanist tradition" (Lacan 1966: 114). As a consequence, some argue that Lacan brought "the discourse of psychoanalysis out of its modernist and into its post-modern phase" (Sussman 1990: 142).

It follows that the problem of an introduction to Lacan's life and work is not the *whole* of his corpus, as Jacques Derrida (1974) rightly says of Hegel, but rather the insatiable *hole* that informs it, the gap which opens the truth of the "subject presumed to know" to a yawning abyss. For truth is now conceived as a rift that can never be patched or, if you prefer, bridged by any finite subject. And thus death, or "being-toward-death" (*Sein-zum-Tode*), is recognized as a limit experience, the horizon which (un)structures human existence as alienation from one's self (or ego). Such are the repercussions of Kojève's influential lectures in France between 1933 and 1939: namely, the inauguration of a philosophy based on the critical power of negation (see Borch-Jacobsen 1997).

It is, in fact, the stinking corpse of "Man" that Lacan draped in psychoanalytic clothing. For while Freud spoke of analytic neutrality (only, mind you, to forget it immediately), Lacan spoke of the analytic *space of death*. According to Lacan, the silent analyst signifies to the patient an empty void, lack, death, the Real: "The analyst intervenes concretely in the dialectic of analysis by pretending he is dead, by cadaverizing his position" (1966: 140). In short, the analyst "makes [*présentifie*] death present." Thus transference onto the analyst, or onto the fictitious ideal of a grounding superego, becomes logically impossible: there is no-body and no-thing to reflect or reinforce one's shattered, essentially false ego. "Any statement of authority," according to Lacan, "has no other guarantee than its very enunciation, and it is pointless for it to seek it in another signifier, which could not appear outside this locus in any way" (1966: 310). As a result, our modern Oedipus is less blinded by the rational light of day than deafened by the hollow fiction that is mastery, truth, closure, subjectivity, and so on. Or again, here in the twilight of the idols, the patient's transference (to Lacan, Freud, the history of philosophy, etc.) is broken and replaced with the fragmentary signifier, finally set loose from its father-signified. It is precisely in this way that the name *Jacques Lacan* always signified the dead letter of truth for a prescription that could never be filled. Thus we have finally passed from the false certainty of consciousness (stereotypified as American thinking) to the unconquerable gap or hole in our infinitely circulating desires.

Just the same, one begins to wonder whether we have also checked into what Georg Lukács once called the Grand Hôtel Abyss: "It is a hotel provided with every comfort, but resting on the edge of the abyss, of nothingness, of the absurd. The daily contemplation of the abyss, in between excellent meals or artistic entertainments, can only enhance the resident's enjoyment of this superlative comfort" (in Bottomore 1984: 34). For indeed it remains to be seen whether the transference onto Freud and Lacan, onto the psychoanalytic family in general, can be broken, or if it really amounts to an exchange of one delusion for another. After all, having found the place of Truth empty in light of the deaths of God and Man, Lacan nonetheless continued to play the role of resurrected father; like Freud, Lacan occupied a privileged reference point in the transmission of psychoanalytic knowledge. As Roudinesco admits of Lacan, "The more he revealed that the subject was not master in its own home, the more he believed his ideas belonged to him alone" (1990: 390). In other words, with the *example* of Lacan (and his followers, the little Lacans) we are confronted with what Borch-Jacobsen calls "an I-the-autoanalyst-who-autoinstitutes-myself-as-me-the-analysis, me-the-psychoanalysts, as an I-who-leaves-my-ego-to-those-who-claim-to-descend-from-me, the-Freudian-cause" (1993: 7).[7] Lacan was, that is, caught in the bind of every Master disdainful of his unworthy Slaves; "The Master's attitude," as Kojève rightly suggests, "is an existential impasse" (1939: 19). Thus caught in the grip of an "infinite transference" that "never lets go" (Roustang 1983: 60), we risk staring into the (Hotel) abyss only to have Freud and Lacan stare back, the "footnotes" of the psychoanalytic horde having re-turned to the master hypnotists who (rather conveniently) countersign and authenticate the "truth" of the entire procedure. In this context it cannot be surprising that "people who had come to Lacan because of his critique of the 'subject supposed to know' would turn into the most rigid, dogmatic, intolerant disciples; leftist radicals who had been attracted by Lacan's subversive aspects would become ultraconformist bureaucrats of the Lacanian school; free spirits would start reading the *Écrits* as if it was the Bible" (Borch-Jacobsen 1994).[8]

Like son, like father. For this is of course an old story, one that Freud and his followers repeated to perfection. The "apostle" Paul Federn is reported to have said that "There is only one other book that is read and has been read with such care and diligence as one should devote to reading Freud's dream book, that is the Bible" (in Sterba 1982: 128). Similarly, when in 1937 Freud remarked that his patient Smiley Blanton was always carrying around "some printed material," Blanton simply pointed to Freud's dream book under his arm and stated: "Yes, this is my bible. I carry it and reread it every year" (Blanton 1971: 92–93). Such was, as Maurice Natenberg suggests, the "evangelizing influence" of the very dreamy Dream Book (1955: 162)—*The Interpretation of Dreams*. Predictably, when someone had the audacity to question the great man, Freud could respond with blunt indignation: "You know *Schmarn* [shit] about psychoanalysis. You don't have the right to query my interpretation" (in Dufresne 1996b: 593).

If the neutral mirror of psychoanalysis has become or has always been a vertiginous looking glass, the *Écrits* and Dream Book being new and old testaments, then perhaps Lacan and Freud have served up nothing but an authoritarian prescription that resolves, or dissolves, all fragmented subjectivities in the group effect of the psychoanalytic cause. For finally, in the end, if you can't *be* your own subject, you can always become someone else's. As always, the price of admission is submission to an other's mission. Or as Theodor Adorno nicely put it: "The psycho-analyst's wisdom finally becomes what the Fascist unconscious of the horror magazines takes it for: a technique by which one particular racket among others binds suffering and helpless people irrevocably to itself, in order to command and exploit them" (1951: 64).

CHAPTER 2

The Heterogeneous 'Beyond'

AN INTRODUCTION TO THE DEAD AND DYING

French philosophy, under the banner of Lacanian psychoanalysis and its variations, has been now for decades France's greatest cultural export to the West—the Viennese plague in elaborate philosophical disguise. But if the theme of death really is at the heart of the French reception of Freud, as suggested above, we should at least figure out what death meant for Freud in his own life and work. Of course, it is never quite that simple, since what is deemed "Freud's" is always mediated through a complex and distorting process of interpretation and reinterpretation: a repetition, then, always beyond what Freud said, might have said, should have said, or didn't bother to say. Such interpretations are constantly layered upon the crushed original, like ruins piled one on top of the other over the course of history. And as meanings are found, lost, forgotten, and ignored, one thing always remains the same: the psychoanalytic edifice continues to expand ever outward.

Any return to Freud, in this case to the circumstances of *Beyond the Pleasure Principle*, is thus conditioned upon a working-through of this mass—which I would suggest is also a mess—of interpretive efforts that have bombarded the field with hints, assertions, denials, rejections, additions, revisions, and so on. Any rigorous return to Freud's view of death, in other words, is always already a return to the reception of this body of work at the hands of his followers, friends, foes, and critics.

What immediately follows is more or less a work of review and reconstruction, an archaeology of *BPP* in general, and of the theory of the death drive in particular. To this end I survey, all too quickly I'm sure, the many readings that have circulated about Freud's 1920 publication, *Beyond the Pleasure Principle,* a text wherein he first introduced to psychoanalysis a "repetition compulsion," *Wiederholungszwang,* beyond the pleasure principle and, with it, a new dualistic theory of the life and death drives. In the following sections I explore the different reactions to *BPP,* from the biographical to the deconstructive. But I first of all want to begin with a general preamble on Freud's predecessors, and the early reception that *BPP* has earned across disciplines among its interested observers. If the end is always in a constant state of deferral, always receding into the distance, then it is only appropriate that what passes as a beginning should keep on beginning over and over again.

In Medias Res: Given, Taken, Denied, and Forgotten 'Beyond's

> I am still heavily booked up, but at the same time I am writing the essay "Beyond the Pleasure Principle," and, as in all instances, I am hoping for your understanding, which has not yet abandoned me in any situation. In it I am saying many things that are quite unclear, out of which the reader has to make the right thing. Sometimes one can't do otherwise.
> —Sigmund Freud to Sandor Ferenczi, March 31, 1919[1]

However much disagreement *BPP* continues to generate, everyone seems to agree that it is Freud's most speculative work, if not, as Ernest Jones suggests, his most "profoundly philosophic" one (1957: 41). In his official three-volume biography of Freud (1953–57), Jones contends that the Freud of *BPP* "displayed a boldness of speculation that was unique in all his writings; nothing that he wrote elsewhere can be compared with it" (1957: 266). Speaking of "this extraordinary text of Freud's," Lacan states plainly, and correctly, that it is "unbelievably ambiguous, almost confused" (1954–55: 37). Similarly, French analyst Jean Laplanche remarks that *BPP* "remains the most fascinating and baffling text of the entire Freudian *corpus.* Never had Freud shown himself to be as profoundly *free* and as audacious as in that vast metapsychological, metaphysical, metabiological fresco" (1970: 106).

Yet however audacious and singular *BPP* may seem, it was obviously not produced ex nihilo; like each of Freud's works, it must be placed within its historical and theoretical context. At least one commentator has argued in this regard that *BPP* is not as sharply divergent a text as is normally suggested in the secondary literature. The "little curve or fork" Freud added to psychoanalysis in 1920, writes analyst Gregory Zilboorg (1959: 5), "did not overthrow any old psychoanalytic regime nor did it establish any new one. It was not even a small village revolution" (9). In his 1959 introduction to the Bantam (formerly Liveright) edition of *BPP*, Zilboorg correctly reminds us that the text is reflected in Freud's earliest biological and, later, cultural texts, that is, in texts written before 1897 and after 1920. Indeed, even as Freud describes in *BPP* the compulsion to repeat, the text is itself an uncanny repetition of some old pre-psychoanalytic ideas, refurbished in the name of something brand new for psychoanalysis.

While Zilboorg is undoubtedly correct in his assessment, he underestimates just how "new," indeed radical, these old thoughts have remained—not only for psychoanalysts committed to Freud's seminal id psychology of the early 1900's, but for generations of admiring theorists desperate for another baffling text upon which to cut their teeth or, more simply, to appropriate to their own, often peculiar, ends. Among theorists, of course, the more obscure and "free" Freud could be, the more intrigued, if spellbound, they have generally remained—a strange but not unusual fact about the delirious production and reception of psychoanalysis after Freud.

Freud grew very attached to his new dualism, especially the death drive, later admitting that "I can no longer think in any other way" (1930: 119). As he put it in *BPP*: "We make this assumption [about the existence of a death drive] thus carelessly because it does not seem to *be* an assumption" (1920a: 44). Years later, he would bluntly mock those who rejected the death-drive theory, echoing Goethe's line that:

> "little children do not like it" when there is talk of the inborn human inclination to "badness," to aggressiveness and destructiveness, and so to cruelty as well. God has made them in the image of His own perfection; nobody wants to be reminded how hard it is to reconcile the undeniable existence of evil . . . with His all-powerfulness or His all-goodness. (1930: 120)

Despite Freud's commitment to the death drive, it is true that at times he gave the appearance of being less dogmatic about it than about some other innovations during his long career. This tolerant side perhaps reflects Freud's ambivalence about the theory, especially in the beginning, but it is more likely a good example of his seductive style of argumentation: rhetorically he admits the weakness of his (manifest) arguments the better to substantiate his (latent) position. For example, about his new speculations Freud qualifies in *BPP* that "I am not convinced myself and . . . do not seek to persuade other people to believe in them" (1920a: 59). Elsewhere in this work Freud even cautions his reader to "consider or dismiss [what follows] according to his individual predilection" (24). It is possible that by this time in his career Freud realized that he was not entirely free to adjust his creation to fit his personal fancies; psychoanalysis had evidently become a hard piece of a shared reality. Confronted by disciples who were often, as Martin Peck aptly puts it, "More Freudian than is Freud himself" (1930: 53), Freud was more than ever inclined to smooth the way into his new views. As he concedes at one point, much of his essay is "speculation, often far-fetched speculation" (1920a: 24).

That Freud, at least on the surface, initially doubted his own commitment to the innovations of *BPP* led Jones to suggest, a bit dubiously, that "while writing it Freud had no audience in mind beyond himself" (1957: 266; cf. de M'Uzan 1977).[2] In a letter of June 16, 1920, to Max Eitingon, Freud admits that "many people will shake their heads over it" (in Jones 1957: 40). It is also true that in later years Freud continued to dampen the enthusiasm that his followers occasionally showed for the "findings" of *BPP*. In a letter of June 17, 1937, to Princess Marie Bonaparte, Freud writes: "Please do not overestimate my remarks about the destructive instinct. They were only tossed off and should be carefully thought over if you propose to use them publicly" (in Jones 1957: 465). Freud even suggests that *BPP* had become too popular and, for that reason, was probably wrongheaded. In a letter to Eitingon, March 27, 1921, Freud writes with his characteristic irony, "For *Beyond* I have been sufficiently punished. It is very popular, is bringing me lots of letters and expressions of praise. I must have done something very stupid there" (in Schur 1972: 343). "On this last point," historian Ronald Clark chortles, "he may have been right" (1980: 432).

If Freud himself could express public and private caution about the death drive, both during and after its inception, we cannot be surprised that his speculative revisions were often rejected by many observers, including his most loyal followers. For Wilhelm Reich, although the death drive began as a tentative hypothesis, it "was not only not given up—it led to nothing good. Some analysts even contend that they have direct evidence of the death instinct" (1952: 232, n. 11). Reich has a point. According to Ferenczi, Freud himself came to believe that epilepsy "express[ed] the frenzy of a tendency to self-destruction" (1929: 102); and Ferenczi, always the eager disciple, thought he could corroborate this mistaken idea (102–103). It is understandable that more commentators rejected than accepted Freud's theory. In a typical assessment, William McDougall concludes that Freud's notion of a death drive is "the most bizarre monster of all his gallery of monsters" (1936: 64). Years later Ernest Becker would echo this sentiment, concluding that the death-drive theory "can now be securely relegated to the dust bin of history" (1973: 99; cf. Sulloway 1979: 394).

On the other hand, like so much Freudian theory, the idea of a death drive seems immune to criticism. An untestable piece of mythology, it has entered popular psychology just as assuredly as the "Freudian slip." It is, for example, often recalled when thoughts turn to the Second World War. In a recent article in the *New Yorker*, novelist John Updike states "that this disagreeable mythology, proposed in 1932 [*sic*], gathered credibility as Hitler rose to power the next year" (1996: 64). As the French analyst Jean-Bertrand Pontalis rightly suggests, "It is as though the metaphors of *Beyond the Pleasure Principle* have become, fifty years later, those of our culture" (1981a: 193).

If Freud's revisionism was hard to accept among his followers, this was in part because they were less free to fiddle with psychoanalysis than Freud was himself. As Freud's colleague, the Italian analyst Edoardo Weiss, put it: "We wonder how Freud would have reacted had another analyst reached these modified concepts before he did himself" (1970: 13). Many analysts did not expect or appreciate that the sixty-three-year-old Freud, apparently bored during the war years, had single-handedly renovated the analytic kitchen. As Freud states in a letter of July 8, 1915, to his American supporter James Jackson Putnam: "I myself am using the break in my [clinical] work at this time to finish off a book containing a collection of twelve psychological essays" (Freud 1960: 103). The changes in psychoanalytic doctrine came at a time when the old views had finally gained some currency amongst the paying public. By the 1920's psychoanalysis was internationally recognized, Freud himself was famous, and business was improving. Many of the early radicals of psychoanalysis—including an assortment of outsiders, dilettantes, and social misfits—had been replaced by more conservative, even opportunistic, practitioners. It was with this lattermost thought in mind that Freud and his Viennese colleagues regularly questioned the motives of American doctors looking, so it seemed, for quick training that they would sell to the highest bidder back home. In the wake of the First World War, the unstable European economy was not an ideal context for changing a winning business formula. Moreover, it was generally felt that the problems of sexuality were the primary business of a psychoanalytic science—not death, which was traditionally the province of literature and philosophy.

No doubt the sociopolitical conditions of the time encouraged Freud to follow this path of greatest resistance. Analyst Bruno Bettelheim (1990: 6) argues that Freud's brooding, introspective attitude was a characteristic of the Viennese cultural elite shaken by the decline of the Austrian empire. As power shifted to Berlin and elsewhere, the Viennese became increasingly inclined "to withdraw their attention from the wider world and turn inward instead." "In this unique Viennese culture," Bettelheim attests, "the strongest inner powers were thanatos and eros, death and sex" (12).

Yet if withdrawal from the world of power politics reflected the "despair" (15) of the cultured Viennese at the end of the nineteenth century, a morbid kind of introspection was already a well-established theme of romantic literature, beginning with Jean Paul and E.T.A. Hoffmann. Like many others, Freud was greatly influenced by the unsettling works of Hoffmann. Hoffmann's short story "The Sandman" is discussed in Freud's essay "The 'Uncanny'" (1919), which Freud rewrote and published during the same period as *BPP*. In this essay Freud grapples with the *unheimlich*, or uncanny, impression that a double, a *Doppelgänger*, can make on a person. Predictably, Freud tries to uncover the original meaning of this impression in the universal psychology of children. Our ideas about the double, he writes, "have sprung from the soil of unbounded self-love, from the primary narcissism which dominates the mind of the child and of primitive man. But when this state has been surmounted, the 'double' reverses its aspect. From having been an assurance of immortality [e.g., the soul], it becomes the uncanny harbinger of death" (1919b: 235).

While traceable to the Egyptians (235; cf. Rawcliffe 1952: 115), the theme of the double became for the Victorian era a sign of "divided" or "double consciousness"—as found, for example, in Robert Louis Stevenson's *The Strange Case of Dr. Jekyll and Mr. Hyde* (1886). Indeed, the character of Hyde is a personification of the unconscious, if not a split-off piece of the death drive at war with the life drive, that is, with Jekyll:

> The powers of Hyde seemed to have grown with the sickliness of Jekyll. And certainly the hate that now divided them was equal on each side. With Jekyll, it was a thing of vital instinct. He had now seen the full deformity of that creature that shared with him some of the phenomena of consciousness, and was co-heir with him to death: and beyond these links of community, which in themselves made the most poignant part of his distress, he thought Hyde, for all his energy of life, as of something not only hellish but inorganic. This was the shocking thing; that the slime of the pit seemed to utter cries and voices; that the amorphous dust gesticulated and sinned; that what was dead, and had no shape, should usurp the offices of life. (159)

This popular view of subconscious activity and dissociated personality was, however, inherited directly from the theories of magnetism introduced by Franz Anton Mesmer, and later expanded upon by his student, the Marquis de Puységur. "It was a startling concept," writes historian Adam Crabtree (1985: 5) of double consciousness. "It meant that every human being was double, with what people thought of as the 'I' only a part of their whole self."

Doubling is among the most pervasive themes of romantic literature, as outlined so well by Freud's student Otto Rank in his book *The Double: A Psychoanalytic Study* (1925). Not incidentally, Rank's book was derived from his essay of 1914, "Der Doppelgänger," a piece that influenced Freud's own work "The 'Uncanny' " (1919). Fascinated by and fearful of one version or another of the split or altered ego, the double was a psychological problem that plagued the arts in general. But it was also an inspiration for the contemporary theoretical and clinical research conducted on split personalities. This attitude, according to which the arts were essential material for the science of the mind, is nicely captured by Rank, who writes:

> Up to this point [in the analysis], it has been a question either of a physical double . . . or of a likeness which has been detached from the ego and become an individual being (shadow, reflection, portrait). Now we come upon the representationally opposite form of expression of the same psychic constellation: the representation, by one and the same person, of two distinct beings separated by amnesia. These cases of double-consciousness have also been observed clinically. (1925: 19–20)

The pervasiveness of these observations, which resonate so uncannily with current preoccupations with the doubling (and multiplying) found in dissociative disorders, were high and low parts of a culture that made Freud's discourse of repetition both possible and (artistically, socially, and scientifically) relevant. This connection surely exposes an underappreciated aspect of his motivation when theorizing the compulsive repetition of the death drive.

If Freud's way of thinking was indebted to the great figures of literature, from the Greek tragedians to the German poet Friedrich von Schiller,[3] it is more simply the case that his ideas were prefigured by a broad intellectual context that included such writers as Gotthilf Heinrich von Schubert and Novalis. Among other things, a strict belief in the ubiquity of polarities in the world characterized the *Naturphilosophie* expounded by German Romantics (see Ellenberger 1970: 202–204). Von Schubert, for example, felt that the longing for death and love could not be separated in living beings (Ibid.: 205). Freud, of course, knew that he was treading on some old territory; as he says to Bonaparte, "there is so little [that is] new" in the death-drive theory (in Jones 1957: 465). Henri Ellenberger (1970: 514) points out that two Russians, A. Tokarsky and Elie Metchnikoff, had already advanced notions that seem relevant to Freud's work, although they "viewed the death instinct simply as a wish to die." John Kerr (1993: 499) has similarly argued that Freud may have gleaned some of his ideas from Metchnikoff's 1903 text, *Rhythm of Life*. A biologist and founder of immunology, Metchnikoff produced in this work a biologically based polemic against religion and the fear of death. In his masterful sweep across the literature, Ellenberger also reminds us that the theme of death was a major preoccupation of the nineteenth-century intelligentsia: "It followed a tradition going back to Hobbes and popularized by Darwin and the social Darwinians, by Lombroso, and by Nietzsche" (1970: 515). It is not so surprising, then, that followers of Freud committed to a scientistic version of psychoanalysis have been and continue to be uncomfortable with this humanistic inheritance.

Closer to home, Freud encountered—and to some extent avoided—this cultural preoccupation with death, as it appeared in the work of three analytic followers: Alfred Adler, Wilhelm Stekel, and Sabina Spielrein. In a position that became increasingly incompatible with Freud's, Adler believed that the search for power captured the essence of psychic life, including sexual and Oedipal dynamics. This view, which coincided with Adler's interest in Nietzsche's (loosely) psychological idea of the "will to power," led him to postulate the now popular idea of the "inferiority complex." What Adler came to call Individual Psychology was, according to one commentator, "one of the first existential psychologies" (Hauser 1961: 70). But, essentially, Adler posited sociality as a cause of neurosis, something that fits badly with Freud's instinct-driven psychology. In this respect (as we will see later), Adler's views anticipated to some extent the neo-Freudian focus on external reality rather than inner fantasies and unseen (biological or animistic) forces.

Adler and Freud's friendship had almost run its course by 1911, when Adler and his adherents left Freud's group to found the Society for Free Psychoanalysis. Years later, in 1923, Freud appended a footnote about Adler to his case study of Little Hans, "Analysis of a Phobia in a Five-Year-Old Boy" (1909). While Freud once discounted the "existence of a separate aggressive instinct," he now modified that position: "Since then I have myself been obliged to assert the existence of an 'aggressive instinct', but it is different from Adler's. I prefer to call it the 'destructive' or 'death instinct' "(1909: 140, n. 2). Although Adler's theory of aggressivity is not really the same as Freud's—as Jones suggests, it "was more sociological than psychological" (1957: 274)—it is interesting that Freud felt obliged to confront, and to this extent acknowledge, his connection to Adler on this score. As he put it in *Civilization and Its Discontents*: "I remember my own defensive attitude when the idea of an instinct of destruction first emerged in psycho-analytic literature, and how long it took before I became receptive to it" (1930: 120).

Stekel's views on aggressivity are closer to Freud's. Stekel was, in fact, perturbed by Freud's apparently changed opinion about the functions of death, destruction, and aggressivity in the organization of mental life. Until 1920 Freud gave little attention to death, which was eclipsed by his consuming interest in sexuality. As Jones mentions, Stekel "had in 1909 used the word *Thanatos* to signify a death wish" (1957: 273) and felt that Freud had lifted the idea directly from his own studies. Stekel thus complained in his autobiography (1950: 138): "Freud later adopted some of my discoveries without mentioning my name. Even the fact that in my first edition [of *Causes of Nervousness*] I had defined anxiety as the reaction of the life instinct against the upsurge of the death instinct was not mentioned in his later books, and many people believe that the death instinct is Freud's discovery" (138; cf. Clark 1980: 432). It is certainly interesting that Freud could acknowledge his differences with Adler but not with Stekel. In any case, Freud eventually excised many of the references to Adler and Stekel that he had once liberally sprinkled throughout his essays (Roazen 1975: 207, 217). At the height of his troubles with these two dissidents, he wrote in a letter to Ferenczi that "Adler is a little Fliess come to life again. And his appendage Stekel is at least called Wilhelm" (in Jones 1955: 130). And Freud, as always, wasn't likely to forgive the turncoats. Upon hearing in the early 1930's that Stekel still spoke highly of him, Freud remarked sharply: "Very nice of Stekel. He's always ready to forgive me for the things he did to me" (in Dufresne 1996b: 599).

On the basis of some recent discoveries, Spielrein's role in the history of psychoanalysis has generated much more interest than that of either Adler or Stekel. Yet there is still fundamental disagreement about her importance for the development of Freud's death-drive theory. In November 1911, Spielrein read to the Vienna Psychoanalytical Society a paper entitled "Destruction as the Cause of Coming Into Being." Apparently the paper was a failure with most members, except for Freud and Victor Tausk (see Appignanesi and Forrester 1992: 216), who were theoretically more sophisticated and adventurous than the others. But as Freud says of Spielrein in a letter to Jung, dated March 21, 1912, "Her destructive drive is not much to my liking, because I believe it is personally conditioned" (Freud and Jung 1974: 494). Years later, in a footnote in *BPP*, Freud recorded his debt to Spielrein's essay, which appeared in print in 1912. At the same time, however, Freud claimed that her essay "is unfortunately not entirely clear to me" (1920a: 55, n. 1).

This tactic is characteristic of Freud, who could give with one hand while he took with the other. In fact, it sometimes seems as though Freud chose his predecessors with special care, the better to dispose of their intellectual claims to priority later on. This is certainly the impression one gets from reading John Kerr's *A Most Dangerous Method* (1993). Kerr argues that Freud overstates his debt to Spielrein concerning the death drive. In fact, according to Kerr, "There is no death instinct in [Spielrein's paper]. Neither the term nor the idea appears there" (502). So why did Freud cite Spielrein? It is possible that Freud acknowledged his debt to Spielrein precisely because she was not a real competitor in the world of analysis.[4] Or perhaps he used Spielrein to put his followers off the scent of his true debts. Either way, his acknowledgment of her work does seem like another slap in the face of his one-time followers Adler and Stekel.

Yet if a death instinct or drive isn't found in Spielrein's text, it is still accurate to say, as John Forrester (1996) does, that the role of *destruction* ties not only Freud and Spielrein together, but also Freud and Jung. Accordingly, in *Freud's Women* Appignanesi and Forrester offer a rather different conclusion from the one offered by Kerr (1992: 215–19). The authors remind us that Spielrein may not have mentioned the death drive in her published essay of 1912, but she did discuss it during her spoken presentation of 1911. Moreover, according to the Minutes of the Vienna Psychoanalytical Society, Spielrein, herself a Russian, couched her discussion of a death instinct explicitly in terms of Metchnikoff's biological speculations (see Nunberg and Federn 1962–75, 3: 329–35). Jung suggests as much in a letter to Freud where he denies personal responsibility for her ideas, claiming instead that they were "home-grown" (Freud and Jung 1974: 471). In other words, if Freud gleaned his ideas about the death drive from Metchnikoff, as Kerr in fact contends, he surely did so through Spielrein's influence. At the time of her presentation, it is true, Freud thought that she had unduly subordinated psychology to biology, something "no more acceptable than a dependency on philosophy, physiology, or brain anatomy" (469). But as it turned out, Freud was just as smitten with these forms of dependency and returned to them most decisively in *BPP*—as we will see later.

Perhaps, then, Freud acknowledged a very real debt to Spielrein, even though he qualified and, to that extent, distorted it somewhat. If so, this distortion may not have been tied simply, or only, to his usual obsession over scientific priority, but to his complicated relationship with Jung. For Jung too was influenced by Spielrein, his first analytic patient and also his illicit lover. According to Appignanesi and Forrester, "Both Freud and Jung underplayed Spielrein's influence on them, Jung because she knew more of his inner personal and conceptual development than anyone, Freud because he associated her ideas with Jung and repudiated in advance any influence from so dangerous a source" (1992: 220).

Despite his efforts, it is obvious that Freud hardly exorcised Jung by writing *Beyond the Pleasure Principle*. If the new metapsychology had "as its point of departure a sharp distinction between ego instincts, which we equated with death instincts, and sexual instincts, which we equated with life instincts" (Freud 1920a: 52–53), this dualism was completely undone by the extremity of the death-drive theory itself. Why? Because Freud made of life or Eros a mere "detour" along the "circuitous path" leading to death (39). "It is life," as Derrida (1980: 355) puts it, "that resembles an accident of death or an excess of death." That Freud assigned an almost sovereign role to the death drive has not gone unnoticed in the literature (see Jones 1957: 272), where it has been characterized as the "dominant force" (Chessick 1989: 546), as "absolute" (Blumenberg 1985: 91), and as the "almost universal principle behind all drives" (Laplanche 1989: 51). Or as Laplanche and Pontalis state in *The Language of Psycho-Analysis*: "What is designated here [by *Todestrieb*] is more than any particular *type* of instinct—it is rather that factor which determines the actual *principle* of all instinct" (1973: 102; their emphasis).

Consequently, as the philosopher Herbert Marcuse rightly says, "The monism of sexuality . . . now seems to turn into its opposite: into a monism of death" (1955a: 28). Or as Gilles Deleuze and Felix Guattari (1972: 331) similarly put it in their influential *Anti-Oedipus*, Freud's new dualism was in fact "the liquidation of the libido." These conclusions are of course ironic, since part of Freud's reason for establishing his dualism more forcefully was Jung's "hasty judgement" in erecting a monistic view of instinct around libido (Freud 1920a: 52–53). Writing with a new "combative vigor," as Zilboorg (1959: 3) puts it, Freud was "still combatting his opponents [in *BPP*] rather than trying to instruct his proponents." Freud certainly felt that his revision of the instinct theory was "even more definitely dualistic than before" (1920a: 53)—by which he meant his old pairings of love and hunger, and the sexual and self-preservative instincts. Yet Freud's attempt to ostracize Jung's generalized libido theory—to annul it in the eyes of psychoanalysis—with a "generalized" death drive, only mirrored in reverse that very theory. As such, Jung's monistic vision of libido remains the essential supplement, the counterpart, to Freud's death drive and, consequently, the true structural partner to Freud's uneasy dualism of 1920: Jung/Freud, life/death (see Derrida 1980: 366–67). And actually this conclusion seems to fit a pattern in Freud's life: his treatment of dissident analysts was often characterized by a tendency to put them to work as the other, as opposites, in a romantic battle between good and evil.[5] Enemies, as both Nietzsche and Freud liked to say, can be more useful than friends.

And, indeed, the death-drive theory probably made Freud more enemies than allies within the analytic establishment. For if some of Freud's followers agreed with or even recognized themselves in the death-drive theory, most of his earliest colleagues, trained to be "libido hunters and detectives" (Sterba 1982: 75), were particularly disinclined to revise the "classical"

Freudian view that subsumed aggressivity under the rubric of sexuality. Analyst Richard Sterba summarizes the situation this way:

> In 1914, Freud, in his paper on narcissism, had extended the dynamic deployment of libidinous forces into the realm of the ego, which up until then was considered the agency that defended itself against the unacceptable libido manifestations. No wonder that some of the Viennese analysts had a hard time accepting the aggressive drive as an independent dynamic force. They continued to consider aggression a reaction to frustration, caused by external . . . prohibitions. (1982: 75)

For the Freud of *Beyond the Pleasure Principle*, aggression was detached from sexuality and formalized as its own primary *Instinkt* or, as he more typically put it, *Trieb* (drive).[6] As such it owed little to "external prohibitions," which assume a secondary or derivative status in his overall theory. Younger analysts, finding a new venue for their own ambitions, were obviously more willing and able to adopt Freud's revisions than the older generation of analysts. Nonetheless, a few older analysts followed Freud. Paul Federn, for example, eventually accepted *BPP* and, as Weiss (1970: 13) suggests, "considered the death instinct cathexis as a third kind of teleologically directed cathexis, namely, towards death and destruction" (cf. Sterba 1982: 76). And an analyst as influential as Melanie Klein remained deeply committed to the theory of innate instinctual impulses throughout her life, making it the cornerstone of her theoretical work.

It is interesting that Freud never bothered to name the aggressive and destructive energy of the death drive, as he did when he called the energy of the life drive "libido." With this in mind, Federn called this new energy force "mortido," while some others, such as Charles Brenner (1973: 22), elected the word "destrudo" for this purpose. Theorists after Freud have generally ignored these particular additions, although the word *Thanatos* has found widespread acceptance. It is interesting and perhaps a "little odd," as Jones (1957: 273) puts it, that Freud himself did not adopt this Greek word for death as the structural partner to his often-used "Eros," the Greek god of love.[7] Although it has become an established part of psychoanalese, Freud would apparently use the word *Thanatos* only in conversation. This oddity is explained by Roazen (1975: 218), who suggests that Freud did not formally adopt the word because Stekel had already used it in print.

While the trail of Freud's intellectual debts is an endless fascination to scholars, it is often of little or no interest to practitioners of psychoanalysis. Clearly the intellectual coherence of Freud's theory is not a primary concern for most therapists who are, perhaps understandably, more concerned with practical results. Consequently, it is no surprise that American "ego psychologists," for example, hardly understand that their own theory is based on the much-despised theories of *Beyond the Pleasure Principle*. It is easy to forget that Freud's late "structural" theory of the mind, introduced in *The Ego and the Id* (1923), was a continuation of a dialogue that began with *BPP*, if not much earlier. Yet as Freud indicates with the very first words of the preface to *The Ego and the Id*: "The present discussions are a further development of some trains of thought which I opened up in *Beyond the Pleasure Principle*" (1923a: 12; see Robert 1964: 335). For example, the moral agency Freud called the "superego," *Über-ich*, was meant to invoke the dark, self-destructive powers of the masochistic death drive. Despite hype to the contrary, the superego is not just the introjection of social taboos and historical traditions. As Freud suggests, "Following our view of sadism, we should say that the destructive component had entrenched itself in the super-ego and turned against the ego. What is now holding sway in the super-ego is, as it were, a pure culture of the death instinct, and in fact it often enough succeeds in driving the ego to death" (1923a: 53). As we will see again and again, the role of society is seriously delimited by Freud's instinct or drive theory. Nonetheless, eager dabblers in Freudian theory often take bits and pieces from different phases in Freud's thought to create, piling absurdity upon absurdity, theoretical monsters after their own image.

As many critics are quick to point out, sometimes a bit defensively, Freud never simply abandoned his "science" of sexuality for a philosophy of death. How could he? In theory, at least, the study of sexuality formed and still forms the basis of clinical work. According to Freud in the *New Introductory Lectures* of 1933, "We are not asserting that death is the only aim of life; we are not overlooking the fact that there is life as well as death" (1933a: 107). And certainly in other places Freud recalls that "eternal Eros" would (perhaps) balance his negativistic image of man (see 1930: 145; 1937: 246). Yet, to echo Nietzsche in his *Beyond Good and Evil*, this is a "perilous perhaps" that Freud invokes—and sometimes without much force or gusto. A confusion often arises on this point, because the Freud of *Beyond the Pleasure Principle* postulates a theory that conflicts with the old one in striking and possibly irreconcilable ways. First of all, death for Freud became an integral *part of life*; worse, death was conceived as the beginning and end of life, perhaps even its essence. Again, death seems to dominate life and sexuality. For this reason the death drive is a *meta*-theory, and also a threat, that undermines the theory, practice, and business of psychoanalysis from within. The death-drive theory is rotten to the core of psychoanalysis.

In this respect, the collective resentment is at times almost audible: *If only Freud had died before his annoying new revisions of 1920.* "Had his work come to an end" before 1919, Jones writes, "then we should have possessed a well-rounded account of psychoanalysis" (1957: 265). The death drive is the *non plus ultra*, the ultimate extreme of psychoanalytic theorizations. As such, *Beyond the Pleasure Principle* has been experienced (and rightly so) as a self-inflicted trauma to Freud and psychoanalysis, that is, as a bit of nasty repetition of some unresolved (theoretical and practical) problems stemming back as far as 1892. To these I will turn in a later section.

The worst readers are those who behave like plundering troops: they take away a few things they can use, dirty and confound the remainder, and revile the whole.
—Friedrich Nietzsche, *Assorted Opinions and Maxims*[8]

If, just the same, *BPP* has become an almost unavoidable reference point among fashionable theorists, one has to wonder where all the embarrassment has gone; philosophers, literary critics, feminists, and postmodernists of all stripes continue to drop vague references to this text, although at one time few would have dared—or bothered. As Freud himself suggests, such popularity should make us wonder what has happened to this theory, and what mechanism lies at the bottom of its endless recurrence. I should say once again that theorists—with the possible exception of the deconstructionists—rarely cite *Beyond the Pleasure Principle* as a traumatic rupture point in the history of psychoanalysis. Instead, the essay is almost always used as just another piece of scaffolding in the building of some other edifice, some other more or less delirious project.

The continued interest in the death-drive theory, or in what passes for it, is in part perpetuated by a general disinterest in the untenable biological side of Freud's argument. Outside of a handful of historians of science, it is decidedly unfashionable to attend to this confusing aspect of Freud's troubled legacy. On the contrary, it has proven far more profitable for theorists to strip *BPP* of the broad historico-intellectual context within which Freud produced psychoanalysis, and re-cover it with some elaborate, if eccentric, tapestries. One unfortunate result of this trend is that the truly fascinating heterogeneous aspects of the text have become more and more difficult to discern in an equally confused and heterogeneous literature—especially in works written by theorists unwilling to consult secondary texts outside their own niche. Alas, secondary literature has long garnered a bad name among the most self-consciously brilliant of theorists, whose work is produced without reference, *à la française*, apparently ex nihilo. As a consequence, even as readers find little or nothing of Freud in these texts, the truly provocative and enduring *problems* of *BPP* are repeatedly effaced or ignored. From my perspective, such theorists risk becoming a part of the very machine they ought to be examining with more care.

Against this tendency, I want to give the multiple profundities and banalities of *BPP* the space they need to resonate against each other across the primary and secondary literature. My aim in this regard is to emphasize what is arguably the most provocative aspect of psychoanalysis: Freud's audacious attempt to synthesize disparate theories, bits and pieces scavenged from different fields, in the creation of an autobiographically based scientific theory of human nature. If, for a change, we allow these bits and pieces of speculation to pile upon one another, in *Beyond* and beyond, the heterogeneous elements resonate at such a pitch that everything "psychoanalytic" is ripped apart from the absurd "inside" of interpretation. The repetition of these themes is the death in, and the death of, psychoanalysis: to put it in the mechanistic terms that Freud preferred, references across a body of literature multiply without discharge, repeating at the textual level the death drive that Freud described at work on the cellular level. Writing Freud to death in this way seems to me a most faithful end to psychoanalysis, where the edifice constructed is given up to the great flow of references that become at last nothing but a pile of theories, and perhaps a great heap of nonsense.

Biographical 'Beyonds'

If I have already taken small steps away from theory proper by introducing the broad cultural-political-personal context within which psychoanalysis was produced and consumed, biographers and historians have taken it much further down this sometimes provocative and almost always bumpy road. Certainly Freud's own far-reaching speculations have encouraged others, with some justification, to do the same in their own work. As David Bakan puts it, "If a great man writes what appears to be nonsense, as Freud's writings on the death instinct have sometimes been regarded even by psychoanalysts, it behooves us to look again to see what might lie underneath the facade" (1966: 155; cf. Jones 1957: 278).

It is rather significant, I think, that Freud's most speculative and abstract text is widely thought to have another, far more subjective, side. Yet this is true of the entire Freudian corpus, which is deeply autobiographical. It is often forgotten, at times conveniently, by those who traffic exclusively in psychoanalytic theory, that Freud was thinking of his dissidents—Jung, Adler, Stekel, and Reich, among others—when he wrote on paranoia, the Schreber case, The Rat Man, the history of psychoanalysis, world prehistory and anthropology, civilization and its discontents, group psychology, interminable analyses, and so on. Theorists with two hands in the philosophic pot have had difficulty paying adequate attention to what may seem the all too human, base considerations of a biographical history; theorists tend to keep their hands clean of the messy details of everyday life, even as they shy away from clinical "discoveries" and "evidence." Still, it is theoretically naive and a bit ironic when commentators of psychoanalysis ignore the unbreakable continuity between Freud's work and his life or, more radically, between fantasy and reality, autobiographical theory and biographical histories. Each side, if there are indeed discernable sides, inflects and disrupts the other.

In their varied attempts to fashion life histories from dry facts and dates, Freud biographers have often advanced a subjective interpretation of *Beyond the Pleasure Principle* (see Jones 1957: 44; Robert 1964: 323–38). Of paramount concern in this regard are the ominous events of the First World War, a time when the Freuds suffered privations at home and worried about their soldier-sons, Ernst and Martin. Certainly the war reinforced Freud's pessimistic view of mankind, which led directly to his essays "Thoughts for the Times on War and Death" (1915) and "On Transience" (1916). In a letter to Fredrick van Eeden in late 1914, Freud openly laments the pitiable state of human nature:

> I venture, under the impact of the war to remind you [that] . . . the primitive savage and evil impulses of mankind have not vanished in any of its individual members. . . . Our intellect is a feeble and dependent thing, a plaything and tool of our instincts and affects. . . . You will have to admit that psychoanalysis has been right in both its theses. (1915b: 301–302 (appendix); see also Freud and Andreas-Salomé 1966: 21)

During this same period, as Ilse Grubrich-Simitis (1987: 77) suggests, Freud would engage in an "almost cheerful war imagery" in his writing, especially in his personal correspondence. Freud wrote to Ferenczi on December 15, 1914, about his metapsychological efforts during that time: "I am living, as my brother says, in my private trench; I speculate and write, and after hard battles have got safely through the first line of riddles and difficulties" (Freud and Ferenczi 1996: 36). But however much Freud adapted to the new situation, it is likely, as both Bruno Bettelheim and Erich Fromm contend, that the war disturbed Freud's attachment to the old Austro-Hungarian empire. Fromm even argues that the war "constitutes the dividing line within the development of Freud's theory of aggressivity" (1973: 440; cf. Burston 1991: 197).

Freud began to write *Beyond the Pleasure Principle* not long after the war, in March 1919, completing it by the middle of July 1920 and publishing it with the International Psychoanalytic Press by the end of the year. In January 1920 Freud's friend, colleague, and key financial supporter Anton von Freund succumbed to cancer. Although Freund's death was expected, Freud writes that it was "for our cause, a heavy loss, for me a keen pain, but one I could assimilate in the course of the last months" (in Gay 1988: 391). With this admission in mind, some suggest that Freud "assimilated" the pain of Freund's illness and death into his new theories of that time. As Gay suggests of Freud, "work was also a way of coping" with life's hardships (390).

Only a few days after Freund's death, on January 25, 1920, Freud's favored "Sunday child," Sophie Halberstadt, died of influenzal pneumonia. To his friend, the Swiss pastor and lay analyst Oskar Pfister, Freud writes that Sophie's death was "a heavy narcissistic insult." During Hilda Doolittle's (H.D.'s) analysis with Freud from 1932 to 1933, she recalled the Spanish influenza of 1920, which she, unlike Sophie, had managed to survive (and with child). Freud openly lamented to H.D. the loss of his daughter: " 'She is here,' he said, and he showed me a tiny locket that he wore, fastened to his watch-chain" (Doolittle 1974: 128). Freud understandably thought it monstrous for a parent to outlive a child; years later he seemed relieved when his own mother finally died, thus clearing the way for his own (guilt-free) death.

Fritz Wittels, Freud's first biographer (and also an analyst), was the first to connect in writing the general atmosphere of death and mourning in Freud's life to the theoretical ruminations of *Beyond the Pleasure Principle*. Wittels writes: "When Freud made this communication [about the death drive] to an attentive world, he was under the impress of the death of a blooming daughter whom he had lost after he had had to worry about the life of several of his nearest relatives, who had gone to war" (1924: 251). As Gay responds, "It was a reductionist explanation, but most plausible" (1988: 395). By the 1920's, though, Freud had long developed a keen sense for his own place in world history, and had taken steps to preempt such dangerous speculation. He enlisted Max Eitingon, who was by then a member of

Freud's inner circle and wealthy benefactor of the cause, to certify in a letter that *BPP* was nearly complete when Freund and Sophie had died in January. On July 18, 1920, Freud writes: "The *Beyond* is finally finished. You will be able to certify that it was half finished when Sophie was alive and flourishing" (in Schur 1972: 329). As Jones reflects, this "rather curious request" indicates that Freud was already aware, if uncomfortable, with the subjective aspects of his theory (1957: 40). Naturally Jones felt that Freud had protested his innocence a bit too much by conspiring to find an outside source to verify his objectivity.

On December 18, 1923, Freud sent Wittels a list of corrections to consider should a second edition of the biography ever appear. Among this list was Freud's direct response to Wittels's suggestion that the death drive was motivated by subjective factors in his life. Freud writes:

> That [idea] seems to me most interesting, and I regard it as a warning. Beyond question, if I had myself been analyzing another person in such circumstances, I should have presumed the existence of a connection between my daughter's death and the train of thought presented in *Beyond the Pleasure Principle*. But the inference that such a sequence exists would have been false.... What seems true is not always the truth. (1924a: 287, n. 1; see also Jones 1957: 40–41)

Freud's dismissal of Wittels's speculation is not very convincing. For although he had already published his paper "The 'Uncanny' " in 1919, which anticipated some of his findings in *BPP*—most specifically, the phenomena of doubling and of "repetition compulsion"—the notion of a death drive did not appear until *after* Freund and Sophie had died, that is, after January 1920.[9] Rather, the death-drive theory first appears in letters to Eitingon, dated February 12 and 20, 1920, after which time Freud revised *BPP* accordingly (see Schur 1972: 329).

Whatever "warning" Freud had in mind when Wittels revealed his biographical detective work, Freud could never shake loose the subjective interpretation of *BPP* during his own lifetime. These themes continue to influence the current literature as well. For instance, Elizabeth Bronfen writes: "The situation, then, is one of Freud doing as much work as he can in an effort to restore his wounded narcissism.... Writing about death seems to become a way of regaining control after the disruption of death, of reassuring continuity in the face of discontinuity, of mastering the absence of the Sunday-child" (1989: 964). According to Bronfen, Sophie's death threw Freud more completely than ever into the arms of Lady Psychoanalysis. With a French twist to her reading, Bronfen only adds that Freud exchanged the real loss of his daughter for the symbolism inherent within language itself. In short, he displaced his loss (Sophie's death) onto a "chain of substitutions" and signifiers found in *Beyond the Pleasure Principle* (960). Or again, Sophie lives on, transformed in the pages of Freud's text *as the text itself*—textually inscribed, although not materially described as such. As Freud himself put it: "*la séance continue*" (in Schur 1972: 330). This textual reading is partly supported by a letter of condolence Freud wrote to Ludwig Binswanger on April 12, 1929. There Freud admits that they "will never find a substitute" for their dearly departed: "No matter what may fill the gap, even if it be filled completely, it nevertheless remains something else. And actually this is how it should be. It is the only way to perpetuate that love which we do not want to relinquish" (Freud 1960: 386).

Another plausible biographical explanation for the appearance in Freud's work of the death drive can be found in Paul Roazen's controversial book of 1969, *Brother Animal*. Roazen tells the now well-known story of Victor Tausk's complicated relationship with Freud and his eventual suicide on July 3, 1919.[10] The relationship between Tausk and Freud is fascinating, in large part because the dangers of transference fit so well with the themes of doubling and death in psychoanalysis. According to Roazen, Freud was often annoyed by Tausk's ability to complete ideas only partially formed by himself. With his gifted intellect, combined with an equally strong emotional tie to Freud, Tausk impeded Freud's creative process. As a *Doppelgänger* lurking in the shadows, Tausk seemed able to read Freud's thoughts and act upon them before Freud, always a plodder, had a chance to act himself. In a way, Tausk enacted the uncanny truth of telepathy, what Freud would later call "thought transference." Roazen thus writes:

> Freud had been intrigued by the psychology of death for some time, as had a whole tradition within German literature. But his explicit postulation of an instinct of primitive destructiveness came simultaneously with Tausk's suicide.... Could Tausk have been acting out Freud's newest, or just barely burgeoning, idea? Or perhaps the notion of a death instinct represented another way for Freud to deny any responsibility for Tausk's suicide. (1969: 143)

Roazen has a point. While Freud was able to deny the role that Freund's and especially Sophie's deaths might have played in his hypothesis of a death drive—since large parts of *BPP* were indeed written before they died—he certainly could not deny the possible relevance of Tausk's suicide, which occurred in the summer of 1919. In fact, in a letter of August 1, 1919, to Lou Andreas-Salomé, Freud discusses Tausk's suicide only to conclude with a remark about his new ideas about death: "For my old age I have chosen the theme of death; I have stumbled on a remarkable notion based on my theory of the instincts, and now I must read all kinds of things relevant to it, e.g., Schopenhauer, for the first time" (Freud and Andreas-Salomé 1966: 99). Tausk's last act would have been the most *unheimlich* of all if, as Roazen suggests, he anticipated Freud's theory through an identification to the point of death—that is, by anticipating and becoming the very proof for which Freud was looking. If so, by killing himself Tausk gave himself up to the still unformed theory of the death drive, thus once again beating Freud to the punch.

Yet Freud took special care to exclude Tausk from *BPP*, thus rejecting the gift, the sacrifice, of his follower's life. For according to Freud, any force that negates the path that biology is determined to follow—including even those forces that superficially appear to do the work of the death drive—is really a force of *sociality*. According to what he always admits is an "extreme view," Eros operates "to assure that the organism shall follow its own path to death." By this Freud means that it will follow a path that is "immanent in the organism itself" (1920a: 39). Or again: "The organism wishes to die only in its own fashion." "Hence arises the paradoxical situation," Freud claims, "that the living organism struggles most energetically against events (dangers, in fact) which might help it to attain its life's aim rapidly—by a kind of short-circuit." Suicide, in other words, turns out to be an unnatural and inauthentic act that defeats the circuitous path that each life is destined to follow. Suicide is not an end approved in advance by the life history stored up ontogenetically and slated for a particular and idiosyncratic discharge; suicide only interrupts a preordained sequence of events given, as it were, in advance. Quite simply, the choice of suicide remains a nasty piece of sociality, which is what Freud means when he discusses sadism and masochism in his late work: one wishes another dead (sadism), but kills one's self instead (masochism).

It is a peculiar and rather morbid fact that suicides punctuate the history of psychoanalysis. These tragedies are worth recalling. In addition to Tausk, the following early figures in the movement took their own lives: Edward Bibring, Paul Federn, Johann Honegger, Max Kahane, Karl Landauer, Monroe Meyer, Sophie Morgenstern, Martin Peck, Tatiana Rosenthal, Karl Schrötter, Herbert Silberer, Eugenia Sokolnicka, Karin Stephen, and Wilhelm Stekel (Roazen 1992: 243; Sulloway 1979: 482). Freud himself contemplated suicide when he suspected he had cancer of the jaw, and made preparations with his physician (at that time, Felix Deutsch) to end his life if necessary: "For what I intend to do, I need a doctor. If you take it for cancer, I must find a way to disappear from this world with decency" (in Roazen

1975: 492). It was probably for this reason that Deutsch, who had indeed confirmed Freud's cancer in 1923, kept the bad news from Freud for some time. As it happened, though, Freud faced his personal tragedy with considerable stoicism. One of his admiring biographers, the historian Giovanni Costigan, has even woven this courage into the fabric of *BPP*. "It is curious," Costigan claims, "that Freud apparently failed to recognize that his tenacious clinging to life was a prime illustration of the basic theory in *Beyond the Pleasure Principle*: the determination of the organism to die in its own way at the duly appointed hour, without permitting the interference of external agencies such as disease or accident" (1965: 230).

While the topic of suicide appears in *BPP*, it has received scant attention in the literature. One of the few exceptions is Hans Blumenberg, who explores the specific relevance of Freud's passing objection to suicide found in the essay and, in turn, substantiates Roazen's assertion. Blumenberg argues that the postulate of a "conversion of instinct" is a rationalization that gave Freud some much needed emotional distance from Tausk's suicide: according to Freud's view, Blumenberg writes, "one who kills himself, kills himself instead of another, at whom his death wish was directed" (1985: 95). From the analytic perspective, that is, Tausk primarily wanted to kill Freud, and turned his aggression inward only secondarily. As Sachs says of Freud, "Suicide meant to him . . . the shirking of a task, an attempt to escape in the midst of action" (1945: 147).[11] From this somewhat convenient and unsympathetic perspective, Freud had no need to feel guilty about the murderous Tausk, whom he had rejected as a prospective patient just months before. "It really seems," Freud writes in *The New Introductory Lectures* of 1933, "as though it is necessary for us to destroy some other thing or person in order not to destroy ourselves, in order to guard against the impulse to self-destruction. A sad disclosure indeed for the moralist!" (1933a: 105). As always, Freud turned the tables with an interpretive reversal of the most likely—dare I say, the most commonsensical?—order of things.

Freud's contempt for, and insensitivity to, such human suffering was sometimes shocking, as Roazen amply demonstrates in *Brother Animal*. To Lou Andreas-Salomé, who was once Tausk's lover, Freud poured his venom: "I do not really miss him [Tausk]; I had long taken him to be useless, indeed a threat to the future" (in Roazen 1969: 140). Elsewhere Freud writes, "Despite appreciation of his talent, [I have] no real sympathy in me" (Freud and Ferenczi 1996: 363). We find a pattern here. Sachs recounts a time when he observed Freud as "the news came that someone with whom he had been on friendly terms for years had committed suicide. I found him strangely unmoved by such a tragic event" (1945: 147). Clearly Freud could be callous, if not cold-hearted. According to Sandor Rado, who was with Freud when the news of Karl Abraham's death came, "Freud's mourning was over after five minutes" (in Roazen and Swerdloff 1995: 90).

In any case, Blumenberg seems to support Roazen's contention that Freud's theoretical formulation of a death drive was really a way of denying responsibility for Tausk's suicide. He writes: "Of course the death instinct had its own logical force in the development and completion of Freud's total myth; but the point in time, so close to a catastrophe [Tausk's suicide] in which Freud was involved in so many ways, may also have suited his need for consolation, a need that the new dualism of the system of instincts could satisfy" (1985: 95). For Blumenberg, then, the "myth" of psychoanalysis "becomes helpful to the survivor, as a means of exempting himself from traumatic impact." Even more tantalizing is his suggestion that "the success of Freud's myths is the result of, among other things, the fact that they are the most complete guidelines to the formulation of excuses that have been offered since Origen."

The death drive became for Freud a repository into which he could dump everything that didn't fit well in the categories of sexuality or libido. It was, in effect, a "rhetorical strategy," whereby blame and responsibility could be assigned always elsewhere (Kerr 1993: 500). At the same time, cut off from any referent save itself, the death drive became increasingly less autobiographical *or* biological; in short, it became efficient and silent, sublime and ridiculous.[12] It was, in short, a principle without example (see Deleuze and Guattari 1972: 332).

Take, for instance, the clinical viability of the death-drive theory, the most scandalous instance being that of the "negative therapeutic reaction." According to this bit of remarkable double-think, a patient (or rather, a part of the patient's ego) may be under the impress of an overly severe superego— the purveyor of the death drive—and thus be singularly responsible for the failure of the therapy. "People in whom this unconscious sense of guilt is excessively strong betray themselves in analytic treatment by the negative therapeutic reaction which is so disagreeable from the prognostic point of view" (1933a: 109). In other words, while blame, just like aggression, might theoretically fall on one of two shoulders—analyst's or patient's—it was in practice dispensed to "bad" patients alone as the burden of an emotional and/or intellectual failure, weakness, or symptom. Or worse, it became a part of their biology, a constitutional problem. As Wilhelm Reich quite properly complained, the death drive thus did away with the necessity for considering the *sociological* side of neurotic disorders:

Such formulations have made any further thinking unnecessary. If one was not able to cure, the death instinct could be blamed. When people committed murder, it was in order to go to prison; when children stole, it was to obtain relief from a conscience that troubled them. I marvel today at the energy that was expended at that time on the discussion of such opinions. (1952: 213)

If resignation is at the bottom of the mystery of the new drive, the historian of psychology Daniel Burston adds that it was also "a confession of impotence in the face of the baffling complexities of mental illness" (1991: 199). If the devil is behind the bad conscience of the repentant Christian, Freud obviously finds a new place for him in his psychology: first in the Inferno he called the unconscious, then in the death drive he called demonic, and finally in the superego he called repressive and overly harsh. But in each case, and in any case, the devil was for Freud always on the side of the *patient*. And for one absolutely unimpeachable reason: Freud himself couldn't have been in the wrong.

Commentators do not hesitate to point out a few more biographically based explanations for the dark turn in Freud's thinking. It has been argued, even by Freud, that psychoanalysis owes something to the fact that he was Jewish. "To profess belief in this new theory," Freud writes, "called for a certain degree of readiness to accept a position of solitary opposition—a position with which no one is more familiar than a Jew" (in Bakan 1958: 43). Some scholars, beginning most coherently with David Bakan, have pursued a possible connection between psychoanalysis and Judaism.[13] Harold Bloom, for example, has recently argued that Freud's use of negation, *Verneinung*, which according to some is tied up with his lifelong penchant for dualism, is in fact a reflection of his Jewish background. The death drive is not, Bloom therefore contends (1987: 150–52), simply reducible to Hegelian dialectics, an idea mostly promulgated in the French literature (and among its progeny), but is part and parcel of Freud's participation in a Jewish tradition concerned with forgetting, repression, and memory.

A more simple explanation offered by biographers, usually in passing, is that the death-drive theory is a reflection of Freud's crankiness in old age. As Freud entered old age in the 1920's, he certainly became more pessimistic about people and even about the therapeutic value of psychoanalysis. In a similar vein, some go a bit further and cite the death in 1923 of Freud's favorite grandson, Heinz Rudolf—the younger son of his favorite daughter, Sophie. As Lionel Trilling puts it, "Freud believed that the death of little Heinz marked the end of his affectional life" (1987: 19).[14] In this same year, Freud also learned of his own cancer of the jaw, from which he would eventually die in 1939. Freud's long battle with cancer makes his withdrawal from psychoanalytic functions understandable, since his private life became a time of painful convalescence; in total, Freud suffered from thirty-three painful operations on his mouth, and was forced to wear a prosthesis, which could make talking difficult. Some observers have thus reflected on the possible connection between Freud's sickness and his late theorizations. Rudolf Ekstein, for example, summarizes the situation thus: "Freud's oral cravings, the guilt connected with them, the beginning stages of the fatal illness, his feelings about aging, found their projective expressions in the theory that described the eternal struggle between Thanatos and Eros" (1949: 213).

Of course, it takes a bit of creative manipulation to connect the sad events of 1923 with *Beyond the Pleasure Principle* of 1920—or, more simply, a mistake. As Roazen (1975: xxii; 1995: 129, 139) found during his interviews with the surviving members of Freud's inner and outer circle, many elderly analysts, such as Robert Jokl, would confuse the chronology of events, believing that Freud's death-drive theory was in fact a "compensation" for his cancer. Still, it is possible that there is a connection between Freud's *later* texts and his cancer, or between his pessimism and the death of his grandson Heinz. No one denies that Freud, by the thirties, had turned away from people and embraced a deep pessimism about human nature. For example, in *Civilization and Its Discontents* (1930) Freud concludes that the potential for unrestricted human happiness will always be compromised by our socially repressed sexuality *and* aggressivity. "If civilization," he writes, "imposes such great sacrifices not only on man's sexuality but on his aggressivity, we can understand better why it is hard for him to be happy in that civilization" (1930: 115). Or again, it is the aggressive instincts "that make human communal life difficult and threaten its survival" (1933a: 110). For the old Freud, civilized man is truly placed between the proverbial rock and a hard place.

Despite the apparent illogic of the argument, at least one commentator has managed to make an intelligent case for the idea that Freud's cancer of 1923 was actually inflected in his theorizations of 1920. In *The Duality of Human Existence*, psychologist David Bakan connects Freud's cancer to the postulation of a death drive by means of Freud's work on narcissism (cf. Derrida 1980: 365, 388). Pointing to some of the circumstantial evidence we have already discussed, Bakan suggests that

> there are connections between Freud's notion of the death instinct and the fact that these works were written at a time when one might presume that the processes associated with the development of cancer may have been active in him.

A secondary hypothesis—nay, a suspicion—which the data suggests is that these writings may also have been representative of Freud's efforts to manage and counteract these very same forces, that his writings reflect a certain amount of self-analysis and therapy. (1966: 158; his emphasis)

Bakan claims that Freud really did know in 1920, on some level, that he had cancer, and that *Beyond the Pleasure Principle* is thus an elaborate rationalization or even justification of this fact.

Bakan correctly notes that Freud equated cancer with narcissism during his fairly esoteric discussion of cellular development in chapter six of *BPP*. In a parenthesis added in 1921, Freud writes: "The cells of the malignant neoplasms which destroy the organism should also perhaps be described as narcissistic in this same sense: pathology is prepared to regard their germs as innate and to ascribe embryonic attributes to them" (1920a: 50; see Bakan 1966: 162). Bakan's detective work gets even more intriguing when he refers to the speculations of Freud's friend Georg Groddeck. Groddeck, one of the founders of psychosomatic medicine, ponders in *The Book of the It* the possibility that cancer may be psychologically determined (Bakan 1966: 163). Freud had read and admired this book, and openly referred to Groddeck in *The Ego and the Id* (1923).

There are, then, a few compelling clues with which Bakan weaves his tale. Like the death drive that, according to Freud, functions in silence, cancer does most of its work undetected; and just as the compulsive repetitions of a trauma symptomatically represent the death drive for Freud, cancerous cells multiply, killing the host, as it were, from the inside out. Cancer, in effect, becomes for Bakan the ultimate expression of a silent force that defies the operations of the pleasure principle. At the same time—and, indeed, like so much psychoanalytic interpretation—Bakan makes a coherent case for what must remain a fascinating, but tendentious, piece of speculation. Those wielding Occam's razor will more simply state that Freud may have written *BPP* against the backdrop of cancer's work, not as it silently attacked his own mouth, but as it quite obviously finished off his friend Freund in early 1920.

It may be worth mentioning that Bakan is not completely alone in his suspicion that Freud's dark mood, which apparently expressed itself in the new theory, was related (if unconsciously) to his cancer. Wilhelm Reich explicitly draws a line between Freud's growing resignation in the early 1920's and the development of his cancer. Unlike Giovanni Costigan, who claims that Freud's heroic battle with cancer was evidence of a death drive at war with life, Reich argues that Freud had conceded to the forces of death. In an interview with Kurt Eissler, Reich states that Freud was "full of zest and zeal" in 1919, but "something happened" around 1924: "Now, cancer, in my research ... is a disease following emotional resignation—a bioenergetic shrinking, a giving up of hope.... Now that hooks up with Freud: Why did he develop cancer just at that time? Freud began to resign.... I didn't see it then, and, peculiarly enough, the conflict between us began about that time" (1952: 23).

As interesting as Reich's speculation is, it is surely more reasonable to reverse the causal order and assume that Freud's cancer was the cause of his resignation. In addition, Reich confuses the relevant dates: the supposed cancer-causing conflict between Freud and Reich actually began in 1927, a few years after Freud was diagnosed with cancer. Again, if Freud was unhappy in 1924, it seems more reasonable to assume it was a result of his cancer and not the cause of it. It is interesting, though, that Freud himself (for a time) entertained the possibility that a poor flow o f libidinal energy may promote cancer. Encouraged by Paul Federn and others, he actually undertook on November 17, 1923, an operation on his testicles that was supposed to rejuvenate his energy supply and battle the cancer.[15] "This extraordinary accomplishment," Sharon Romm writes of the Steinach procedure, "was supposed to transpire merely by ligating the vas deferens, the duct which conveys sperm from the testicle to the seminal vesicle" (1983: 73). The supposed connection between this procedure and psychoanalysis was readily acknowledged by some Freudians. Discussing the procedure, Herman Nunberg, for example, claimed that "what Freud had long since disclosed through objective research by psychological methods is now gradually confirmed through biology" (1955: 54; cf. 186). As Roazen surmises, "The idea was to overcome the forces of death by mobilizing the life instinct" (1975: 491). Nowadays the Steinach procedure, otherwise known as a vasectomy (Romm 1983: 77), is performed for less grandiose reasons.

Reich also drew a bead between Freud's unhappy sex life with Martha and the development of his cancer: "There is little doubt that Freud was very much dissatisfied genitally. Both his resignation and his cancer are evidence [sic] of that" (1952: 33). As we will see a bit later, Reich argues that genital satisfaction is a crucial component of mental health. Reich even rationalized the location of Freud's cancer in his mouth to his character being " 'bitingly' polite" (34). It is, of course, probably true that chomping down on a cigar year after year may contribute to mouth cancer. But whether Freud's *character* helped cause the sickness to grow in that particular location is clearly another matter altogether.[16] If, finally, there is anything growing out of control in this scenario, it is surely the cancerous absurdity that can sometimes claim interpretation.

It should be no surprise to learn that the historico-biographical explanation of *BPP* is often followed by a psychological one. Psychoanalytic case studies are, after all, histories of psychological findings. It is in this mode that Freud's personal physician from 1928 to 1939, Max Schur, contends that *BPP* "had multiple determinants in [Freud's] inner life" (Schur 1972: 321).

It is well known that Freud suffered from what he himself called *Todesangst*, an anxiety about death and dying, that went beyond the anxieties we might chalk up to hard times. As it happens, the specter of death played a long and sometimes subtle role in the history of analysis. Freud's seminal book on dreams—the sometime (depending upon who you consult) harbinger of psychoanalysis—was attempted as a response to his father's death in 1896. In that year Freud began collecting antiquities (eventually of Greek, Roman, Egyptian, Etruscan, and Far Eastern varieties), an objectification of his long interest in archaeology and ancient or "dead" cultures. Not incidentally, a large portion of these objects of art were of funerary origin. As Lynn Gamwell suggests: "To consider that [Freud] began his collection in some sense as a reaction to his father's death seems unavoidable; not only the timing but also the content of Freud's early collecting suggests its strong connection with the loss of his father" (1989: 23, 26). Similarly, Jones reminds us that "the theme of death, the dread of it and the wish for it, had always been a continual preoccupation of Freud's mind as far back as we know anything about it" (1957: 42).

After his father's death, Freud seems to have channeled this dread into an anxiety about the future of psychoanalysis. To French analyst (and patient) Maryse Choisy, Freud once remarked, "What will they do with my theory after my death? Will it still resemble my basic thoughts?" (in Choisy 1963: 5). His concern is understandable. For having put his entire existence into psychoanalysis, its future became synonymous with his own; it was his best chance for immortality. It is well known, in addition, that Freud's fear of death was reinforced by his superstitious belief in dark portents, especially of the numerological sort. Freud combined a lifelong interest in Fliess's characteristically romantic theory of human periodicity with his own cabalistic belief in the magic of numbers to prophesy his own death at various dates throughout his life. According to this "necrological bookkeeping" (Pontalis 1981a: 186), Freud at different times in his life feared the numbers forty-one, forty-two, fifty-one, sixty-one, sixty-two, and eighty-one and one-half, and thought he would die at various dates in his life—in 1918, for example, when he was aged sixty-two (cf. Schur 1972: 159). But, like every Chicken Little, he was always able to prophesize the next date not long after the last one expired. Freud was also attracted by the number seven, and many of his works have this many chapters—including *BPP* (see Derrida 1980: 329–30; Mahony 1987: 49–50). It is likely, then, that Fliess's views about periodicity were absorbed into Freud's discourse on repetition in *BPP* (Mannoni 1968: 38).

Predictably, then, many have reasoned that Freud's dealings with death border on the obsessive. As Freud once said to Smiley Blanton, "I think about the possibility of death every day" (in Blanton 1971: 48, 111). Apparently Freud "had the disconcerting"—some will say laughable—"habit of parting with the words 'Goodbye; you may never see me again' " (in Jones 1957: 279). Given the details of this potentially rich "case history," it is thus no wonder that some biographer-analysts propound what I would call a "neurotic" reading of *Beyond the Pleasure Principle* to supplement or supersede the "biographical." Actually, the two readings are almost always combined, sometimes to the point of pathography or unwitting parody. Jones, for example, argues that Freud's style of exposition in *BPP* is itself grounds for considering "some personal and profound source" at work behind the scenes (1957: 266). About Freud's dualism Jones speculates that "it must have sprung from some depths in Freud's mentality, from some offshoot of his Oedipus complex, perhaps the opposition between the masculine and the feminine side of his nature" (267).

A more involved example relevant to the supposed neurotic content of *BPP* concerns two episodes, in 1909 and 1912, in which Freud fainted in Jung's presence. In the first, Freud fainted after becoming annoyed by Jung's incessant discussion of corpses and mummification. "Afterwards," Jung states, "[Freud] said to me that he was convinced that all this chatter about corpses meant I had death-wishes towards him" (Jung 1961: 156). In the second episode, which occurred at a psychoanalytic gathering (or "congress") in Munich, Freud fainted when Jung defended the practice among Egyptian pharaohs of replacing their father's name, etched on public monuments, with their own (157). Still smarting from the news that Jung and another Swiss analyst, Franz Rilkin, had failed to properly acknowledge his work in their recent publications, Freud became vexed over Jung's apparent lack of respect for his priority as the true father of psychoanalysis. Freud in effect feared that Jung was ready, willing, and able to assume the father's place; that he was an uncanny double awaiting the father's death—and the sooner the better. After Freud awoke from his fainting spell, having been carried to a couch in a nearby lounge by the robust Jung, he lamented aloud: "How sweet it must be to die" (in Jones 1953: 317). According to Maurice Natenberg's lively psychobiography, this "farcical episode" seems to indicate that Freud was "at bottom only a nervously distraught personality" (1955: 177). It is certainly true that Freud would have encountered similar "cases" of melodrama in his own therapeutic practice, and would have known how to play the part of hysterical lover. Jones, too, thought that Freud's remark about the sweetness of death was strange, "another indication that the idea of dying had some esoteric meaning for him" (1953: 317).

Freud himself, always quick to self-analysis or, what was often the same thing, self-exculpation, connects the 1912 fainting episode to "some [unexamined] piece of unruly homosexual feeling" in his mental life (Freud and Jones 1993: 182). Interestingly enough, Freud mentions that his reaction to Jung was a repetition of a similar episode he had experienced in Fliess's presence ten years earlier—near the end of their friendship, and in the very same room in Munich. At that time, Freud was apparently compelled on more than one occasion to retreat from the table where he sat with Fliess—lest he faint. Once again, the repetition of these symptoms seems to indicate the sort of neurotic compulsion Freud described in *BPP* as the most decisive reason for adopting the notion of a death drive.

Such examples are the kind of thing that fuels Max Schur's *Freud: Living and Dying*, proving that historians of any stripe will use or not use analysis, whichever suits their own ends. In Schur's case, the subjective interpretation is pursued as a strategy to minimize the theoretical importance of *BPP* in the grand scheme of things truly psychoanalytic. With his hands on previously restricted materials, Schur draws a portrait of Freud's depression and shaky theory-building. Beginning with the circularity of Freud's reasoning—a logic according to which the death drive and its expressions (such as repetition compulsion) prove nothing but each other (1972: 323, 325)—Schur ends by preserving the classical view of the pleasure principle, namely, a view unencumbered by the wild speculations of *BPP*. "Could it be," Schur thus concludes, "that uncovering a 'death instinct' permitted Freud literally to *live* with the reality of death" that he confronted in 1920 (332)? If so, *BPP* has value not as a scientific work, Schur assures the reader, but as an artistic one (342). In other words, Schur uses psychoanalysis to save psychoanalysis from itself, that is, from a wild, unstable, and neurotic Freud. To his considerable credit, though, Schur is uniquely attuned to the dangers that Freud's metapsychology does present to psychoanalysis—dangers that I will outline in detail in Chapter 3.

While the stage for *BPP* was set by Freud's earlier forays into metapsychology—in the *Project for a Scientific Psychology* (1895), in chapter 7 of *The Interpretation of Dreams* (1900), in the metapsychological papers of 1915, and in "The 'Uncanny,'" refurbished in 1918–19—analytic and nonanalytic detectives alike cannot be blamed for exploring, and then exploiting, the infinitely rich "neurotic" side of Freud's unusual theorizations in *BPP*. It really is too tempting, if not entirely appropriate given the role of subjectivity in psychoanalysis, to have a try at interpretation.

Yet such understandable temptation can easily become delirium (assuming it isn't already). My favorite example of a wildly delirious interpretive venture that touches on *BPP* is found in Paul Scagnelli's *Deadly Dr. Freud* (1994). A clinical psychologist by training, Scagnelli has reviewed much of the secondary literature on psychoanalysis to weave a coherent but outlandish tale about Freud. Basically Scagnelli supplements the "neurotic *Beyond*" with its psychotic reflection, arguing that Freud arranged to have his half-brother Emmanuel killed in 1914, in part because he had identified so fully with the assassination of Franz Ferdinand in 1913 (424–32). Emmanuel did die from falling off a train. Similarly, Scagnelli argues that Freud identified with the assassin of Austrian Prime Minister Stürgh in 1917, Friedrich Adler—a former resident of Freud's home at Berggasse 19 and the son of socialist leader Victor Adler. In March 1919, the month Freud began writing *BPP*, Freud arranged (Scagnelli argues) for the kidnapping and murder of Emmanuel's son, John. John did disappear, never to be seen again. For Scagnelli, then, the new death-drive theory signals a "bizarre switch which sometimes accompanies a 'snapped mind,' i.e., as a reflection of pathological mental processes" (426). Here is his thesis, in a nutshell: "Freud's creation of the death instinct theory was provoked by deranged ideation connected with his ancient death wishes towards his greatest rival in life, his nephew John—and as a reaction to arranging for John's disappearance and murder in the early months of 1919" (429).

What is so disturbing about this tale is not just the tale itself, but the way in which Scagnelli weaves the well-known "facts" into this paranoid tapestry. To be more precise, what is disturbing is the uncanny resemblance this tale has to other, apparently legitimate, histories of the analytic movement. In this way Scagnelli represents in the extreme the same problem that we find elsewhere in the history of psychoanalysis: where do we draw a line between fact and fantasy? And just as important, *when* do we draw that line? Invariably, where and when the line is drawn is less a function of the facts than of partisan interests.[17]

The line between reasonable and absurd, true and false, interpretation goes to the heart of the history of psychoanalysis, including the history of the reception of Freud's theories. It is a problem for all historiography, but it is a special epistemological problem for Freud—as Lacan was among the first to really confront (see Bougnoux 1997). After all, the "truth" of fantasy, of the individual subject, is not likely to be the truth itself—assuming for the moment that such a thing exists—even though Freud himself failed to abandon a connection between analysis and the recovery of actual memories. Similarly, when biographers and historians try to arrange the theory to fit the life, or vice versa, things get very tricky indeed: it is hard to know where the facts end and where unsubstantiated fantasy begins. The situation gets even more complicated when the historian is him or herself an analyst, or when the historian wittingly or not adopts an analytic perspective of the facts. *Given the rules of psychoanalysis*, the history of psychoanalysis is an abyss from which there is no recourse, save maybe one: repeat the stories, yes, but never believe a word of anything.

This may be as good a place as any to draw a line in the sand of poor and, say, less poor interpretation. I want to turn now to Freud's biologism, which at first glance will probably seem a more secure foundation for unpacking the essential truths of *Beyond the Pleasure Principle*. One thing at least is certain: the intellectualism of the debate around biology is a notch or two above that normally associated with what I have for shorthand called the "biographical *Beyond*."

Biological 'Beyond's

> Psycho-analysis, like every psychology, in its attempt to dig to the depths must strike somewhere on the rock of the organic.
> —Sandor Ferenczi, "The Problem of Acceptance of Unpleasant Ideas—Advances in Knowledge of the Sense of Reality"[18]

Freud's recourse to biological speculation is among the most striking and potentially dumbfounding features of his discussion of the death drive in *Beyond the Pleasure Principle*. Among other things, Freud acknowledges experimental work on cellular reproduction and decay, openly professes his attraction to the mechanistic view of mental functioning, and invokes the old theories of recapitulation and Lamarckian inheritance. Freud clearly thought of his own speculations on the death drive as a fresh stimulus for the field of biology, about which he was unusually optimistic. "Biology," he says at one point, "is truly a land of unlimited possibilities. We may expect it to give us the most surprising information and we cannot guess what answers it will return in a few dozen years to the questions we have put to it" (1920a: 60). Or, as Freud admits only one year before his death,

> we may be struck by the fact that we have so often been obliged to venture beyond the frontiers of the science of psychology. The phenomena with which we are dealing do not belong to psychology alone; they have an organic and

biological side as well, and accordingly . . . we have also made some important biological discoveries and have not been able to avoid framing new biological hypotheses. (1940: 195)

Incredibly, and despite Freud's professed lifelong interest, it was not until Frank Sulloway's work appeared that the biological foundation of psychoanalysis received any sustained attention in the literature. In his comprehensive *Freud, Biologist of the Mind: Beyond the Psychoanalytic Legend*, Sulloway makes short shrift of the biographical *Beyond* outlined above, effectively consigning it to the myth-making tendencies of biographers—partisan or otherwise. For Sulloway, a historian of science, the subjective interpretation of Freud's work only perpetuates in disguised form the psychoanalytic attitude and, more importantly, contributes to misinformation about Freud's essential biologism. Sulloway is certainly right to find the biographical literature irredeemably contaminated and thus compromised by a myth-making tendency among exponents of psychoanalysis, who often whitewash whatever doesn't fit their particular view of history—a tendency that is quite evident when it comes to Freud's biological speculations in *BPP*. It is also true, more simply, that *BPP* is a far more intellectually interesting and coherent work from the perspective of biology.

Against the biographical reduction of *BPP*, Sulloway argues that logic and reason "supply the real key to [the appearance of] his death-instinct theory" (1979: 395). With this in mind Sulloway makes a good case that *BPP* was not written in a theoretical vacuum but as a long overdue response to three problems or "inconsistencies" that confound the metapsychology of Freud's middle period (see ibid.: 395–99). According to this important perspective, Freud devised his new dualism to rectify, first of all, the nagging suspicion that his theory of narcissism (ca. 1911–14) had undone much of the difference between self-preservative (ego) instincts and sexual (libidinal or object) instincts. For with narcissism both self-love and self-preservation work together rather than against each other. By 1915 Freud recognized this "problem" and tried to resolve it with a new distinction between love and hate. Yet until he subsumed self-preservation and sexuality under the banner of Eros, against which he posited a death drive, all instinct seemed like a variation on the theme of libidinal energy. "If the self-preservative instincts too are of a libidinal nature," Freud writes, "are there perhaps no other instincts whatever but the libidinal ones? At all events there are none other visible" (1920a: 52). Freud's subsequent postulation of a psyche structured by a universal and eternal battle between noisy life and silent death thus reestablished the sort of dualistic vision he always held as a conviction, intuition or, less charitably, as a prejudice.

The second problem that Freud resolved with *BPP* centers upon the fundamental role of repetition in psychoanalysis. Repetition plays an essential role in Freud's basic theory. According to the standard interpretation, dreams, symptoms, neuroses, and transference neuroses are meaningful because they repeat in the present fragments of unresolved conflict from the repressed past. To repeat something in the present, to "act it out," is understood by Freud as a prelude to *remembering* something from the past: emotion, in other words, can precede conscious understanding. Until 1920 Freud argued that such repetition is governed by the pleasure principle, namely, by our innate urge to experience the pleasurable discharge of energy through cathartic acts. Freud is famous, in this regard, for his claim that dreams are always the pleasurable fulfillment of our repressed (and therefore unconscious) wishes. Following the usual reversals of psychoanalytic interpretation, Freud argued that even "bad" dreams are a kind of self-inflicted punishment that prove his essential point: confronted by the illicit pleasures of a dream, the dreamer reacts with guilt and turns pleasure into unpleasure, clear and distinct dream imagery into distorted and censored jumbles. As he would later argue, socially inspired self-punishment (conscience, the superego) gets in the way of our natural urge for instant and unmediated gratification.

By 1920 Freud needed to account for the disturbing fact that some experiences—in apparent disregard for his theory of pleasure—appear to be governed by a "compulsion to repeat" unpleasant or traumatic experiences from the past. That is, certain experiences seemed governed by a repetition that did not *discharge* energy, but *stored it up* within the psychic apparatus; the experiences thus went beyond the pleasure principle. Freud, careful to preserve psychoanalysis from his extreme metapsychological speculations, stresses that this compulsion is less in *contradiction* to the rule of the pleasure principle, than it is older and also *independent* of that rule. Such dreams, Freud states, "afford us a view of the mental apparatus which, though it does not contradict the pleasure principle, is nevertheless independent of it and seems to be more primitive than the purpose of gaining pleasure and avoiding unpleasure" (1920a: 32, 35). While he surely could have, Freud did not try to dispatch with (or wish away) phenomena that spoiled his theory—as he did with the example of bad dreams.

Probably the first tangible evidence of Freud's change of heart about a beyond of the pleasure principle came in September 1915, when he observed the play of his grandson Ernst (see Jones 1957: 267). Freud thought that little Ernst's game with a cotton spool was psychoanalytically meaningful, that is, symptomatic, and thus amenable to interpretation. A major part of Ernst's game consisted of repeatedly tossing the spool away (over a bed) and pulling it back again. Freud first of all interpreted this activity as a game of mastery, one in which the boy reenacted the disturbing absence/presence of his mother Sophie. To this he added the supposition that the noises Ernst made while playing the game were also meaningful: in his native German Ernst said something like *fort* (gone) when he threw the spool away, and *da* (here) when he pulled it back. Cast as a meaningful game of repetition, Freud ultimately postulated a "daemonic" force at work which was not entirely amenable to the governing rule of pleasure as understood by psychoanalysis. As such, the drive or impulse for mastery, *Bemächtigungstrieb*, gave way to the more original impulse for destruction. A few years later this scenario appeared in *Beyond the Pleasure Principle*, and the mantra *fort/da* has ever since become a classic reference point for child therapists looking for an empirical basis for their own speculations, and for theorists (especially from France) impressed by Freud's interpretive prowess.

A more powerful instance of an "exception" to the usual rule of pleasurable discharge came with the "traumatic neuroses," such as those produced by the great American train wrecks of the nineteenth century, but also those cases of "war trauma" (or shell shock) found among soldiers in the First World War. As psychologist Raymond Fancher suggests, post-traumatic dreams associated with war are often "caused by 'close calls' [what Freud called "surprise"] rather than situations resulting in actual physical injury. The death or injury of a close comrade, while the patient himself was miraculously spared, was a frequent precipitating trauma in World War I" (1973: 181). Those with a physical injury are apparently less disposed to experience the retrospective trauma of shell shock; for, in Freud's mechanistic language, the shock was discharged physically, across the musculature. Given the international forum provided by the war, Freud was motivated to account theoretically—that is, psychoanalytically—for the fact of war trauma. Indeed, the war was a convenient forum for psychiatric research and, as Fancher suggests, war trauma was "a special embarrassment" for Freud's theories. As a result, Freud postulated a new, unforeseen, masochistic force—one independent of, and yet opposed to, libido—that seemed to circumvent or go beyond the pleasure principle: the death drive.

Finally, Sulloway notes a third (internal, logical) reason for Freud's *BPP*. Although Freud had already accounted for the patient's regression to an earlier object (for example, a breast), he had trouble explaining "regression-in-aim" (for example, to the "oral phase" of psychosexual development). Without a primary regressive force, something like a purely negative death drive, Freud could not explain how one regressed backward toward neurosis. In this last respect Freud may have been protecting his Oedipal story, based as it is on the primal father of his anthropological fantasies, against the threat of Jung's matricentric view. Jung had challenged Freud with his own focus on pre-Oedipal dynamics, which rested on a mother-child relation rather than on a father-child one. The threat Jung posed to Freud's tragic version of psychoanalysis had become especially apparent when it was in part repeated in Ferenczi's and Rank's deviations of the twenties—according to which the mother-child bond was a major concern. Freud, in other words, had good reason for identifying the present-day mechanism that rationalized such a "regression-in-aim," and was not very interested in the idea that it was connected with the question of the mother. Or more exactly yet, for Freud the child's "most primitive object-choice" was always, and without exception, the father (Freud 1918: 27).

FREUDIAN METASCENE

> All physical and physiological phenomena require a *meta-physical* (i.e., psychological) explanation and all psychological phenomena a meta-psychological (i.e., physical) one.
> —Sandor Ferenczi,
> *Thalassa: A Theory of Genitality*[19]

Beyond the Pleasure Principle is without question a metabiological treatise based on turn-of-the-century assumptions about energy and discharge, assumptions Freud first put to work in the psycho-physicalistic theory of mental functioning with which he dabbled during the 1890's. More exactly, the radical new death-drive theory recalled the outdated biologism of Freud's early, abandoned, and posthumously published *Project for a Scientific Psychology* (1895). At the time of the *Project* Freud sought refuge in the materialism of his former teachers—not, as some wistfully contend, as a *retreat* from the wild speculation that surfaced during his intense correspondence with Wilhelm Fliess, but as its culmination. The *Project* was written during a particularly turbulent time in Freud's life. Freud wrote to Fliess about his ideas for a scientific psychology, spoke to him in person during a "congress" in late 1895, and began composing the first chapter of his work on the train ride home from a visit with Fliess in Berlin. But while Fliess encouraged Freud, the direction of his thought may also owe something to Freud's unsettled, perhaps even altered, state of mind. According to historian of medicine E. M. Thornton, Freud's experimentation with cocaine is reflected in his impressive productivity during the 1890's, and in the near cosmological proportions of the *Project* (1983: 229–30).

It is certainly true that Freud's scientific psychology is a metapsychological and metaphysical concoction of rather baroque proportions. As historian Richard Webster puts it, "Although Freud described his model of mind in remorselessly scientific language, it remained no less speculative in its nature than any of his other metapsychological structures" (1995: 173). Like his early work on aphasia, Freud tried to create in the *Project*—what he privately called his "Psychology for Neurologists" (Freud and Fliess 1985: 127)—a "metapsychological" synthesis of two apparently disparate fields, that of neurology and psychology, even as he borrowed heavily from physics and cerebral physiology. The word "metapsychology" first appears in a letter of 1896 to Fliess; it is not until *The Psychopathology of Everyday Life* in 1901 that Freud formally committed the word to print, and not until 1915 that the word became an unavoidable part of psychoanalytic conceptualization.

During his metapsychological work of 1915 Freud wrote twelve essays, each intended as one part of a large book on metapsychology, but destroyed the last seven;[20] fortunately, one essay was recently discovered by Ilse Grubrich-Simitis among the papers of Sandor Ferenczi. By "metapsychology" Freud meant the three interrelated aspects of analytic theory: the psychic energy of the "dynamic" aspect, the conscious/unconscious distinction of the "topographical" aspect, and the quantitative side of psychic energy of the "economic" aspect. By and large these are dry, obtuse, and uninspiring works. As Freud ironically admits in a letter of November 9, 1915, "All these works suffer from the lack of good cheer in which I wrote them and from their function as a kind of sedative" (Freud and Andreas-Salomé 1966: 35). Although Freud did produce the twelve essays, by 1919 he still considered the metapsychology unwritten. He qualified in a letter to Lou Andreas-Salomé that "if I still have ten years to live and remain capable of work in this period ... then I promise to make further contributions to it. A first example of this will be found in an essay of mine entitled *Beyond the Pleasure Principle*" (95). Unlike his first sustained attempt at a general theory of psychoanalysis, Freud appears to have enjoyed writing *BPP*: "I am amusing myself greatly with a work, *Beyond the Pleasure Principle*," Freud confessed to Ferenczi in March 1919 (Freud and Ferenczi 1996: 340). His cheerful attitude was no doubt influenced by what he considered a breakthrough in his thinking. As noted, while his metapsychological efforts of 1915 are tied up with his early distinction between sexual and ego instincts, the later metapsychology of *BPP* is based solely on the new dualism of life and death drives.

Given the evolution of analytic doctrine and practice, Freud's late, almost illicit, interest in metapsychology has been a challenge for intellectual historians. Freud's early hope that neurology might provide grounds for mapping a scientific psychology was a dismal failure. His lingering interest in this psycho-physicalist work has thus been hard to reconcile with the apparent *psychological* emphasis of psychoanalysis. After all, according to the official history of psychoanalysis, it is not neurology but psychology that defines Freud's unique contribution to medicine and psychotherapy. But obviously the contradiction is resolved once it is realized that Freud never abandoned his old scientific aspirations at all. As J. C. Flugel rightly suggests, although Freud's late formulations may be phrased in the language of psychology, he never had "in mind any clear-cut distinction between the psychological, physiological and biological spheres as we departmentalise them for the purpose of current scientific disciplines" (1955: 102). For this reason it is not wise to differentiate too dogmatically the apparent inside of psychoanalysis from its heretical outside—a tendency that undermines even the most sophisticated of analyses (see Laplanche 1970: 110).

Among partisan historians the biologically derived ideas of *BPP* are recycled from an age better forgotten or, at least, minimized. As Sulloway (1979) argues, many analytic historians have done their best to downplay the fact that Freud's turn toward psychology was grounded upon his early studies in biology and neurology. To take a rather harmless example, French analyst-historian Octave Mannoni contends that Freud's career in psychology was "established on a play on words" (1968: 14). While Mannoni is not wrong exactly, his clever remark suffers from an ahistorical bias. Based on nineteenth-century notions of mental illness, a neurologist like Freud was *expected* to have some stake in the study of "nervous affliction." Neurologists were interested in nervous disorders such as hysteria and neurasthenia[21] because they were, quite simply, considered to be somatic in origin. As historian of medicine Edward Shorter states, "*Nervous* had meant a physical affliction of the nerves in the brain and spinal cord. Later this term would also mean 'of emotional origin' " (1985: 142). The origin of modern psychotherapy is quite clearly predicated upon this dubious slippage of registers. Fin-de-siècle neurology was part of a "century-long deception" by patients and neurologists to locate mental illness in the body, literally in the "nerves"; a deception inspired by the narrow psychiatric view of madness of the time, and by the much-feared psychiatric institute (Shorter 1996). Historically speaking, then, Freud's choice of career cannot be explained away by a "play on words," which is a slick way around the bedrock of psychobiology that grounds the earliest efforts of psychotherapy at the turn of the last century.

Although the appearance of the abridged *Project for a Scientific Psychology* in 1950 forced the analytic community to confront the old (some would say repressed) biology, apologists for the psychological Freud still emphasize that Freud had in any case dropped the unfinished *Project*, albeit after a time of great elation; the work was an aberration that Freud himself regretted and he promptly destroyed the manuscript. Freud's biological views were, Jones thus contends, "incidental to his work rather than deliberate" (1957: 314). The original *Project* notebooks were only saved for posterity because Freud had sent copies to Fliess, which were eventually procured and protected (from Freud, among others) in the 1930's by Marie Bonaparte.

If it is relatively easy to dismiss the *Project* as an aberration in the overall development of psychoanalysis, or more simply yet as prepsychoanalytic, it is much more difficult to dismiss *Beyond the Pleasure Principle*. As a public endorsement of some old metabiological speculations, *BPP* is bound to be an anachronistic embarrassment for most of Freud's followers, a relic of an outmoded scientific paradigm. *BPP* has indeed been experienced by the analytic establishment as a trauma of a poorly discharged biologism, a biologism that haunted psychoanalysis from the beginning (ca. 1897–1900) or, more rigorously, from before the supposed beginning (ca. 1892–97).

Probably the leading idea behind both the *Project for a Scientific Psychology* and *Beyond the Pleasure Principle* is that of the "constancy principle." Already in his remarks collected as "Sketches for the 'Preliminary Communication' of 1893,"[22] in which Freud reiterated his theory of repression, we find the following formulation: "*The nervous system endeavours to keep constant something in its functional relations that we may describe as the 'sum of excitation.' It puts this precondition of health into effect by disposing associatively of every sensible accretion of excitation* [Erregungszuwachs] *or by discharging it by appropriate motor reaction*" (1892: 153–54; his emphasis). This idea received its first public endorsement in the "Preliminary Communication" of 1893, which was collected in *Studies on Hysteria* (1895), written by Breuer and Freud. In their editors' introduction, James and Alix Strachey correctly surmise that "the essential theoretical position underlying the *Studies* is that the clinical necessity for abreacting [i.e., reenacting and discharging] affects and the pathogenic results of its becoming strangulated are explained by the much more general tendency (expressed in the principle of constancy) to keep the quantity of excitation constant" (in Freud 1895b: xx). Abreaction is a notion that Breuer first identified in his treatment of Bertha Pappenheim, which is discussed in *Studies on Hysteria*—the ur-case of psychoanalysis, famously known as "Anna O."

The theory of constancy is intimately tied to Freud's somewhat bizarre view of pleasure and unpleasure. Always conceived from an "economic" perspective, the constancy principle states that quantifiable energy (a sort of endogenous electricity[23]) must be "bound" together and discharged in a manner amenable to the pleasure principle; amenable, that is, to the organism's unending search for pleasurable release and general stability. Freud states very clearly in *Beyond the Pleasure Principle* that the constancy principle "is only another way of stating the pleasure principle" (1920a: 9). "The pleasure principle," he repeats, "follows from the principle of constancy: actually the latter principle was inferred from the facts which forced us to adopt the pleasure principle" (9). Although a few years later he would qualify this equation between the principles of constancy and pleasure-unpleasure (1924b: 159–60), constancy and pleasure remain intimately connected in his early and late work. At no point did Freud deny that the satiation of energy (or affect) is what most accurately defines pleasure.

Freud's view of constancy fit well enough into his personal and professional views about sexuality. He more or less thought of pleasurable discharge as the "little death," so often described by poets, that defines orgasmic release during intercourse. In *The Ego and the Id* (1923) he writes:

> The ejection of the sexual substances in the sexual act corresponds in a sense to the separation of soma and germ-plasm [described by August Weissmann]. This accounts for the likeness of the condition that follows complete sexual satisfaction to dying, and for the fact that death coincides with the act of copulation in some of the lower animals. These creatures die in the act of reproduction because, after Eros has been eliminated through the process of satisfaction [i.e., discharge], the death instinct has a free hand for accomplishing its purposes. (1923a: 47)

If "ejection of the sexual substances" is generally cathartic, it follows that there is a connection between poorly discharged energy and the onset of neuroses, or even, as noted above, of some more serious physical illness like cancer. This idea was reflected in Freud's attitude toward contraception, according to which strategies such as coitus interruptus interfere with the free and absolute discharge, the "decathexis," of pent-up energy. As he is reported to have once said, "A condom is a tissue-plate against infection, and an armor-plate against enjoyment" (in Roazen 1995: 26). In addition, and like so many of his contemporaries of the time (see Bonomi 1997), Freud thought that masturbation—that "one major habit" (Freud and Fliess 1985: 287)—could also cause depression and a host of strange, inexplicable ailments. "In typical cases of neurasthenia," Freud reports in a paper on the role of sexuality in the etiology of the neurosis, "a history of regular masturbation or persistent emissions was found" (1906: 272).[24] So, taken to its logical extreme, the ideal of constancy signified for Freud the ultimate pleasure of death, that is, the orgasmic release from self. As he says in *BPP*, the "fact" of constancy in mental functioning "is one of our strongest reasons for believing in the existence of death instincts" (1920a: 56).

In *BPP*, Freud invokes Barbara Low's "Nirvana Principle" to describe the ideal of tranquil stability implied by the principle of constancy. Freud, however, lifted the idea of constancy—or, as some would later say, echoing American physiologist Walter B. Cannon (1932),[25] "homeostasis"—from the controversial "psycho-physicist" and founder of experimental psychology, Gustav Theodor Fechner. It is in turn possible that Fechner derived his "principle of stability" from the same source as Low: namely, from what Jones, following Maria Dorer, calls "the quietistic teaching of Buddhism" (1957: 270). This is an interesting idea, since Freud's death-drive theory strongly echoes Buddhist notions about nirvana, where the goal of the four stages of meditation (*jhana*) is precisely a return to an "existence" before life (cf. Alexander and Selesnick 1966: 25–26)—a beyond of the pleasure principle.[26] Freud, in fact, was told as much by Yaekichi Yabe, who was the editor of a forty-volume collection of Freud's work in Japanese. During his visit in May 1930, Freud expressed curiosity that *Beyond the Pleasure Principle*, the seventh volume of the collection, was one of the first of his works available in Japan. Yabe justified his decision, stating that "the theory that life tends towards death is a Buddhist idea. Since Buddhism influences Japanese thinking to a great degree, an understanding of psychoanalysis might be easier through this book" (in Freud 1992: 70). Apparently Freud was very pleased,[27] which helps explain why he purchased many Buddhist figures for his collection during the 1930's (Molnar 1992: xxi).

The principle of stability or constancy had been floating around in scientific circles for years, however, long before Freud put it to use as a psychotherapeutic ideal. As Henri Ellenberger (1956: 89–103) tells us, the "principle of the conservation of energy" was first formulated by the physician Robert Mayer in 1842, and was later extended by the physicist-physician Hermann von Helmholtz. Fechner's contemporary Herbert Spenser also proposed an evolutionary theory of "complete equilibrium" in his book of 1855, *The Principles of Psychology*. As Flugel puts it, Spenser believed that all activity "represents an effort of adjustment [or adaptation], which itself aims at the maintenance or re-establishment of equilibrium in the face of varying environmental situations which threaten or disturb it" (1955: 105). For his part, Fechner himself thought that the German astronomer J. C. F. Zollner was the first to formulate the principle of constancy, which he applied, Ellenberger states, "to a theory of the sunspots and of the movements of the comets" (101). It is also true, finally, that a theory of constancy was already evidenced in the Second Law of Thermodynamics, as devised by Lord Kelvin and Max Planck, and in the work of Rudolph Clausius, who in 1865 introduced the theory of entropy to physics. Many years later, in the 1930's, some fashion-conscious analysts were only too eager to attach Freud's death-drive theory to the physical theory of entropy (see Bernfeld and Feitelberg 1931). Yet Fechner was the first to give the principle of constancy a *psychological* meaning. Fechner adopted the principle as the last of his three great laws, all of which resonate with Freud's metapsychological vision: first, that the spiritual world is dominated by *das Lustprinzip*, or the pleasure principle; second, that there is a mechanical relation between spirit and body, what Fechner called his "fundamental psychophysical law"; and third, that pleasure and unpleasure are regulated by the principle of stability.

In BPP, Freud specifically cites a passage from Fechner's work of 1873, *Some Ideas on the History of Creation and the Development of Organisms*, in which a psycho-physical relation is purported between pleasure-unpleasure and stability-instability (1920a: 8). Freud's reliance on Fechner is, in fact, rather pervasive. As Ellenberger expertly summarizes, "Freud took from Fechner the concept of mental energy, the 'topographical' concept of the mind, the principle of pleasure-unpleasure, the principle of constancy, and the principle of repetition" (1970: 218). Not surprisingly, though, Freud's reliance on Fechner has been a source of misgiving for some historians, since Fechner was as much a philosopher-metaphysician as a biologist-psychologist. Fechner, for example, did not simply abandon the previous physical and astronomical theories of constancy. On the contrary, the philosopher of nature felt that stability was just as evident in the repetitious movement of stars as it was in the heart, and in the vagaries of pleasure (217; cf. Ellenberger 1956: 102). If stability was found in repetition, such a situation was itself repeated on all levels in the universe. Fechner's "psychological" work sounds no more acceptable to modern ears: he had, for example, written a work on the psychology of *plant life* (Ellenberger 1956: 92).

Yet, according to revisionist historians, it is this wildly speculative side of Fechner's brain mythology, his *Hirnmythologie*, that provides a clue to Freud's own interpretive follies. As Webster contends, Fechner's legacy provides us with Freud's "*real* intellectual genealogy" (1995: 175–81; his emphasis). According to this view, Freud merely dressed certain "cryptotheological" fictions from the past in the popular positivistic language of the day. Webster writes:

> In the century following the Enlightenment the original terms of this ancient and superstitious physiology gradually disappeared. But the physiological fantasy which the ancients had created survived. What happened in effect was that key terms such as "animal spirits," which too easily disclosed their theistic origins, were translated into modern-sounding "scientific" concepts—in this [i.e., Freud's] case "nervous energy" or "nervous force." These were then discussed

by having recourse to metaphors drawn from electricity or hydraulics so that, almost imperceptibly, the ancient fantasy was reconstructed in terminology appropriate to positivistic science. It was this mechanistic reworking of ancient physiology which Freud inherited from his teachers and adapted to provide an explanation of "hysterical conversion." (179)

Like Fechner, Freud hoped to locate the actual mechanism by which thought impacts on the body, that is, by which psyche is converted into soma. To this end Freud generally worked backward from those cases where the connection between mind and body had somehow failed or misfired—for instance, with a case of hysterical paralysis. The problem, Freud thought, was one of misdirected energy. Mental illness always came down to the so-called "cathexis" (*Besetzung*), the investment, charge, or amperage that ran amok in the body. The reorientation or—more literally—the rewiring of this endogenous energy in the proper direction constituted the cure for Freud in the 1890's, if not for the rest of his life. In this respect Freud was rather conventional in his thinking, which has a long pedigree: Mesmer's theory of animal magnetism from the late 1700's was based on the discovery of electricity; and magnetism gave way to the craze for hypnotism that Freud himself inherited at the beginning of his career, and which pervades his entire oeuvre, albeit covertly (see Borch-Jacobsen 1996a). In other words, even when Freud spoke of the "psycho-neuroses," his thinking was never far from the mechanistic explanation of the "actual neuroses"—those disorders due to sexual practices, such as masturbation, rather than some mental disturbance.

There were of course many others who influenced Freud's psychophysicalistic imagination, including two of his former teachers: Theodor Meynert thought that brain anatomy would provide some answers to the riddle of mental functioning, and Sigmund Exner published a psycho-physicalist account of the mind in 1894, just one year before Freud began his work on the *Project for a Scientific Psychology*. Also important for Freud was the work of John Hughlings Jackson, who wrote (ca. 1880's) about the relation between mind and body and about the benefits of emotional discharge, and August Weissmann, who proposed (ca. 1880's) that organisms are comprised of two parts corresponding to reproduction and death, namely, the germ plasm and the soma. There are, however, perhaps no greater influences on Freud's metapsychological imagination than the biological theories of Ernst Haeckel and Jean-Baptiste Lamarck. Haeckel basically argued that an organism repeats in abbreviated form the previous stages of development of its entire lineage; the human embryo, for example, ontogenetically repeats the entire history of its possibility. This means that the present-day human organism is the embodiment of an ancient history, a biological signifier of a buried past. As such, the scientist who is able to break the code of this biology has a privileged window onto this past and, hence, onto the present. Haeckel's recapitulationist views were, in turn, often attractive to followers of Lamarck's pre-Darwinian view of evolution. Lamarck is known for his claim, first, that life is not immutable but is driven toward always more complex forms of life and, second, that evolution is fueled by the inheritance of acquired characteristics (i.e., experience is transferred to the genotype and passed on to subsequent progeny). This latter claim is basically functionalist: the giraffe, for example, has developed a long neck over time because it has had to stretch it to reach a food source.

As historian-paleontologist Stephen Jay Gould remarks, Haeckel's theory of recapitulation "finds an almost automatic justification under Lamarckian notions of inheritance" (1977: 156; cf. 80–88). This is certainly true of Freud who, despite scientific evidence to the contrary,[28] was entirely convinced by the theories of Haeckel and Lamarck (see 155–66). "Freud," Jones complains of Freud's Lamarckian side, "never gave up a jot of his belief in the inheritance of acquired characters" (1957: 313). In fact, Freud sprinkled the doctrines of recapitulation and acquired characteristics in many of his texts throughout his lifetime—the most striking examples being *Totem and Taboo* (1912) and *Moses and Monotheism* (1939). For many analysts of that time such biological tenets were not problematic. Karl Abraham was only too happy to echo the claim that "psycho-analysis has extended this biogenetic law [of recapitulation] first postulated by Haeckel to the psychic realm" (1920: 134). It is certainly significant that, in the years just preceding *BPP*, Freud and his colleague Sandor Ferenczi had planned to write a joint work, "Lamarck and Psychoanalysis," and for this purpose read widely in the neo-Lamarckian literature (Freud and Ferenczi 1996: 166, 170, 171). As Freud put it to Ferenczi on January 28, 1917, "I have finally received some books on Lamarck. My impression is that we are coming completely into line with the psycho-Lamarckists, such as Pauly" (179). Arguing against Darwin's theory of natural selection, zoologist August Pauly had claimed that evolutionary change was the result of what Sulloway calls "internal physiological needs and the organism's efforts to satisfy such needs" (1979: 274). As Freud tells Abraham in November 1917, the internal explanation for evolutionary change could be made on the ground of the unconscious. In other words, psychoanalysis could provide the most basic explanation for the evolution of the species (Freud and Abraham 1965: 261–62; also in Jones 1957: 312; Sulloway 1979: 275).

Since Freud, always the conquistador, brazenly thought that psychoanalysis could explain the mechanism of evolutionary change, it cannot be surprising that recapitulationist and Lamarckian beliefs are present on the pages of *BPP*. For instance, having just referred to the spawning habits of fish and to the migratory patterns of birds, he lays the foundation of recapitulation upon which he will place his Lamarckian beliefs:

> We are quickly relieved of the necessity for seeking for further examples by the reflection that the most impressive proofs of there being an organic compulsion to repeat lie in the phenomena of heredity and the facts of embryology. We see how the germ of a living animal is obliged in the course of its development to recapitulate (even if only in a transient and abbreviated fashion) the structures of all the forms from which it is sprung, instead of preceding quickly by the shortest path to its final shape. This behaviour is only to a very slight degree attributable to mechanical causes ["energy" from the outside], and the historical explanation cannot accordingly be neglected. (1920a: 37; cf. 1933a: 106)

Freud's basic conclusion is as well known as it is controversial. If all organisms proceed by the shortest path to their "final shape," and if this shape takes a certain amount of time to play itself out, then life is but the length of time it takes for an organism to reach an end that for past generations was reached far more economically. Freud could not have been more clear about this: "An unlimited duration of individual life would become a quite pointless luxury" (1920a: 46). In short, life is the process by which each successive generation becomes more and more extravagant, even unnatural. Every organism is the aggregate of all experiences—biological and historical—that must be compulsively repeated, and therefore discharged, once again in the present. The time of life is, therefore, the time of an always expanding detour, quite literally the time that separates, or the space that grows between, the present and its essential origin. One could say, then, that life is a time of resistance to the inevitability of death. Or one could say that life remains the space between the nothing that came before life and the nothing that follows. And this is more or less what Freud thought: the aim of life is the restoration of an old state of affairs, namely, inanimateness. "If we are to take it as a truth that knows no exception that everything dies for *internal* reasons—becomes inorganic again—then we shall be compelled to say that '*the aim of all life is death*' and, looking backwards, that '*inanimate things existed before living ones*'" (38; his emphasis).

As a good psycho-Lamarckian, Freud also tried to show that while even the most basic organism lives only to die, this drive is temporarily foiled by its brief experience of the world. Freud does not suggest that the impetus for development originates within the organism as a drive for survival, but from without—notably, as an experience of frustration with the external world. All further development is grounded upon this encounter with the outside world, with the cosmos even (Sterba 1949: 157–161), an encounter that repeats and accumulates itself (as the life process) with each successive generation. The organism "learns" life or, rather, life constantly interferes with an immediate and pleasurable death. As historian Brayton Polka puts it, "Thus these guardians of life, too, were originally myrmidons of death" (1989: 312).

The upshot of this is that death becomes for Freud the natural, pleasurable and, above all, *true state* of life. And thus Freud thought of Eros as the real "mischief-maker" in mental life (1923a: 59). One lives only to die—or, according to Freud's Schopenhauerian reworking of Shakespeare, "Thou owest Nature a death" (1900: 205; see Schopenhauer 1844: 569).[29] As that which makes life worth living, death points to a timelessness before *and* after life, both origin *and* goal—that is, to a circle. "*It seems, then, that an instinct is an urge inherent in organic life to restore an earlier state of things*," Freud famously argues, "which the living entity has been obliged to abandon under pressure of external disturbing forces" (1920a: 36; his emphasis). In the beginning was the constancy of inanimateness, from which life began and will return again—just as a salmon returns to spawn along a path that leads to its death, or a bird follows the same migratory path again and again (cf. Freud 1933a: 106). Life begins, just to make this explicit, out of inanimate matter, an idea Freud imported directly from Lamarck's own view of evolution.

As we are beginning to see, death is an actuality which makes of life an impotent potentiality. For, in a way, one is *already dead*, or, more exactly, one is always becoming-dead. And thus life for Freud is much less the opposite of death than it is a matter of *degree*. But to this I will return later.

BIOLOGICAL FRENZY

> "What thou hast inherited from thy fathers,
>   acquire it to make it thine."
> —Johann Wolfgang von Goethe,
>   *Faust*, cited by Freud[30]

While the ironic and paradoxical tone of the death-drive theory is clearly Freud's, the substance of the argument is found—as Freud happily admits in a footnote in *BPP* (1920a: 41–42)—in Ferenczi's paper "Stages in the Development of a Sense of Reality" (1913: 181–203). There Ferenczi argues that evolution is really an illusion, since life ontogenetically stores up past (phylogenetic) developments as stages that are only repeated under a compulsion. The centerpiece of his argument is that human life begins with an ideal state of undisturbed tranquillity (i.e., with constancy): "the period of human life passed in the womb" (185). This so-called "*period of unconditional omnipotence*" (his emphasis) is what drives the child to demand "the return of a state that once existed, those 'good old days' in which they were all-powerful" (186). In the same Lamarckian terms that Freud would later adopt in *BPP*, Ferenczi thus concludes that the "development of the reality-sense" is compelled "not through spontaneous 'striving for development' "—that is, by a forward driving instinct for survival—"but through necessity, through adjustment to a demanded renunciation" of one's original, literally prehistorical, omnipotence (200–201). Freud was attracted to Ferenczi's tale because it fit so well with his own pessimistic belief in renunciation, and because it "proved" that construction or evolution in organic life only masks an essential dissolution or involution. In this way, Ferenczi had neutralized the strictly teleological aspect of evolutionary theory with a brand of materialistic speculation that Freud appropriated for *BPP* (see Sulloway 1979: 399–401).

Ferenczi's wild speculations, like those of Fechner's, reflect a side of Freud's own work that is doubtful to the extreme. Freud and Ferenczi wholeheartedly embraced the phylogenetic view of history, as is evident from their correspondence and from what Freud openly calls their "Lamarckian fantasies" (Freud and Ferenczi 1996: 293). They encouraged each other in this speculative gambit, in much the same way as Freud and Fliess encouraged each other years before. As Gould rightly argues, Freud's metapsychology papers were the result of an exchange "so intense that these works might almost be viewed as a joint effort" (1987: 14). Ferenczi's 1913 paper on the stages of a sense of reality was composed in the wake of Freud's own phylogenetic argument that appeared a year earlier in *Totem and Taboo*. Freud, in turn, followed Ferenczi's suggestion that the events of natural history had impacted upon the psychic health of mankind. Freud was especially intrigued by Ferenczi's idea that the "latency stage" of early puberty was an ontogenetic recapitulation of the Ice Ages (Ferenczi 1913b: 201–202). Characteristically, Ferenczi was eager to draw attention to this dubious prehistory:

> What we may conceive about the *phylogenesis* of the reality-sense can at present be offered only as a scientific prediction. It is to be assumed that we shall some day succeed in bringing the individual stages of development of the ego, and the neurotic regression-types of these, into a parallel with the stages in the racial history of mankind, just as, for instance, Freud found again in the mental life of the savage the characters of the neurosis. (200)

In his unpublished metapsychological essay of 1915, later collected as *A Phylogenetic Fantasy* (1987), Freud enthusiastically recalls Ferenczi's essay and extends it in similar directions. For example, he maps his own Oedipal schema on to Ferenczi's ontogenetic treatment of the Ice Ages—catastrophes that saw "The Coming of Man" (Ferenczi 1924: 69)—concluding that the primal father appeared in human history "as a result of adaptation to [external] exigency" (Freud 1987: 16). The "hard school of the Ice Age," Freud contends, is what had originally made men anxious (Freud and Ferenczi 1996: 66; Freud 1987: 13–14). The genetic inheritance of various experiences with an unforgiving environment thus led, Freud claims, to a "phylogenetic disposition" (1987: 10) toward certain neuroses. "What are now neuroses," Freud writes to Ferenczi in July 1915, "were once phases of the human condition" (1996: 66). Freud is explicit about these stages, which he envisioned as follows: "anxiety hysteria—conversion hysteria—obsessional neurosis—dementia praecox [schizophrenia]—paranoia—melancholia-mania" (66; cf. Freud 1987: 12). That Freud never surrendered his belief in these stages is evidenced, to cite just one example, in "The Future of an Illusion," where religion is explicitly described as a "universal obsessional neurosis" left over from "prehistoric times" (1927: 43).

While Freud incorporated the flavor of this speculation in *BPP*, Ferenczi himself extended this work in his *Thalassa: A Theory of Genitality* (1924). Although Ferenczi claims to have written parts of this work in 1915, and to have presented its central thesis to a small group of colleagues around Freud in 1919 (1), it is clear from his comments and references that he fiddled with it until 1923. It is just as clear that Ferenczi had in no way left Freud's views of psychoanalysis behind in *Thalassa*, which is deeply indebted to Freud's *Beyond the Pleasure Principle*.[31] Just as Freud attempted in his metapsychology essay of 1915, as Ferenczi put it, "the wonderful linking together of *all* types of neuroses, all conceived of as phases in the development of mankind" (Freud and Ferenczi 1996: 67), Ferenczi now proposed a "catastrophe" theory to account for all evolutionary change and psychological development (1924: 69; see Sulloway 1979: 378–81).[32]

As in his "Stages" essay of 1913, Ferenczi claims in *Thalassa* that all life is driven to return to the original state of bliss associated with the mother's womb; a claim echoed by Rank in *The Trauma of Birth* (1924), but to quite different ends. Such "thalassal regression" is apparent, Ferenczi argues, in the physiological facts of sleep, in dreams, in sex, and in death (1924: 20, 73–80). "We shall disclose the stages of the development of sexuality, described by Freud, as uncertain and fumbling yet increasingly outspoken attempts to attain the goal of returning to the maternal womb, whereas we must recognize in the final phases of evolution—in the fully attained genital function, that is—the complete attainment of this goal" (20). That "genital organization" in particular "represents a culminating point in the development of the erotic reality sense" (23) is a function of Ferenczi's rather outrageous conjecture about "the instrumentality of the male organ" (24). According to Ferenczi, the child's "autoplastic" attempts at conjuring up the lost womb—for example, through pre-Oedipal (masturbatory) fantasies—is properly replaced by an "alloplastic" attempt to reunite with the "maternal womb" through intercourse (genitality). At this point Ferenczi echoes Freud's own view of female masochism (which also appeared in 1924), according to which women ultimately find pleasure in their passive position (see also Ferenczi 1995: 40–42). From Ferenczi we learn that the primacy of the male is tied up with his ejaculant, which is symbolically apprehended by both sexes as a "gift." And since both sexes identify with this gift, the female is structured by her unmistakable penis envy—an envy squashed only by procuring a phallus of her own, ideally in the form of a male baby. In this respect Ferenczi argues that gratification is predicated on the "complete identification ... of the entire organism with the executive organ [i.e., the penis]" (1924: 38)—or, to be more exact, with "the genital secretion" (60). Ferenczi even claims that the "sexual secretion" of the male is the "representative of the ego and its double" (18).

Following the logic of an ancient "warfare between the sexes," it is rather obvious that the "woman comes off second best" in Ferenczi's tale (26); she is, as he says, forced to adapt along the lines of her "consolatory character" (58). Even so, Ferenczi makes a virtue of this particular evolutionary path. Unlike the male, who remains biologically "more primitive," the female is organically a "more *finely differentiated being*, that is, one that is adapted to more complex situations" (103–104; his emphasis). Or as he states in his clinical diary of 1932, "The feminine principle, that is, the principle of suffering, is the more intelligent" (1932: 42). So how is the female forced down this path of deathlike "conciliation," rather than lifelike "self-assertion"? Ferenczi claims that male dominance is virtually guaranteed, first of all, by his greater physical strength and, second, by his ability (apparently biological) to fascinate the female "hypnotically" (1924: 31); he later calls these two methods "fright and seduction," and also "father and mother hypnosis" (106). In any case, the "cataleptic" attitude assumed by the entranced subject may be just another instance of womb regression (32);[33] for sleep, hypnotic or otherwise, "is the brother of death" (80). As always, "the goal of coitus" (regardless of how it comes about) is the "attainment of the intrauterine state, with the simultaneous symbolic and real attainment of this goal by the genitalia and the sex cells" (36).

Through this "bioanalytical" reworking of psychoanalysis, a self-styled "*depth biology*" (84; his emphasis), Ferenczi was definitely " 'out-Haeckeling' Haeckel" (Sulloway 1979: 380). For while Haeckel exempted the protective environment of the womb from his theory of recapitulation, Ferenczi made of "the arrangement for the protection of the germ cells" (perigenesis) itself the recapitulation "of the environmental situations which have been experienced during the development of the species" (1924: 46).

To leap the gap between ontogenesis and phylogenesis, Ferenczi employed analytic techniques of interpretation (81–82, 88). From this perspective he put Darwin to one side while he employed "the more psychological concept of Lamarck" (50), according to which there is always a *motive* behind development (cf. 100): "This motive may well be the striving to restore the lost mode of life in a moist *milieu* which at the same time provides a supply of nourishment; in other words, to bring about *the reestablishment of the aquatic mode of life in the form of an existence within the moist and nourishing interior of the mother's body*" (54; his emphasis). According to Ferenczi, the very moisture of the sexual encounter mimics the primal ocean out of which life supposedly began: "The amniotic fluid represents a sea 'introjected,' as it were, into the womb of the mother" (56). He even contends, in an especially ridiculous passage, that a certain fishy odor is the ontogenetic repetition of this phylogenetic origin: "The genital secretion of the female among the higher mammals and in man, the erotically stimulating effect of which . . . may be traceable to infantile reminiscences, possesses a distinctly fishy odour (odour of herring brine) . . . ; this odour of the vagina comes from the same substance (trimethylamine) as the decomposition of fish gives rise to" (57, n. 1; cf. 33).

Life, then, is the adaptive response to a series of historical "catastrophes," after which time the organism goes about reestablishing the "compulsorily abandoned original situation" (66). Yet it is obviously a thin line that separates the naturally occurring catastrophe from the adaptive response; given the inheritance of acquired characteristics, the response is bound to seem uncannily similar to the catastrophe experienced. For this reason it is life itself that seems catastrophic or, better yet, traumatic—a conclusion that follows very naturally in both Freud's and Ferenczi's theories.[34]

Having thus correlated the histories of psychic and natural development, Ferenczi finds in his bleak evolutionary picture evidence for our current-day drive for a return to *"the deathlike repose of the inorganic world"* (63; his emphasis). Life is structured by the death drive:

> To us physicians the "death agony" . . . never presents a serene or peaceful countenance. . . . Perhaps only in our wishful conceptions, themselves governed by the death instinct, is there such a thing as a "natural", gentle death, an untroubled and tranquil manifestation of the death instinct, for in reality it seems as though life has always to end catastrophically, even as it began, in birth, with a catastrophe. (95)

It is, of course, easy to dismiss and ignore these ideas, which has been the usual response. But this approach is a mistake, typically born out of the assumption that Ferenczi's speculations meant little or nothing to Freud. The opposite is closer to the truth. The "deathlike repose of the inorganic world" that characterized for Ferenczi the intrauterine stage of development is obviously tied up with Freud's speculations in *Beyond the Pleasure Principle*; it is also an aspect that some of Freud's most devoted followers would accept and repeat over the years (see Nunberg 1955: 211–13). In a way, Ferenczi merely completed what Freud began, only in more blunt and, consequently, more embarrassing terms. They wrote their respective works during the same period, swapped rough drafts, proposed a joint project on Lamarck and psychoanalysis, and corresponded all the while. We should also not forget that Ferenczi's "Stages in the Development of the Sense of Reality" (1913) essay actually *followed* Freud's *Totem and Taboo* (1912), just as *Thalassa: A Theory of Genitality* (1924) *followed Beyond the Pleasure Principle* (1920); if he wasn't actually influenced by Freud's ideas, which is unlikely, Ferenczi was at the very least liberated by Freud's own speculative excesses.[35] According to Ferenczi, though, things are much simpler still: he claims to be the one who originally posed the death drive to Freud. In what may seem like a strange offering to Freud, Ferenczi claims in his paper of 1926, "To Sigmund Freud on His Seventieth Birthday," the following:

> Once several years ago I myself came forward with the theory that all could be explained by a death-instinct. Freud's verdict was not favourable to the idea, and my faith in him enabled me to bow to his judgement; then one day there appeared *Beyond the Pleasure Principle*, in which his theory of the interplay of death-instincts and life-instincts does far more justice to the manifold facts of psychology and biology than my one-sided conception could do. (1926b: 16)

Questions of priority aside, it is in any case true that Freud's conclusions about a beyond of the pleasure principle in no way preclude the idea of a *before* of existence that could include incubation in the womb. More to the point, Ferenczi's ideas are no more absurd than anything Freud proposed in his published and unpublished metapsychology papers, including his much beloved *BPP*. Both men were basically looking for the primordial phenomenon, what romantic philosophers called *Urphänomene*, that made existence possible (Ellenberger 1970: 203–204). To this end, Ferenczi fully utilized Freud's death-drive theory, what he admiringly called "that supreme simplification" (1926a: 367).

In the period immediately following the publication of *Thalassa*, Ferenczi drifted away from the "neutral" technique of psychoanalysis—which meant that he drifted away from Freud. Claiming that neurotic patients suffer from a lack of love from their parents, Ferenczi proposed that analysts could substitute for this lack during a more active therapy. And thus he began to hug and kiss his patients. Naturally, Freud worried that Ferenczi's kissing technique could, in the hands of less scrupulous practitioners, lead to serious ethical and moral dilemmas. He writes of this slippery slope in a letter to Ferenczi at the end of 1931:

> Now picture what will be the result of publishing your technique. There is no revolutionary who is not driven out of the field by a still more radical one. A number of independent thinkers in matters of technique will say to themselves: why stop at a kiss? Certainly one gets a little further when one adopts "pawing" as well, which after all doesn't make a baby. And then bolder ones will come along who will go further to peeping and showing—and soon we shall have accepted in the technique of analysis the whole repertoire of demivierg-erie and petting parties, resulting in an enormous increase of interest in analysis. (in Jones 1957: 164)[36]

Freud was saved from this newest threat and embarrassment when Ferenczi died of pernicious anemia on May 22, 1933. In his obituary for Ferenczi, Freud discussed their past intimacy, and also spoke glowingly about *Thalassa*. Although more an application of psychoanalysis to the field of biology than a work of analysis proper, Freud considered this book Ferenczi's "most brilliant and most fertile achievement" (1933b: 228). *Thalassa* was, Freud writes, "perhaps the boldest application of psycho-analysis that was ever attempted." Moreover, Freud thought it "probable that some time in the future there really will be a 'bio-analysis,' as Ferenczi has prophesized" (228–29). Yet such praise is double-edged, since Freud was setting Ferenczi up in order to knock him down. To this end Freud applies the precious theory of conservation against Ferenczi: if *Thalassa* represents the pinnacle of analytic work, it was because Ferenczi had nothing more to give—to his science, to his friends and, finally, to himself. Hence he died.

> After this summit of achievement, it came about that our friend slowly drifted away from us. On his return from a period of work in America he seemed to withdraw more and more into solitary work, though he had previously taken the liveliest share in all that happened in analytic circles. . . . Wherever it may have been that the road he had started on would have led him, he could not pursue it to the end. Signs were slowly revealing in him a grave organic destructive process which had probably overshadowed his life for many years already. (229)

No doubt the kissing technique was part of a general regressive trend in his being, part of a "grave organic destructive process" that was activated the moment he spent his true worth on applied psychoanalysis. *Thalassa* was the end of Ferenczi's lively psychoanalytic existence and, thus, the beginning of the end. "Apart from the dangers of his technique," Freud spoke of Ferenczi in October 1931, "I am sorry to know him to be on the track which is scientifically not very productive. The essential thing, however, seems to me to be its neurotically produced regression" (Freud 1992: 111).

Despite Freud's disapproval, it seems likely that Ferenczi's dangerous new technique was grounded in, or at least filtered through, the death-drive theory—a possibility overlooked in the literature. In a more or less forgotten essay of 1929, "The Unwelcome Child and His Death Instinct," Ferenczi outlines the familiar-sounding rationale behind his active technique. As always, life for Ferenczi, as for Freud, is structured by an external compulsion, only in this case by the compulsion Ferenczi calls love:

> The child has to be induced, by means of an immense expenditure of love, tenderness, and care, to forgive his parents for having brought him into the world without any intention on his part; otherwise the destructive instincts begin to stir immediately.... The "life-force"... becomes established only when tactful treatment and upbringing gradually give rise to progressive immunization against physical and psychical injuries. (1929: 105; cf. Ferenczi 1932: 148)

Given Lamarkian inheritance, it makes good sense that we should strive, socially and politically, to establish just the sort of environment that would foster the inheritance of positive attributes. But Freud, unlike Ferenczi, was not interested in the potential effects of a *positive* environment, nor even with the therapeutic effects of analysis, obsessed as he was with a tragic or negative etiology securely entrenched in unprovable prehistory. As Ferenczi writes in his *Clinical Diary* on August 4, 1932, Freud admitted to his closest adherents "that neurotics are a rabble, good only to support us financially and to allow us to learn from their cases: psychoanalysis as a therapy may be worthless" (1932: 185–86; cf. Dufresne 1997a). It follows, then, that the more optimistic Ferenczi was steering therapy away from an interminable analysis of our brutal, deterministic past and toward the imagined or actual problems of sociality—including the experiences of love and hate. Thus did Ferenczi begin to believe, not only that positive experiences might check our brutal past, but that psychoanalysis had made a wrong turn in 1897. As he admitted to Freud in a letter of December 25, 1929, Ferenczi began to accept Freud's more literal, pre-psychoanalytic account of neurosis: namely, the idea that neurosis is caused by a traumatic experience at an early age (see Ferenczi 1932: xii).

It is perhaps ironic that Ferenczi's bioanalytic reworking of psychoanalysis along the lines of Lamarckian inheritance provided the *theoretical* foundation of Freud's *BPP*, even as it exposed the *therapeutic* nihilism of Freud's practice. Although Ferenczi was anything but a jaded therapist, the theory of the death drive consigned analytic therapy to the task of describing our brutal existence, effectively abandoning in advance the hopes of a future. As Marthe Robert recognizes, the death-drive theory "sends therapy very quickly back to a blind fate which it cannot acknowledge without immediately renouncing its claim to cure" (1964: 334). Ferenczi quite rightly recoiled from this dire conclusion and sought to put love back into the picture the only way he knew how: as a recognized, biologically inheritable, ongoing part of human experience, including most especially that experience called therapy. Yet this move was too little, too late: the cast was already set, in large measure due to Ferenczi's own wild speculations. Thus his 1931 pronouncement to Freud, "I am, above all, an empiricist" (Ferenczi 1932: xv), rings very hollow. Clearly Ferenczi's new found distrust of fantasy doesn't fit well with his oldest theoretical commitments.

Despite his good intentions, Ferenczi's reputation in the psychoanalytic world suffered irreparably from his unfashionable interest in the affects and effects of sociality. Naturally, others learned from his apparent mistake and clung ever more dogmatically to a psychological theory of fantasy and psychic reality. A case in point is Ferenczi's one-time analysand Melanie Klein, who more than most based her work on the affects of fantasy. However, it remains to be seen whether even the most dogmatic pursuit of fantasy, such as we find in Klein, can insulate analytic psychology from the effects of a bad, inherently racist, biology. This is especially the case when the theory of fantasy in question is written under the banner of death and aggressivity.

Klein and the "Clinical" 'Beyond'

Melanie Klein is among the few psychoanalysts to adapt Freud's death-drive theory to clinical ends.[37] That she did so in the context of "object relations" theory makes her work a complicated detour in a history of detours, since instinct normally understood is that which undermines, in advance, the self-sufficiency of the object world. Things are further complicated by the fact that Klein's theory of object relations is predicated on some rather fanciful speculations about the infant's earliest relation to the world. First of all, how does one empirically corroborate a psychoanalytic theory of *unconscious fantasy*, what Klein distinguishes as "phantasy,"[38] that exists beyond or, more exactly, before language acquisition? The problem is fundamental: the child analyst on the trail of phantasy must not only do all the interpreting but most of the talking as well. Such a procedure is bound to raise disturbing questions, since the analyst is liable to read his or her own thoughts into the child, thereby corroborating nothing more than his or her own preconceptions—or, as it were, the preconceptions of some others.

In Klein's case, these others, these primary objects, are none other than Freud, Ferenczi, and Karl Abraham. To tell the story of Klein's use of the death-drive theory is to recount the story of her relation to these founding fathers of psychoanalysis. At the same time, it is to recount the story, at once technical and ethical, of how analytic speculations—about phantasy, and about the processes that enable phantasy, such as projection and introjection—compromise the supposed objectivity of clinical observations from the outset.

HISTORICAL RELATIONS

Just as Freud held weekly meetings with interested colleagues from around Vienna, establishing in 1906 the Vienna Psychoanalytic Society, Ferenczi established in 1913 the Hungarian Psychoanalytical Society in his hometown of Budapest. Ferenczi's organization initially attracted a small group of followers, including Sandor Rado, but eventually gained the attention of such notable figures as Anton von Freund, Franz Alexander, Geza Roheim, Michael Balint, and Melanie Klein. As president of the Society, Ferenczi quite naturally set the tone and parameter of the meetings. Consequently we cannot be surprised to learn from Rado, the Society's secretary, that wild biological speculation dominated their discussions. "We had unending discussions," Rado states, "about how the human species had emerged from the ocean and how in particular the genital apparatus and the uterus, as well as the baby, developed" (in Roazen and Swerdloff 1995: 39). These interests, as suggested above, were set in motion by the free exchange of ideas in Freud and Ferenczi's correspondence. Clearly Ferenczi's unique proximity to Freud the man, as well as to Freud's most speculative, unedited thoughts, is what determined the abstract direction of Society interests, including the feelings of giddy enthusiasm for metabiological speculation found therein.

Whether Klein attended the early Society meetings is unclear, although her interest in Freud's work dates almost from the time of its inception. Klein claims to have read Freud's short work "On Dreams" (1901) in 1914, and soon thereafter began an analysis with Ferenczi.[39] According to biographer Phyllis Grosskurth (1986: 70), Klein may have attended meetings of the Hungarian Society during the early days of her analysis. This, in fact, is likely given the informal nature of institutional psychoanalysis in those days; for instance, Klein's fifteen-year-old daughter, Melitta, was allowed to attend Society meetings in 1919 (72).[40] But even if Klein did not attend the early meetings, she would have absorbed the speculative atmosphere that characterized the Hungarian Society.

We do know that Klein was engaged in extraanalytic activities by 1918. On September 28 and 29 of that year she attended the Fifth International Psycho-Analytic Congress, which was held in Budapest. The congress was an important event for psychoanalysis because of the First World War, where psychoanalysis was gaining ground as a promising method for treating the war neuroses. Freud was understandably excited by the new prospects and made a point of declaring at the congress that Budapest had become during the war a center of psychoanalytic activities. He was only too happy to leave behind the memory of the last center of such activity, namely, Jung's Zurich.

At the congress Klein heard Freud deliver his essay "Lines of Advance in Psycho-Analytic Therapy" (1919). "I remember vividly," Klein writes in her unpublished autobiography, "how impressed I was [with Freud] and how the wish to devote myself to psychoanalysis was strengthened by this impression" (in Grosskurth 1986: 71). Klein must have been just as impressed to learn that Ferenczi, who remained her analyst until 1919, was elected to be president of the International Psycho-Analytic Association at the same congress.

During her analysis, Ferenczi encouraged Klein to explore the possibilities of child analysis, probably for two reasons. First of all, Freud's theories about psychopathology were based on assumptions about infantile sexuality and unconscious processes that were never tested empirically. Rather characteristically, Freud worked backward from his ideas to their clinical corroboration in his patients' behaviors and "memories." His earliest significant discussion of *actual* children came only with the analysis of five-year-old "Little Hans," Herbert Graf. But in fact the "analysis" was informally conducted by the boy's father, Max Graf, who reported his findings to Freud. Freud discussed this first case of child analysis in 1907 and again in 1908 (see 1908b), publishing the case study in 1909. It was, furthermore, only in 1915 that he imported a new section on "The Sexual Researches of Children" into his standard work on sexuality, the *Three Essays on the Theory of Sexuality* (see 1905b: 194–97), originally published in 1905. In short, the fundamental work of child analysis was only attempted years after Freud began publishing cases of psychoanalysis.[41] Freud was aware of these evidential lacunae in his theory, and evidently asked some of his close adherents, such as Max Graf, to compile observations of their own children to this end. Ferenczi himself contributed to this group project, publishing in 1913 his own case study of a five-year-old boy, "Arpád," entitled "A Little Chanticleer." While Little Hans was purportedly scared of horses, Arpád was scared of cocks. Thus it makes sense that Ferenczi encouraged Klein to consider the mostly untapped field of child analysis.

It is, of course, rather strange that empirical corroboration of metapsychological ideas was more or less beneath Freud's own interest. This prejudice for abstract (if unprovable) theories brings us to the second reason for why Ferenczi would have encouraged Klein in particular to consider a career in child analysis. Lacking university credentials, the seemingly less challenging field of child analysis was perfect for Klein's (presumably modest) talents. As Helene Deutsch once sneered, Klein was merely "a housewife with fantasies" (in Roazen 1985: 255). Similarly, most male analysts at that time tended to feel that child analysis was best suited for women, as it was a sort of "domestic" application of psychoanalysis.[42] Work with children was work for women, just as work with adults was work for men.

It is thus no accident that Ferenczi, as Klein put it, "drew my attention to my great gift for understanding children and my interest in them, and he very much encouraged my idea of devoting myself to analysis, particularly child-analysis. I had, of course, three children of my own at the time" (in Grosskurth 1986: 74). "It is to him," Klein states of Ferenczi in *The Psycho-Analysis of Children*, "that I owe the foundations from which my work as an analyst developed" (1932: x–xi). When Klein began her analysis with Ferenczi in her early thirties, she was already married with children. According to Grosskurth (1986: 72), she entered analysis because she was depressed, possibly because of her mother's death in 1914.[43] Of her analysis with Ferenczi, Klein admits that she "had a very strong positive transference" (Ibid.). Since this was a therapeutic analysis and not a training analysis, her interest in the psychoanalysis of children was no doubt a crucial aspect of her therapy. Becoming an analyst has long been, for better and for worse, one way of dealing with a personal problem—even though it amounts to extending the process of analysis indefinitely. It is therefore likely that Freud's and Ferenczi's ideas held both emotional and careerist attractions for Klein during these early years. With the encouragement of Ferenczi and Klein's Hungarian colleagues, Klein presented "The Development of a Child" to the Society in July 1919 (Grosskurth 1986: 75), and was thereupon made a full member of the Society. That is, she became a recognized psychoanalyst.

Klein's close association with Ferenczi lasted for about six years, coming to an end soon after the collapse of the Austro-Hungarian empire into its component parts (see Grosskurth 1986: 82; Sayers 1991: 212–13). In Hungary the Bolshevik revolution under Bela Kun was favorably disposed to psychoanalysis and Ferenczi was even made a university professor of psychoanalysis. But with the anti-Semitic counterrevolution in late 1919, psychoanalysis fell out of official favor. Among much else, Ferenczi lost his new post and Klein left Budapest, eventually making her way to the Berlin Psychoanalytic Society and Institute.

The Berlin Society under Karl Abraham was rather unlike its Hungarian counterpart. Abraham was a more disciplined, scientific figure than Ferenczi, and concentrated on establishing Berlin as a powerhouse of analytic training and research.[44] Among those who passed through the Berlin Society during the 1920's were Rado, Alexander, Hanns Sachs, Alix Strachey, Edward Glover, Theodor Reik, Ernst Simmel, Helene Deutsch, and the child analyst Hermine von Hug-Hellmuth.[45]

As opposed to the far-fetched metabiological theories of Freud and Ferenczi, Abraham plodded along the less controversial paths already established by Freud. Most important for Klein was his research into the psychosexual stages of development, and into the processes of introjection and projection. Although Abraham never cites Freud's *Beyond the Pleasure Principle*, he expands the destructive side of Freud's libido theory. As Klein put it in her essay of 1957, "Envy and Gratitude," Abraham "explored the roots of destructive impulses and applied this understanding to the aetiology of mental disturbances more specifically than had ever been done before. It appears to me that although he had not made use of Freud's concept of the life and death instincts, his clinical work . . . was based on this insight which was taking him in that direction" (177; cf. Heimann and Isaacs 1991: 699–700). Like Abraham, Klein would continue to examine the clinical or, more accurately, the *social* side of Freud's death-drive theory: that is, not so much the death drive itself, but its representative, the destructive impulse, *Destruktionstrieb*.

Klein entered analysis with Abraham, probably near the beginning of 1924, and later credited him as a major influence on her research into child analysis. "I should say," Klein writes, "that A. [Abraham] represents the link between my own work and F.'s [Freud's]" (in Grosskurth 1986: 109). Professionally, the sensible Abraham pushed Klein further in the direction of object relations; personally, he shielded her from the wary skepticism of her Berlin colleagues. Klein's apprenticeship under Abraham was, however, cut short by his illness in 1925; Abraham died unexpectedly on December 25, 1925, possibly from "undiagnosed lung cancer" (Clark 1980: 462–63). Just a few weeks later Klein relocated to England, which seemed more hospitable to child analysis. There she became a major source of controversy, her views eventually splitting the British Psycho-Analytical Society into three groups: the Anna Freud group, the Klein group, and the middle or uncommitted group.

OBJECT LESSONS (IN INSTINCT THEORY)

> I want further to call attention to the fact that free thinking, unadapted to reality—that is to say, phantasy—is in itself an important source of pleasure. Children play with thoughts as with toys and just on that account logical thinking, in accordance with reality, replaces only gradually this pleasure-giving play.
> —Karl Abraham, "Psycho-Analytical Views on Some Characteristics of Early Infantile Thinking"[46]

Klein arrived in Berlin at the beginning of 1921 and quickly made her mark as a child analyst. Most important was her development of play therapy in 1922–23, an innovation that has since become the hallmark of most psychotherapeutic efforts with children.[47] Taking a page out of *Beyond the Pleasure Principle*, where Freud has eighteen-month-old Ernst playing a diabolical game of absence and presence with a spool, Klein claimed that child's play at a nonverbal, pre-Oedipal age can be symbolically, even historically, meaningful. In "The Psychological Foundations of Child Analysis," Klein writes:

> The child expresses its phantasies, its wishes and its actual experiences in a symbolic way through play and games. In doing so, it makes use of the same archaic and phylogenetically-acquired mode of expression, the same language, as it were, that we are familiar with in dreams; and we can only fully understand this language if we approach it in the same way Freud has taught us to approach the language of dreams. . . . If we make use of this play technique we soon find that the child brings as many associations to the separate elements of its play as adults do to the separate elements of their dreams. (1926: 7–8; cf. Klein 1955: 122–40)

Following the Freud of *BPP*, Klein also claimed that "phantasies in the service of the repetition-compulsion" are critical for analysis, comprising as they do the "primitive mechanism" of psychic life (1926: 10).

Obviously the "talking cure" had to be refashioned somehow for child analysis, and play seemed to do the trick. But if child's play provided a suitable script for interpretation, transference continued to provide an ideal medium for its psychoanalysis. On this score Klein disagreed with Anna Freud, who claimed in her "Introduction to the Technique of the Analysis of Children" that while "the child indeed enters into the liveliest relations with the analyst ... it forms no transference neurosis" (1926: 33). Indeed, for Anna Freud, "The child is not, like the adult, ready to produce a new edition of its love-relationships, because, as one might say, the old edition is not yet exhausted" (34). Klein felt rather differently, and in 1932 countered: "My observations have taught me that children, too, develop a transference-neurosis analogous to that of grown up persons, so long as we employ a method which is the equivalent of adult analysis" (xvi). Or as she claimed more emphatically in "The Technique of Early Analysis," collected in *The Psycho-Analysis of Children* (1932), children are more or less predisposed to produce a "spontaneous transference" on account of "acute," constitutional bouts with anxiety (24). Such anxiety, she was to repeat in 1958, was a reflection of the innate "danger [felt by the infant] of being destroyed by the death instinct" (237). Obviously the presence of transference in children, constitutionally given at birth, was essential if Klein's interpretation of their play was to be considered properly psychoanalytic and, hence, universally true.

According to Ernest Jones, Klein deserves "the credit of carrying psycho-analysis to where it principally belongs—the heart of the child" (1975: 338).[48] In fact, since child analysis was the missing beat in Freud's theoretical corpus, Klein found herself in a privileged position among some psychoanalysts. While Anna Freud denied that full-blown analytic technique could (or should) be applied to children, correctly admitting for that reason that her own pedagogical efforts were bound to seem like "wild analysis" (A. Freud 1926: 51), Klein laid claim to unconscious material that was supposedly next to the real thing, namely, next to the primary processes themselves.[49] According to this view infants live in close proximity to their unconscious, a golden era they leave behind only as they mature and socialize. As Abraham put it in a short essay of 1923, "We see that, in childhood, thinking is far more influenced by the instinctive life than in riper years" (90). Klein took full advantage of this shibboleth of psychoanalytic thinking and claimed, rather audaciously, "In child-analysis we are able to get back to experiences and fixations which, in the analysis of adults can often only be reconstructed, whereas the child shows them to us as immediate representations" (1926: 9). Klein thus positioned herself as the most Freudian of all Freudians, the analyst most able to plumb the murky depths of "psychic reality."

Obviously method is nothing without material and Klein certainly claimed to have found a lot of it in her practice. She agreed with Freud's claim that children exhibit an "instinct for knowledge or research," *Wisstrieb* (1905b: 194). But while Freud's children were obsessed with sexuality—their need to know, for example, where babies come from—Klein's infants were obsessed, and immediately so, with aggression—their need to know, for example, where the "part object" called a breast comes from. In this respect she followed Abraham's (1924) reworking of Freud's theory of psychosexual development, announced in an essay on the development of the libido, according to which both libidinal and destructive aspects are fused together at each phase; for example, Abraham subdivided the oral phase into its "sucking" and "biting" moments. Of the "ambivalent character" of infantile phantasies, Abraham wrote: "They involve on the one hand a total or partial incorporation of the mother, that is, an act of positive desire; and on the other, her castration or death, that is, a negative desire tending to her destruction" (463). Or as Ferenczi more simply argued in 1926, the breast "has become *an object of love and hate*, of hate because of its being temporarily unobtainable, and of love because after this loss it offers a still more intense satisfaction" (371; his emphasis). We can already see here the outline of what was later to become known, with Winnicott especially, as the "good-enough mother." Accordingly, Klein describes an early "phase of maximal sadism" (1981: xiii) that finds the child anxiously chomping away at, and introjecting, the breast, even as he or she projects its death drive outward as aggression toward Mommy. As Klein put it in an essay of 1933:

> To begin with, the breast of the mother is the object of his [the infant's] constant desire, and therefore this is the first thing to be introjected. In phantasy the child sucks the breast into himself, chews it up and swallows it; thus he feels that he has actually got it there, that he possesses the mother's breast within himself, in both its good and bad aspects. (in 1981: 291)

Klein came to believe that the child's initial, destructive paranoia gives way to guilt and to the "drive to make reparation" with the injured mother of his or her phantasy. Echoing to some extent Freud's work on mourning (see Freud 1917b), Klein basically thought that guilt was contingent upon the child's new recognition of the mother as a "whole object," and called the drive for reparation the "depressive position." "The drive to make reparation," Klein writes, "can be regarded as a consequence of greater insight into psychic reality and of growing synthesis, for it shows a more realistic response to the feelings of grief, guilt and fear of loss resulting from the aggression against the loved object" (1946: 14). Or as Ferenczi put it, the child develops a greater "knowledge of the sense of reality" (1926a: 366–79), what he specifically calls "the art of reckoning" (378). Proper development thus became for Klein a matter of introjecting more good than bad objects, the accumulation of good "internal objects" imbuing all subsequent phantasies (and their projections) in a more positive, loving light. As she claimed in an essay of 1958, introjection "combats the death instinct because it leads to the ego taking in something life-giving (first of all food) and thus binding the death instinct working within" (238).

Klein was not alone in assigning a structuring role to the processes of introjection and projection. That the child filters the external world through phantasy (or, more loosely, through subjectivity) is part of what Ferenczi had already called the "stages in the development of the sense of reality." Like Freud and Abraham, Klein was obviously influenced by Ferenczi's 1913 essay of that name, which became the test run for his psycho-Lamarkian fantasies, later published in *Thalassa*. Among other things, Ferenczi proposed that children believe in the magical omnipotence of their own thoughts, essentially failing to distinguish between thought and deed, fantasy and reality. Such confusion, for Ferenczi, is a natural consequence of introjection and projection. As he states:

> [The child] has to distinguish between certain perfidious things, which do not obey his will, as an outer world, and on the other side of his ego; i.e., between the subjective psychical contents (feelings) and the objectified ones (sensations). I once called [ca. 1909] these stages the *Introjection Phase* of the psyche, since in it all experiences are still incorporated into the ego, and the later one the *Projection Phase*. One might also, following this terminology, speak of the omnipotence stage as the introjection stage, the reality stage as the projection stage, of the development of the ego. (1913b: 192)[50]

Freud echoed Ferenczi's claims in "Instincts and Their Vicissitudes" (1915), and in "Negation" (1925), and again in *Civilization and Its Discontents* (1930). For example, in "Negation" he claims that "the original pleasure-ego wants to introject into itself everything that is good and to eject from itself everything that is bad. What is bad, what is alien to the ego and what is external are, to begin with, identical" (1925b: 237). Both Ferenczi and Freud felt that developing a sense of reality is complicated by the infant's inability to perceive the external world *as* the external world, that is, as independent of its perception. As Freud and Bullitt state, "To reconcile himself to the world of reality is naturally one of the chief tasks of every human being. This task is not an easy one for a child. Not one of the desires of his libido can find full satisfaction in the real world" (1966: 42). For Freud, the problem was quite simple: "The antithesis between subjective and objective does not exist at first" (1925b: 237). What exists is rather a state of narcissism that is abandoned only unenthusiastically with an act of negation, what Ferenczi calls "a transition-phase between ignoring and accepting reality" (1926: 367).

Despite the clear influence of Freud, Ferenczi, and Abraham on Klein's way of thinking, the literature often bends over backward to emphasize her original deviations from doctrine—which is fair enough. We are reminded that Freud made of the Oedipus complex the deciding moment in psychosexual development around the age of four, while Klein pushed everything back to the first months of life; or that Freud spoke of an aftereffect or deferred action, *Nachträglichkeit*, according to which childhood experiences become affective (or traumatic) "memories" only much later in life, while Klein spoke rather ambitiously about prophylaxis. In Klein's opinion, at least in the early years of her practice, child analysis could protect adults from becoming neurotic in the first place, thus nipping the troublesome affect in the proverbial bud. It is worth noting that many other analysts, including Abraham (1920: 130) and Jones (Freud and Jones 1993: 579, 617), shared this therapeutic ambition. It is also said of Klein that by focusing on the earliest months of life—by remaking Freud's theory of psychosexual "phases" of development in terms of her own theories of paranoid-schizoid and depressive "positions"— she was among the first to open Freud's patriarchal conceptions to the decisive role of mothering in child development and character formation.

This last claim is both true and false, though in my opinion it is rather more false than true. Klein may have amended Freud's ideas, and she was undeniably a leader in the push—beginning especially in the 1930's, but already evident, as Robert Kramer (1996: 3–47) argues, in the mostly forgotten works of Otto Rank (see, for example, 1926a and 1926b)—to include mothering in the psychology of child development. Yet she also maintained what I consider (and will later discuss at length) Freud's most precious and debilitating metapsychological assumption: the idea that the environment (e.g., seduction) doesn't matter as much as an instinctually based fantasy life or, as Klein recast it, as much as unconscious phantasy. Indeed, although Klein introduced a theory of object relations to help account for child development, her theory was always written from the side of instinct, nature, constitutionality.

It's not that Klein ignored an etiology based on the outer world of objective relations. In "The Development of a Child," first delivered in 1919, Klein held that sexual enlightenment, for example, could lessen the neurotic impulses of children. However, and even though Freud himself considered this idea in "The Sexual Enlightenment of Children" (1907), such a view is not properly psychoanalytic—as Anton von Freund informed Klein after her presentation of this idea to the Hungarian Society (Grosskurth 1986: 77–78). In 1908 Freud spoke more characteristically of the child's unconscious resistance to treatment, in his essay "On the Sexual Theories of Children." Or as he stated even more emphatically in his "Analysis Terminable and

Interminable," the hopes for prophylaxis through sexual enlightenment, while admirable, were "greatly over-estimated." "After such enlightenment," he cautioned, "children know something they did not know before, but they make no use of the new knowledge that has been presented to them" (1937: 233–34). This tension in Freud's work between liberalism (enlightenment) and analysis (resignation) was repeated most dramatically by Klein during the years of 1919 and 1921. As French analyst Jean-Bertrand Pontalis points out, Klein began with the therapeutic role of education—the proactive flip side of the seduction theory—but quickly reversed her focus so that "everything seems to emanate from the child, given over to his inner demons: his 'development' depends solely on the results of a completely interior fight, between good and bad objects, between Eros and Thanatos" (1981b: 101; see also 98–99).

As Klein learned her trade, it was perhaps inevitable that she too would reject the environment as either the cause *or* cure of psychopathology. It is not that external reality doesn't matter, as Kleinians like to insist, but that reality as such is always already subject to, and dependent upon, "psychic reality." As Klein claimed in her second effort of 1921, "The Child's Resistance to Enlightenment," this time presented to the Berlin Society: "We learn from the analysis of neurotics that only a part of the injuries resulting from repression can be traced to wrong environmental or other prejudicial external conditions. Another and very important part is due to an attitude on the part of the child, present from the very tenderest years" (27). Klein added this chastened conclusion as the second, properly psychoanalytic, half of her old essay "The Development of a Child" and never looked back. As she said of envy many years later, when it became the destructive rock-bottom of her etiological vision: "I consider that envy is an oral-sadistic and anal-sadistic expression of destructive impulses, operative from the beginning of life, and that it has a constitutional basis" (1957: 176).

These beliefs, adapted from Freud, Ferenczi, and Abraham, have far-ranging implications. For example, because external influences are always filtered through phantasy, even conscience owes much to inner determinants. According to Klein, conscience develops by a long process of ingesting and spitting up the world, beginning with the breast (see Klein 1952: 49; 1958: 239). In this respect Klein was influenced by Freud's later claims, the implications of which he failed to draw entirely. In particular, Freud claimed in *The Ego and the Id* (1923) that the punishing superego develops as a reflection of the death drive, meaning that society has only a secondary importance in the development of conscience. In short, both the Freud of

Beyond the Pleasure Principle and Klein felt that experience of the world doesn't necessarily correspond with the acute feelings of guilt with which we may suffer. As Freud put it in 1930, "Experience shows . . . that the severity of the super-ego which a child develops in no way corresponds to the severity of treatment which he has himself met with" (1930: 130). To this particular statement Freud appended a rare acknowledgment, in the form of a footnote, to Klein's work in this area.[51]

Freud's rejection of the environment as a cause of psychopathology is reflected in his biologically based instinct theory. Thus it cannot be surprising that Klein's own treatment of object relations repeats Freud's disdain for the object world and concurrent advocacy of a biologically determined nether-world. In fact, for both Freud and Klein the oxymoronic world of (individual) "psychic reality" is a neat benchmark against which they could measure all human behavior or, as Freud put it in 1921, all *Massenpsychologie*, group psychology. In other words, Klein's theory of unconscious phantasy is the direct, albeit twisted, descendent of Freud's unchecked metabiological speculations: she openly shared Freud's and Ferenczi's belief in phylogenesis and archaic inheritance, Abraham's belief in the constitutionality of psychosexual character development, and Ferenczi's specific claims about the child's acquisition of a sense of reality. A case in point is her attempt in 1923 to buttress the wild claims of Ferenczi's *Thalassa*. While discussing little Fritz's anxiety while walking to school, Klein appends the following footnote to "The Role of the School in the Libidinal Development of the Child":

> [In my essay "Early Analysis," 1923,] I worked out in more detail how Fritz's numerous phantasies about his mother's womb, procreation and birth concealed the most intense and strongly repressed wish to enter his mother's womb by means of coitus. Ferenczi had put forward the suggestion in his Congress paper, "Thalassa," that in the unconscious, return to the maternal body seems only to be possible by means of coitus, and he set up an hypothesis that deduces this recurrently demonstrable [sic] phantasy from phylogenetic evolutionary sources. (1923: 61)

So what is the upshot? Although Klein may not have understood Freud's and Ferenczi's complex bio-logic, as some have argued (see Grosskurth 1986: 108), it is obvious that she absorbed—or, if you prefer, introjected—the spirit of their psycho-Lamarkian conclusions. It is therefore rather unimportant that she couched her own interpretation of the old metabiology in the so-called "psychological" terms of phantasy; or that she claimed to find, first, infantile phantasies of a libidinal nature, then phantasies of a destructive nature, and then phantasies of a more relational nature.

Whatever she may have "discovered" in her clinical practice, she was at bottom an instinct theorist who came of age under the influence of Freud's *Beyond the Pleasure Principle* and its many aftereffects.

CON-PHUSION; OR, HOW FANTASY
BECOMES PHANTASTIC

Of course, Klein had good reason for grounding her clinical observations in a theory of innate human nature. The tragic, loosely Christian, notion that we are born into a life shaped by destructive "unconscious phantasies" made corroboration of her theories not only impossible but unnecessary. Just like Freud's instinct theory, unconscious phantasy is a hidden first cause outside or beyond empirical considerations. And so, as we are starting to see, Klein was no more of an empiricist than Freud—a great irony given the rhetoric of clinical observation that is supposed to distinguish her particular discourse. Despite a touch of equivocation, analysts Jay Greenberg and Stephen Mitchell summarize the situation rather well:

> Klein's views on infancy are, for the most part [sic], *not* based directly on work with "preoedipal" children. Her youngest patient was 2¾ years of age, and most of the children she uses as examples are considerably older, comfortably within the oedipal range as Freud had defined it. The presumption of oedipal impulses within the first two years, despite what Klein acknowledges is little overt indication of such impulses, derives from the content of such fantasies in older children, particularly the predominance of oral themes. The early dating is based on the premise that orality is the central libidinal component within the first year of life ([Klein] 1932, p. 212). Klein was extrapolating back from the data of older children to their earliest years, much in the way Freud had used data from adults to determine infantile experiences in general. (1983: 123, n.)

Evidently the more things changed with Klein, the more they stayed essentially the same as Freud: Klein made theoretical pronouncements about the contents of unconscious infantile phantasy life that she then proceeded to apply to children during therapy.

Let me be more explicit still. Klein based her theories on the unconscious phantasies of infancy for a very specific reason, the same reason, I will argue later, that Freud held on so tightly to a biologically based instinct theory: namely, if these phantasies are found from the beginning of life at the level of *predispositions*, then all of Klein's clinical observations are bound to be true. For such a theory defends, in advance, all clinical "findings" from the charge that they were contaminated by prior expectations and bad technique. Indeed, since Klein's child-patients were supposed to be in transcendent, mystical contact with the unconscious—that is, with the hidden truth of consciousness—there was literally no allowance for error, for social or mimetic behavior, that might compromise objectivity. In this respect Klein tried to have her cake and eat it too, as when she claimed with astonishing naivete: "It is surprising how easily children will sometimes accept the interpretation and even show unmistakable pleasure in doing so. The reason probably is that in certain strata of their minds, communication between the conscious and the unconscious is as yet comparatively easy, so that the way back to the unconscious is much simpler to find" (1926: 8). Instead of supposing that children's minds are extremely pliable—which, of course, they are—Klein invoked a hidden "strata" that did the dirty work which is, surely, of her own doing.

This criticism is supported by a simple, if stunning, fact. The children with whom Klein apparently "discovered," for example, thalassal regressive trends were not just any children. Rather, they were her own children: "Fritz," for instance, was none other than her five-year-old son Erich (Pontalis 1981: 98; Grosskurth 1986: 95–96).[52] Needless to say, this unscrupulous use of her own children as guinea pigs for the cause of psychoanalysis puts her efforts in a bad light.[53] Over the years, it is true, Klein was able to attract a larger sample of children from which to test her ridiculous theories. Yet it would be a mistake to conclude from this fact that her findings became increasingly more objective. For not only was her epistemic foundation built on sand but even her so-called experience amounted to nothing—or to less than nothing. Why? Because the majority of her early case studies, from which we know she derived *all* of her basic principles, came from within psychoanalysis as the children of *other analysts*. This delirious family romance began in Berlin and continued in England. Ernest Jones, for example, invited Klein to England in 1926 at least in part because he wanted her to analyze his own children, Mervyn and Gwenith. As Jones wrote to Freud in a letter of May 16, 1927: "Though we had brought them up as wisely as we knew how, neither child escaped neurosis, which analysis showed, as usual [!], to be much more serious than appeared" (Freud and Jones 1993: 617). Jones claimed that Mervyn was "introverted" and suffered from "sexual inversion," while Gwenith suffered from "intense guilt and a definite obsessional neurosis." As a result of the analysis, Jones thought that the children were "in every way freer, and are constantly gay and happy." Later on Jones's wife, Katherine, was also analyzed by Klein, thus closing the circuit of this questionable family affair.

So what, if anything, is the moral of this story? To begin with, children who are psychoanalyzed become the objects of psychoanalytic research, that is, they become research subjects and patients. Worse, they become fantastic *projects*, the child's unconscious phantasies being nothing more than the analyst's conscious wish fulfilled, a cultural artifact that owes nothing to human nature and everything to the theoretical, therapeutic, and normative culture of psychoanalysis. What we find in Klein is, in other words, a disturbing tendency to sacrifice children to the theories, desires, and fantasies she dreamed up under the name of psychoanalysis. As such, "phantasy" is merely the name for her own fantasy life as reflected in the eyes of loving and hating, devouring and spitting, patients. This is of course a troubling conclusion, all the more so because we are discussing children rather than consensual adults. Most disturbing of all are those children who—having identified with, introjected, or swallowed whole the doctrine of psychoanalysis—have indeed exhibited signs of a death drive à la Klein.

About these hapless victims of a botched therapeutic regimen we are left to ponder a number of questions. First, for example, what sort of "object relations" have these children been subjected to within the analytic scene? Second, what sort of analyst is the lesser of two evils, the sadistic or the masochistic analyst? And, finally, what sort of guardian delivers a child up to the trauma called psychoanalysis, the aftereffects of which are likely to do far more harm than good?

By insisting on the continuity of Freud's metabiological speculations, not only across his oeuvre, but as they are reflected in the works of his predecessors and followers, such as Ferenczi and Klein, one gets a fairly accurate picture about just how wild, how *meta*, the Freudian scene really was. Surely it affords the critic some much-needed insight into Freud's own practice, and into his so-called philosophical or metaphysical impulse in *Beyond the Pleasure Principle*. Unfortunately, in most cases the philosophically inspired literature on Freud's death-drive theory seems barely cognizant of the biological context of his argument, or of the bizarre uses to which it has been put—the surfaces of which I have just scratched in the last two sections.

On the other hand there seems to have been, so to speak, bigger fish to fry. In the next section I want to turn more carefully to the philosophical literature on *BPP*, in particular to its appropriation to a dialectical and politically motivated way of thinking about the grand struggles of life and death. This turn begins with a preamble about Freud's relation to philosophy in general and to Nietzsche in particular, and is followed by a closer examination of Hegelian and Marxist ways of interpreting the psychic conflict that lies at the heart of Freudian interpretation.

Philosophical 'Beyond's

> Did not Goethe, indeed, say that a bad theory was better than none at all?
> —Sandor Ferenczi, *Thalassa: A Theory of Genitality*[54]

Just as some commentators are smitten with either the biographical or biological takes on *Beyond the Pleasure Principle*, another group, perhaps the most prolific of all, obviously prefers the philosophical. Read with a twist of Continental philosophy, Freud's metapsychological "speculations" are most often subsumed from this perspective under the rubric of philosophical reflection (see Jones 1957: 41) or metaphysics. And, actually, this may not be too far-fetched an idea, since Freud himself conceived that through the "psychology of the unconscious" he might "transform metaphysics into metapsychology" (Freud 1901b: 259).

Some contend that *BPP* in particular reflects Freud's "Continental weakness, illustrated by Hegel and Marx, for espousing dialectical theories" (Clark 1980: 433). For others, such as French philosopher Jean Hyppolite, the theories of *BPP* are more simply a "woolly philosophy" (in Lacan 1954–55: 67). It is certainly from within the Continental tradition that many theorists want to locate Freud, a fact that is all the more delirious as it slams one theoretical project, itself comprised of disparate bits and pieces of theory, against some others. For example, French philosopher Gilles Deleuze enthusiastically refers to *BPP* as the "masterpiece" wherein Freud "engaged most directly—and how penetratingly—in specifically philosophical reflection" (1991: 111). By reflection, Deleuze means to invoke the "transcendental" philosophy of Immanuel Kant: "that is to say [a philosophy] concerned with a particular kind of investigation of the question of principles."[55] No matter that Freud referred to Kant very sparingly indeed. Predictably, it was this nonscientific side of Freud's work that worried English analyst Ernest Jones, who also thought that Freud's notion of a repetition compulsion assumed "transcendental significance" in *BPP* (1957: 271, 275; cf. Freud and Jones 1993: 667).

Just as *BPP* marks a return to Freud's earliest professional interest in biology, his speculation about the death drive also marks a return to some of his earliest personal interests in cultural and philosophical questions. "In the works of my later years," Freud writes in "An Autobiographical Study," "I have given free rein to the inclination, which I kept down for so long, for speculation" (1925a: 57). According to an interesting suggestion by Bakan (1958), Freud returned to philosophical questions at an age when Jewish men are expected to consider such matters for the first time. As a young man Freud certainly imagined a time when old age would give him an excuse to dabble in philosophical matters: "Philosophy, which I have always pictured as my goal and refuge in my old age, gains every day in attraction" (in Jones 1957: 41). As it turns out, Freud is known to have read at least some of the works of Plato, Aristotle, David Hume, Arthur Schopenhauer, Ludwig Feuerbach, Friedrich Nietzsche, Franz Brentano, and Henry Thomas Buckle.

He also squashed this youthful interest and later qualified, sometimes to the point of distortion, his "regressive" attraction to philosophy. In words placed in smaller type in the original edition of his "Autobiographical Study," Freud adds this disclaimer: "Even when I have moved away from observation, I have carefully avoided any contact with philosophy proper. This avoidance has been greatly facilitated by constitutional incapacity" (1925a: 59). Throughout his career, Freud's fear of being associated with philosophy seems to have encouraged him to use psychoanalysis for the same polemical ends that he officially eschewed. Like artists, philosophers were subject to the analyst's all-knowing, often condescending, gaze. For instance, in "The Claims of Psycho-Analysis to Scientific Interest," Freud writes:

> There is yet another way in which philosophy can derive a stimulus from psycho-analysis, and that is by itself becoming a subject of psycho-analytic research. Philosophical theories and systems have been the work of a small number of men of striking individuality. In no science does the personality of the scientific worker play anything like so large a part as in philosophy. And now for the first time psycho-analysis enables us to construct a "psychography" of a personality. (1913a: 179)

Of course, Freud might just as well have been writing about psychoanalysis in this passage devoted to subjective motivations. That he nonetheless recognized the shaky ground upon which he was treading is established by his following admission that such work is really "not the business of psychoanalysis," claiming self-interestedly that although "a theory is psychologically determined does not in the least invalidate its scientific truth."

Freud's avoidance of philosophy registered the hostile climate within which the pursuit of speculative philosophy was derided in his youth, especially during the 1870's, under the constant ridicule of a zealous materialism.

As Fritz Wittels puts it, Freud "grew up in a dreary epoch of philosophy, in the midst of the roar and stork of battle, a veritable intoxication of science by facts" (1931: 52). Yet it was also a time, as noted above, of great speculative thinking among the nature philosophers, such as Fechner. Thus Freud seems to have remained conflicted by his illicit attraction to philosophy. For example, near the beginning of *BPP* he states that the long history of philosophical work on pleasure is "of no concern" to psychoanalysis, referring instead to the "facts of daily observation" which comprise the essence of scientific work (1920a: 7). As always, Freud gives and takes away any question of debt within the space of a few sentences:

> Priority and originality are not among the aims that psycho-analytic work sets itself; and the impressions that underlie the hypothesis of the pleasure principle are so obvious that they can scarcely be overlooked. On the other hand we would readily express our gratitude to any philosophical or psychological theory which was able to inform us of the meaning of the feelings of pleasure and unpleasure which act so imperatively upon us. But on this point we are, alas, offered nothing to our purpose. (7)

Freud audaciously states that priority is of no concern even as he dismisses the substance of that priority, in effect claiming that the prior philosophical work on pleasure is "obvious" to the point of banality; or again, he would gladly accept some help from either philosophy or psychology, but they offer "nothing" except the obvious and the self-evident. Evidently, if priority is not a problem for Freud, it is because there is nothing philosophers can teach him that he doesn't already know.

Despite Freud's avowed disdain and "constitutional incapacity" for philosophy, *BPP* arrives "unwittingly" in chapter 6 "into the harbour of Schopenhauer's philosophy" (49–50). As Jones puts it, Freud "was surrendering the old control and allowing his thoughts to soar to far distant regions" (1957: 41). Like many others, Schopenhauer helped prepare the foundation for Freud's understanding of sexuality (the will to live) and the unconscious (see Young and Brook 1994). Moreover, and despite some claims to the contrary (107), Freud did lift the general tenor of the death-drive theory from Schopenhauer. Freud was probably thinking of the following passage near the end of the second volume of *The World As Will and Representation*:

> Dying is certainly to be regarded as the real aim of life; at the moment of dying, everything is decided which through the whole course of life was only prepared and introduced. Death is the result, the *résumé*, of life, or the total sum expressing at one stroke all the instruction given by life in detail and piecemeal, namely that the whole striving, the phenomenon of which is life, was a vain,

fruitless, and self-contradictory effort, to have returned from which is a deliverance. (1844: 637)

Death, as Schopenhauer adds, "crowns the instruction given him by life." Or as Freud put it the *New Introductory Lectures* of 1932–33, "From the concurrent and opposing action of these two [the life and death drives] proceed the phenomena of life which are brought to an end by death" (1933a: 107). Freud's strategy for dealing with this philosophical port of call is then rationalized in familiar terms:

> You may shrug your shoulders and say: "That isn't natural science, it's Schopenhauer's philosophy!" But, Ladies and Gentlemen, why should not a bold thinker have guessed something that is afterwards confirmed by sober and painstaking detailed research? Moreover, there is nothing that has not been said already, and similar things had been said by many people before Schopenhauer. (107)

And by these other thanatographers, Freud may have meant the litany of similar "guesses"—from Plutarch to Lord Byron—about life and death found in Schopenhauer's discussion "On the Vanity and Suffering of Life" (see 1844: 585–87). If so, Freud used Schopenhauer's erudition against him, erasing Schopenhauer's originality and, to that extent, his own debt to his work.

Many scholars have noted Freud's almost obsessive denial of priority—however much his rhetoric suggests otherwise—which in this case is surely based on the close proximity of his work to that of Schopenhauer and Nietzsche. As Jacques Derrida puts it, "Schopenhauer's and Nietzsche's words and 'notions' resemble psychoanalytic discourse to the point of being mistaken for it.... And because of the resemblance, because of the all too natural imputation of inheritance, this affiliation must at all costs be avoided" (1980: 266). And thus the father of psychoanalysis attempted to erect his own theoretical ground without recourse to the history of philosophy.

Freud was certainly more comfortable citing as authorities the great poets, especially Shakespeare and Goethe. "We are accustomed to think," Freud writes of the death drive, "that such is the fact, and we are strengthened in our thought by the writings of our poets" (1920a: 44–45). Indeed, having reviewed the biological literature and found it generally unable to confirm *or* reject his own hypothesis about the instinct to "*restore an earlier state of things*" (57; his emphasis), Freud finds solace in "myth rather than a scientific explanation." According to the philosopher Rodolphe Gasché, Freud's recourse to myth is precisely that which "lies beyond the philosophic and the metatheoretical speculative" (1974: 200). In particular, Freud invokes

Plato's myth about the origin of life in the unity of opposites that was subsequently cut in two by Zeus; it is a myth, then, that explains the unexplainable, namely, sexual difference. As Derrida (1980) rightly suggests, Freud engages in an operation that allows him to sidestep Plato and Socrates for Greek mythology and poetry. Freud, in fact, cites Plato only to cite the poet Aristophanes: "What I have in mind," Freud writes, "is the theory which Plato put into the mouth of Aristophanes in the *Symposium*" (1920a: 57). Although recognized elsewhere (see 1905b: 134), in *BPP* Freud does not refer to Socrates's discourse on Eros, which is also described by Plato. Furthermore, in a footnote added in 1921 Freud adds insult to injury by stating that the origin of Plato's myth (as told by Aristophanes) "is essentially the same theory to be found in the Upanishads" (1920a: 58, n. 1). "If Freud in his turn erases Socrates," Derrida justly remarks, "it is in order to take the origin away from Plato, and to make him, already, an heir" (1980: 374). It is of course significant that Freud does not return the father of philosophy to the poets in general but to the author of *The Clouds*, Socrates's most vocal and public adversary. "Aristophanes is not just anyone," Derrida reminds us. "Not just for Socrates. Or for Plato. He is the other" (1980: 372).

Perhaps, however, Freud had more trouble dealing with Nietzsche's influence on psychoanalysis than that of any other thinker. Nietzsche had anticipated some of Freud's ideas, such as the chaotic id and the disciplining role of conscience, and considered himself a critical psychologist of his *Zeitgeist*. And so, before I turn to Hegel and Marx and the dialectical interpretation of *BPP*, I want to briefly outline Freud's relation to Nietzsche, which is in some ways relevant to an understanding of a "beyond" of the pleasure principle.

THE NIETZSCHEAN BOND

> Most frequently, finally, I found among young scholars that what lay behind the arrogant contempt of philosophy was the bad aftereffect of—a philosopher to whom they now denied allegiance on the whole without, however, having broken the spell of his cutting evaluation of other philosophers—with the result of an over-all irritation with all philosophy.
> —Friedrich Nietzsche, *Beyond Good and Evil*[56]

In 1905 Eduard Hitschmann presented a paper to the Wednesday Psychological Society on Freud and Nietzsche, and in the years to follow many would repeat this earliest recorded attempt at a genealogy of psychoanalysis. For instance, in a letter to Freud in late 1930, Arnold Zweig wrote to Freud about psychoanalysis and Nietzsche. In a typical surge of enthusiasm, Zweig suggests that he would like to write something about this apparent familial relation:

> To me it seems that you have achieved everything that Nietzsche intuitively felt to be his task, without his really being able to achieve it with his poetic idealism and brilliant inspirations. He tried to explain the birth of tragedy; you have done it in *Totem and Taboo*. He longed for a world beyond Good and Evil; by means of analysis you have discovered a world to which this phrase actually applies. Analysis has reversed all values, it has conquered Christianity, disclosed the true Antichrist, and liberated the spirit of resurgent life from the ascetic ideal. (Freud and Zweig 1970: 23)

A few years later Zweig would repeat, in another gushing letter, that "in you I recognize the man who has carried out all that Nietzsche first dreamt of" (74). Although Freud did not dissuade Zweig from this train of thought, he was not very keen about such speculation either. He made it very clear that he did not want or need to read about Zweig's Freud-Nietzsche project, preferring to pass the torch of memory unlit to another. "You could write it," Freud replies, "when I am no longer here and you are haunted by the memory of me" (25).

Always ready to sidestep questions of intellectual priority, Freud preferred to ignore the connections between his and Nietzsche's work. According to Sterba, Freud once admitted frankly that "He who wants to be original should not have read Nietzsche" (1982: 120). Freud was uncomfortable with the idea that someone might confuse analysis for philosophy and took steps to distance his creation from that questionable tradition. To take one example, he sometimes likened philosophers to psychotics, their work to delusion: "Philosophers no doubt believe that in such studies they are contributing to the development of human thought, but every time there is a psychological or even psychopathological problem behind them" (in Costigan 1965: 226).

Freud strategized that psychoanalysis in an age of science would suffer from an association with philosophy. As a result, he remained a protective father who plotted a course of least resistance for his ideas—even if it meant blinding himself, at convenient junctures, to certain questions of priority and originality. If one keeps in mind this strategy of avoidance—where ignorance, no doubt correctly, is understood as the essential precondition of originality—it is less mysterious to read in the *Minutes of the Vienna Psychoanalytic Society* that Freud "has never been able to study Nietzsche" (Nunberg and Federn 1962–75, 2: 32). Later, around the time that Nietzsche's autobiographical work *Ecce Homo* was posthumously released, an entry records that:

PROF. FREUD first emphasizes his own peculiar relationship to philosophy: its abstract nature is so unpleasant to him, that he has renounced the study of philosophy. He does not know Nietzsche's work; occasional attempts at reading it were smothered by an excess of interest. In spite of the similarities ... Nietzsche's ideas have had no influence whatsoever on his own work.
(Nunberg and Federn 1962–75, 2: 359–60)

If these remarks seem disingenuousness, it is at least fitting that they were made on an April Fool's Day in 1908. And actually Freud does sound playful in his rejection of an excessively interesting Nietzsche—an aspect of his personality that commentators have an increasingly difficult time discerning with the passing years. A less comic though similar sounding response from Freud can be found years later in "An Autobiographical Study," where he admits that Nietzsche, "whose guesses and intuitions often agree in the most astonishing way with the laborious findings of psychoanalysis, was for a long time avoided by me on that account" (1925a: 60).

Even though Freud kept his distance from Nietzsche and philosophy, he did pay his respects on occasion. According to Jones, Freud once stated that Nietzsche "had a more penetrating knowledge of himself than any other man who ever lived or was likely to live" (1955: 344)—certainly high praise from the father of psychoanalysis. But as many have remarked, Freud could not have ignored Nietzsche's ideas, since the latter's reputation had risen considerably in Germany and Austria after his death in 1900. As Sulloway puts it, "Both Schopenhauer's and Nietzsche's ideas were so widely discussed within late-nineteenth-century intellectual circles that Freud could not possibly have escaped a reasonably general education in their doctrines" (1979: 468; Dorer 1932: 62; Ellenberger 1970: 277).

If the cultural context made it hard for Freud to ignore Nietzsche, his disciples made it nearly impossible. Paul Federn, a loyal Freudian, is recorded as stating: "Nietzsche has come so close to our views that we can ask only, 'Where has he not come close?' He intuitively knew a number of Freud's discoveries; he was the first to discover the significance of abreaction, of repression, of flight into illness, of the instincts—the normal as well as the sadistic instincts" (Nunberg and Federn 1962–75, 1: 359; see also Sterba 1982: 120). Freud may have discussed Nietzsche with their mutual friend, the analyst Lou Andreas-Salomé. It is also true that analysts like Alfred Adler and Otto Rank would use Nietzsche as a name with which to rattle Freud. Of Rank, Roazen writes: "It was no accident that in 1926, when Otto Rank was breaking with Freud, he sent as a seventieth birthday gift to Freud the collected works of Nietzsche; nor should we be surprised to hear that Freud is reported not to have appreciated this gift, a reminder from a former student of a spiritual teacher upon whom Freud himself was dependent" (1997: 15). Rank had a firsthand opportunity to witness Freud's reaction to Nietzsche, since he was the secretary who recorded the minutes of the Vienna Psychoanalytic Society.

Beyond the Pleasure Principle itself seems to be a fairly deliberate echo of Nietzsche's great work of 1886, *Beyond Good and Evil*, just as the notion of repetition finds some resonance with Nietzsche's theories of *Zarathustra*. But whereas Nietzsche's "beyond" signals an overcoming of morality, a beyond that explodes the categories of good and evil from within, Freud's use of the word *jenseits*—the noun form of which means "the hereafter"—is arguably quite different. With his title Freud ironically proposed an impossibility that he neither could nor would deliver: the beyond as a "spiritual plane above and beyond ordinary existence" (Kerr 1993: 500). Consequently, Freud's reference to the "beyond" is a misnomer of sorts, primarily because it signifies a "before" of the pleasure principle. The different tone of the word *beyond* in Freud's and Nietzsche's work is reflected in their quite different approach to strife and conflict. Viewed against the *gaya scienza* of Nietzsche's affirmative philosophy, Freud's psychoanalysis is consistently structured by an ethic of resignation and withdrawal; that is, by what Deleuze and Guattari call "the ascetic ideal" (1972: 332). It thus follows, despite Freud's apparent reliance upon Nietzsche in *BPP*, that Freud is closer to Schopenhauer's pessimistic "harbor." Of course, Nietzsche himself was an avid follower of Schopenhauer in his youth, and this may have something to do with Freud's attitude to both thinkers. For, according to many biographers, Freud was familiar with the early works of Nietzsche, which he encountered as a student, but not so much with the later works. By the time Freud was discussing psychoanalysis, he was long inclined to ignore Nietzsche's publications. Consequently, he was probably unfamiliar with the affirmative side of Nietzsche that had turned decisively away from the pessimism of Schopenhauer and the decadence of Richard Wagner.

Nietzsche was, of course, a great critic of Hegel and of dialectics in general, and his notion of a "beyond" was meant as an alternative to the progressive spirit of synthesis. However, the anti-Hegelian side of Nietzsche's influence on Freud was mostly ignored until the French, influenced by Heidegger's reading of Nietzsche (published in the 1960's), began to read Freud and Nietzsche together. Until then, it was much more common for commentators to push Freud in the direction of Hegelian and Marxist dialectics than toward Nietzsche's less systematic, but (arguably) more volatile thoughts. To this more Nietzschean Freud I will turn later, since it only makes sense in the wake of the dialectical interpretation of Freud that began in earnest only in the 1920's and 1930's.

DIALECTICAL 'BEYOND'S

It is certainly true that the dialectical appropriation of *Beyond the Pleasure Principle* often proceeds against the grain of Freud's own text. In fact, psychoanalytic speculations are often put to work for the sorts of ends that Freud himself openly rejected. It follows that a dialectically useful *BPP* almost always turns around a critique or "correction" of Freud's biases, especially his narrow focus on individual psychobiology and concordant disinclination to accord social factors etiological significance.

Although Freud does not seem to have read any Hegel or Marx, he would have in any case encountered their views, like those of Schopenhauer and Nietzsche, in the popular discourse of the time and in the dialectical arguments of authors he would have read. For example, Eduard von Hartmann's work was very well known during Freud's lifetime. In 1869, Hartmann published *The Philosophy of the Unconscious*, which, by 1882, had already appeared in nine editions. Hartmann's main concern in this text is to bridge the distance between Schopenhauer and Hegel with a fresh synthesis of Will and Idea. To this dialectical end, he turns to Friedrich Wilhelm Schelling and posits the existence of an unconscious realm in mental life.

If many have emphasized Freud's debt to early theories of the unconscious, including Hartmann's, few have said much about the possible *philosophical* importance of Hartmann's work for Freud, especially for *BPP*. Ellenberger says nothing about this possibility, finding only that "the main interest in *The Philosophy of the Unconscious* lies not so much in its philosophical theories as in its wealth of supporting material" (1970: 210). But Ellenberger would certainly agree that a tentative line can be drawn between Freud and Hartmann on a popular topic of German Romanticism: namely, death.

Hartmann follows Schopenhauer's supposition that evil and suffering exist on a conscious level (see Copleston 1965: 57–59). As a dialectician, this conclusion implies its opposite for Hartmann, which he finds in Schelling's philosophy: namely, developmental advancement toward a goal must exist at an unconscious level. To these dialectical maneuvers Hartmann adds another, attempting to synthesize Schopenhauer's pessimism with Leibniz's optimism (for example, his claim that this is the best of all possible worlds). Yet, despite the influence of Leibniz, Hartmann's thinking remains—for modern readers, at least—pessimistic overall. The unfolding of consciousness that defines progress for Hartmann does not imply happiness in civilization, but quite the opposite. Hartmann concludes that *peoples in a state of nature* are not more wretched, but *more happy*, than civilized peoples; that the *poor, low*, and *rude* classes are happier than the *rich*, aristocratic, and *cultivated*; that the *stupid* are happier than the *clever*, in general, that the stupid are happier the obtuser is its nervous system, because the excess of pain over pleasure is so much less, and the entanglement in the illusion so much greater. (1869: iii, 115; cf. Ibid.: 76)

As Schopenhauer similarly argued, human reflection not only heightens our sensitivity to the highs, but mostly to the lows, of existence (n.d.: 17–27). Since intelligence from this economic point of view implies unhappiness, Hartmann follows Schopenhauer's conclusion that the lowest organism is "enviable" for its lack of self-consciousness (1869: iii, 76–77). As Schopenhauer puts it, if pleasure is merely the absence (or negative) of suffering, then "the lower animals appear to enjoy a happier destiny than man" (n.d.: 17); it is a thought that reappears throughout *The World As Will and Representation* (1819 and 1844). Hartmann thus envisages a moment of realization when our fellow sufferers will comprehend the pursuit of pleasure as a hopeless "folly," and long instead "only for absolute painlessness, for nothingness, Nirvana" (iii, 117–18). As Frederick Copleston puts it, Hartmann's developmental scheme thus contends that World Spirit wants to extinguish itself in a "cosmic suicide": "What is needed is the greatest possible development of consciousness, so that in the end humanity may understand the folly of volition [i.e., will], commit suicide and, with its own destruction, bring the world-process to an end" (1965: 59).

The connection between aspects of Hartmann's and Freud's dark outlook is striking, cutting across their visions of the life and death drives, Idea and Will, and construction and dissolution, and culminating for both in a bleak economic appraisal of pleasure, pain, and happiness. Both men conclude that death (as a state of nirvana) is strangely preferable to life and that civilized humanity is plagued by the impossibility of happiness. However, the two men do differ slightly in their appraisal of lower and higher organisms. While Freud would have appreciated the irony of Hartmann's verdict that the most civilized are the least happy of all, Freud's more stoical view, perhaps based on therapeutic considerations, implied that such unhappiness or dis-ease (*Unbehagen*) in civilization is an unavoidable and irrefutable price of *Kultur*. In other words Freud was more likely than Hartmann to praise the sickness of self-consciousness, whereas lower life forms were obviously not so capable. Even so, aspects of Freud's metapsychology come dangerously close to the sorts of antisocial or antilife conclusions that are found in Hartmann's philosophy.

Just as Freud himself was part of a culture caught in the undertow of

Hegel's sweep across history, Freudian psychology has subsequently been subject to the deformations of dialectics. While some have analyzed Hegel's dialectics in terms of Freud's views of psychic conflict and dualism (see Robinson 1969: 40–42), others have mapped Hegel's "science of experience" directly onto Freud's psychosexual stages of development. Philosopher Clark Butler (1976) has tried to demonstrate, for example, how Hegel's description of the stages of historical development—from the state of sense-certainty, through self-consciousness, to reason, can be read against Freud's descriptive psychology. To take just one instance, Butler contends that the child's recognition of the mother reflects Hegel's "inverted world," which is followed by an onslaught of desire at the oral stage.

This sometimes strange game of comparative theory has, however, been more passionately played out in the case of Karl Marx and Freud. Among some others, Wilhelm Reich, Erich Fromm, and Herbert Marcuse have tried to reconcile historical materialism and depth psychology—an attempt that probably began with analyst Alfred Adler, a social democrat, who made some tentative overtures in this direction during the early days of the Wednesday Psychological Society (Clark 1980: 306). An important factor in the creation of a Freudian Marxism was the publication in 1932 of Marx's *Economic and Philosophic Manuscripts of 1844* (which only appeared in English in 1959). Against expectations, the young Marx was found steeped in Hegel's philosophy and in the idea of alienation—a slant in his work that opened a new round of debate about Marx, existentialism, and humanism during the thirties.

Marx, of course, felt that he had turned Hegel's idealism on its head to reveal the material or economic conditions of world history. As such, the revolutionary spirit of the slave described in the second section of Hegel's *Phenomenology of Spirit* is famously reinterpreted by Marx as the explosive potential of the proletariat. Some innovators have proposed that Freud's own psychological idealism can be turned on its head to similar good effect. The problem with this conjecture is that Freud's assumptions about society are based on a subjective foundation in the individual's psychic economy whereas Marx's assumptions about individuality are based on an objective foundation in political economy. What is foundational for one is secondary for the other. As John Strachey puts it:

> The principle conclusion to be derived from the study of psycho-analytic theory is, it seems to me, that the emergence of a particular type of consciousness—a particular set of political, religious, scientific, and miscellaneous opinions, a particular ideology, that is to say—must not be conceived of as the passive reflection of a given environment. It must be conceived of rather as the inter-

action of the social environment with certain dynamic, subjective urges within man himself. (1937: 13–14)

From a certain perspective, then, each methodology seems to complete the other, creating in effect a new sociopolitical psychology or, from the other side, a new sociopsychological politics. As we will see, this synthetical view has led to various responses to Freud's death-drive theory of 1920.

Personally and professionally, Freud himself rejected Marxist doctrine and thought of himself as "a liberal of the old school" (Freud and Zweig 1970: 21). While he recognized late in life that neither Marx nor Engels had "denied the influence of ideas and super-ego functions," he nonetheless continued to reserve judgment on the dialectical method itself (in Jones 1957: 345). "As to the 'dialectic,' " Freud writes, "I am no clearer [than before]." That Freud claimed to be mystified by dialectics was probably a reflection of his distaste for metaphysics and his corresponding pretensions to science. "I so rarely feel the need for synthesis. The unity of the world seems to me so self-evident as not to need emphasis. What interests me is the separation and breaking up into its component parts of what would otherwise revert to an inchoate mass" (Freud and Andreas-Salomé 1966: 32). But if Freud never warmed up to Marxism or Bolshevism—claiming in 1933 that "although practical Marxism has mercilessly cleared away all idealistic systems and illusions, it has itself developed illusions which are no less questionable and unprovable than the earlier ones" (1933a: 180; cf. Sterba 1982: 109)—some Marxists were just as convinced that Freud himself was nothing more than a bourgeois scientist. The differences between Freud and Marx are well known but worth spelling out. In the words of Thomas Johnston:

> For Marx, evil is rooted in society; for Freud, evil is rooted in human nature. Both offer answers: Marx would eradicate evil through rebuilding society; Freud would teach us to recognize and cope with psychic evil. When Marx is concerned with psychology at all, his concern is with men in the masses, Freud's concern is with both men in groups and men as individuals. Freud wants to reconcile human wishes to authority, for he assumes a fixed opposition of human wishes and authority. Marx wants to harmonize individual wills with an authoritarian, monolithic, collective will. (1965: 100)

In spite of these serious differences, analysts like Ernst Simmel and Siegfried Bernfeld thought that psychoanalysis and Marxism were complementary doctrines (see Jones 1957: 344). From the other side, even Vladimir Lenin was interested in Freudian ideas, as evidenced by the title of one of his works: *"Left-wing" Communism, An Infantile Disorder* (Johnston 1965: 81).[57] Similarly, Leon Trotsky was attentive to things psychoanalytic, especially to its therapeutic potential. Evidently shaken by the failure of the proletarian revolution,[58] and disgruntled with the Soviet experiment, some Marxists began to feel they had good reason to reconsider Freud's bourgeois science. As Erich Fromm later asked of the complacent proletariat: "Why has their *real* interests as human beings not outweighed their *fictitious* interests produced by all kinds of ideological influences and brain-washing?" (1981: 28). If the problem was no longer the actual material conditions of society, which had been secured in places without effecting significant political change, then perhaps the problem lay with the proletariat itself. In other words, perhaps a vestige of false consciousness remained untouched within the individual's inner economy; or again, perhaps the repressive forces of civilization were still entrenched in the individual's ego structure, which unfortunately lagged behind and complicated the radical possibilities of a new social order. This possibility did not mean that Marxists had changed their minds about the cause of social repression. On the contrary, their attention to individual psychology marked a deepening of that commitment on slightly different grounds, as we find in Herbert Marcuse's work: "The individual reproduces on the deepest level, in his instinctual structure, the values and behavior patterns that serve to maintain domination" (1970: 3). Given this view, psychoanalysis became a possible way of accounting for, and perhaps even alleviating, those inner conflicts that reflected and reinforced the false ideology that was turn-of-the-century capitalism. As Reuben Osborn[59] suggests in an early effort of Freudo-Marxist synthesis, the "real significance" of psychoanalysis seems to lie "in the contribution it makes to the task of freeing society from the trammels of capitalist conditions of production" (1937: 243).

Of course, the entire venture presupposed that Freud and Marx are indeed two halves of a whole, something which usually implies that Freud was a closet dialectician. Osborn is explicit about some of the ways Freudian psychoanalysis appears dialectical (234–50). At bottom, though, everything boils down to a debate about Aristotle's three principles of logic—namely, of identity, contradiction, and of the excluded third. According to some observers, dialectics and psychoanalysis both undermine these principles; still others, like psychoanalyst Ludwig Jekels (1941: 249–53), were not so easily convinced. Perhaps a quick review is in order.

Hegel and Marx argue that truth is actually a historical process fueled by the contradictions that analytic philosophers traditionally eschew; a monstrous truth expressed in, by, and as dialectics. While for Hegel the contradictions of history culminate in absolute knowledge, a state of transcendent consciousness, for Marx that history culminates in communism, a politico-economic state of social equality. The cunning of history is in both cases understood as the revelation of meaning over time.

Now, Freud also seems to eschew the formal logic of traditional philosophy. For Freud, after all, mental life is structured by conflict and, so the story goes, by contradiction. As he once put it, the primary processes are not accessible to conscious thought, "nor are they subject to the critical restrictions of logic, which repudiates some of these processes as invalid and seeks to undo them" (1940: 198). Since logic is cut off from the deep structure of the psyche, namely, from the unconscious, it is also cut off from the inverted truths of psychoanalysis. Freud himself states in "The Claims of Psycho-Analysis to Scientific Interest" that "the hypothesis of unconscious mental activities must compel philosophy to decide one way or the other and, if it accepts the idea, to modify its views on the relation of mind to body" (1913a: 178; cf. 1900, 5: 611–13). Against traditional philosophy, then, Freud's world is populated by psychic monsters after the likeness of Jekyll and Hyde: ego identity is not, therefore, reducible to the laws of reason. Accordingly, Freud explores the ways in which the unconscious ruins the logician's assumptions, for example, by following the unruly examples of symbolism and reversal: in fantasy life representations are not reducible to the external world of reality. So much, then, for classical logic. Based on a philosophy of the unconscious, Freud rather holds that interminable conflict is the greatest reality of our psychic lives.

To the extent that Marxists try to salvage something radical in Freud, they often translate the warring dualisms of psychoanalysis into the language of dialectics. Resolution of conflict thereby becomes a species of "synthesis," of what Hegel more precisely called the moment of *Aufhebung*—the simultaneous preservation and overcoming, sublation or "lifting up," of contradiction in a higher truth. And since conflict exists at the instinctual level for Freud, some Marxists like Osborn have been inclined to appropriate the late dualism of life and death drives to the dialectical method: "That life, as a process, involves the struggle between life and death forces, are almost commonplaces of the dialectical outlook" (1937: 248).

Despite the resemblance, though, there are a number of fairly obvious problems with this view. To begin with, psychic conflict is less defined by contradiction than by frustration. More to the point, Freud's life/death dualism is not dialectical in any meaningful way. Johnston is quite right when he states that "this dualism is not dialecticism. The life and death instincts, for instance, are not synthesized, unless they be synthesized into the life process itself; and that is unsatisfactory, for if the life process be a new thesis, it has no antithesis" (1965: 86). It should also be recalled that the all-important unconscious of psychoanalysis is not easily reducible to any Marxist category. In fact, Marxists are not usually impressed by the idea that there is a nonmaterial basis for understanding reality. In an excellent essay on this subject, Francis Bartlett thus argues, "The unity or interpenetration of opposites [i.e., Marxist and Freudian] means nothing at all if the opposites do not interpenetrate" (1939: 82). In short, the simplistic add-together-and-stir view of Freud and Marx violates their differences, which are not convergent.

Even so, it is worth exploring some of the specific dialectical responses to Freud's late dualism of the life and death drives, in part because such examples place Freud's theory in some much needed relief, even as they end up with their own problems and peculiarities. As I will argue later, I am sympathetic to the Marxist critique that psychoanalysis is far too dismissive of external reality, which it views suspiciously as the enemy (see Dufresne 1996b).

Reich Versus Freud. Wilhelm Reich, the first to recast Freud in Marxist terms with any care, understood that Freudian psychology diverges from dialectical materialism. Thus he flatly rejected Freud's late dualism and the pessimistic evaluation of mankind that goes along with it. Whereas Freud, in *Civilization and Its Discontents* and elsewhere, championed the tragic view of the antisocial individual trapped in society, the romantic Reich felt that human nature was essentially good and was perverted only later on. According to Reich, in fact, Freud's *Civilization* was written in 1929 to counter his Freudo-Marxist politics—which were first presented during lectures in Freud's home—with the biologically based, even "antisexual" arguments derived from *Beyond the Pleasure Principle* (Robinson 1969: 36). As Reich states, "I was the one who was *'unbehaglich in der Kultur,'* " discomforted by civilization (1952: 52), echoing the original German title of Freud's book of 1930.

Reich had first joined the Vienna Psychoanalytic Society in 1920 as a young medical student, eventually becoming well respected for his work on analytic technique and "character analysis." Reich's work at this time is heavily invested in Freud's early libido theory of energy. In 1924, Reich introduced his orgasm theory to his analytic colleagues, which was systematized three years later in *Die Funktion des Orgasmus* (later translated as *Genitality in the Theory and Therapy of Neurosis*). As suggested earlier, Reich argues that dammed-up libido causes neuroses and that relief is possible through orgasm: "Orgastic disturbance is thus the key to an understanding of the energy economy of every such illness. Neuroses are nothing but the attempts of the organism to compensate for the disturbance in the energy equilibrium" (1927: 76). "Orgastic potency" was the goal of his therapeutic practice.

While some analysts, like Richard Sterba, "mockingly" referred to Reich's views as a "genital paradise" (1982: 87), Freud at first merely regarded Reich's preoccupation with a genital basis for neuroses as his *Steckenpferd* or "hobby-horse" (I. O. Reich 1969: 13). For obviously much of what Reich wrote is indebted to Freud's own thoughts about neuroses, especially in the early days of analysis. Reich's theory basically stipulates, as Sterba puts it, that "a perfect orgasm will prevent or cure any form of neurosis" (1982: 87)—for, according to Reich, orgasm discharges the unused or surplus portion of energy in the organism's body. Reich proposes that orgasm occurs as a process of "four beats," wherein lies its therapeutic value: mechanical tension => bioelectric charge => bioelectric discharge => relaxation (1952: 229). As Paul Robinson states of Reich's orgasm theory, "The simplicity and consistency of this vision are at once magnificent and appalling" (1969: 13). Yet, from Reich's perspective, the orgasm theory and character analysis were obviously "consistent extensions of Freud's natural science" (1952: 170).

Even though these ideas resonate with Freud's own economic bias, including his precious theory of constancy, Freud nonetheless rejected Reich's extreme formulation since not all energy was amenable to such a happy solution (orgasm). For instance, *pregenital* drives are not susceptible to orgasmic discharge because they are physically premature. Also, Reich's work reduced the scope of analysis from sexuality broadly conceived to genitality alone. As a consequence, Reich emphasized physical or actual neuroses over the psychoneuroses that (in principle) interested Freud. For this reason, Reich felt that "*psychoanalysis is a psychology of ideas*, while *orgonomy is a science of physical energy*—physical energy inside the organism and outside the organism" (1952: 110; his emphasis).

If Reich promoted a view of libidinal energy more consonant with Freud's early psycho-physicalistic work, it is perhaps not surprising that he felt that the speculative Freud of *BPP* had betrayed the radical potential of his scientific discoveries. Psychoanalysis, Reich writes, "never recovered" from the introduction of the new dualism (213); moreover, the death drive was a "sinful" idea and a crime against life (177). While Reich fell out of favor with Freud by 1927, it was not until the publication of "The Masochistic Character" in 1932 that he finally attacked the death-drive theory directly. In this essay, later collected in *Character Analysis*, Reich argues: "This new theory traced the psychic conflict back to inner elements and more and more eclipsed the supreme role of the frustrating and punishing outer world" (1927–33: 232). On the subject of masochism, Freud had shifted his emphasis from the patient's *fear* of punishment—which would entail object relations—to his or her subjective *need* for punishment; in short,

Freud concluded that "masochism is older than sadism" (1933a: 105). Consequently, as Reich was the first to surmise, "this new formulation blocked the difficult path into the sociology of human suffering," and rather led to a "cultural philosophy of human suffering" (232–33). Indeed, this shift of emphasis from outer to inner in Freud's work is a critical, and insufficiently appreciated, result of *Beyond the Pleasure Principle*, or, more accurately, *BPP* is the culmination of this trend, which is present in all of his work.

Naturally, Freud was angered by Reich's essay on masochism, claiming that it "culminated in the nonsensical statement that what we have called the death instinct is a product of the capitalist system" (in Jones 1957: 166). However, according to Reich's biographer, Reich "believed nothing so idiotic" (Sharaf 1983: 183). In fact, Reich claims that his critique of the death drive does not derive from his Marxist interests (1952: 136).[60] Yet there is no doubt, as Freud suspected, that Reich came to think of any psychoanalytic theory organized around the dualism of life and death drives as just another piece of false ideology—more a projection than a true description of the ways things are in the material world.[61] Against this ideology Reich proposed a "sex-economic sociology" dedicated to a new synthesis of Marx and Freud. "Sex-economic sociology dissolves the contradiction that caused psychoanalysis to forget the social factor and Marxism to forget the animal origin of man" (1970: xxiii).

Reich felt that his work was greater than the sum of its parts—and rightly so, given the differences between Freud and Marx indicated above. Nonetheless, he was always careful to recognize Freud's importance for his version of the Freudo-Marxist synthesis.[62] His growing child was obviously made possible by Freud's new insights, insights, as Reich puts it in *The Mass Psychology of Fascism*, that were unavailable to Marx because he "was a sociologist and not a psychologist, and because at that time scientific psychology did not exist" (1970: 25). But if Marx had a good excuse for ignoring psychology, Freud failed to grasp even the basics of the old sociology. In a letter of March 26, 1934, to his colleague Otto Fenichel, Reich thus states:

> The basic debate between dialectical-materialist and bourgeois psychoanalysts will primarily have to prove where Freud the scientist came into conflict with Freud the bourgeois philosopher; where psychoanalytic research corrected the bourgeois concept of culture and where the bourgeois concept of culture hindered and confused the scientific research and led it astray. "Freud against Freud" is the central theme of our criticism. Not for one moment should we put our consideration for Freud before our consideration for the future of psychoanalysis. (1952: 155)

It is a recurrent theme, even (and sometimes especially) in the dissident literature on psychoanalysis, that the question of who is more Freudian or, in this case, more faithful to the "science" of psychoanalysis invariably comes to the fore during a dispute among competitors. As Reich repeats in an open letter to some like-minded colleagues on December 16, 1934, "I know from experience that there is no better way to serve Freud and psychoanalysis than to separate the scientific [orgasm theory] from the non-scientific [death-instinct theory] within the doctrine of psychoanalysis" (169).

According to sociologist-historian Philip Rieff, part of their different orientation lies in the fact that Freud, despite everything, was a closet philosopher while Reich was implicitly anti-intellectual and antiphilosophical. For Reich, thought itself brought the mind into conflict with the body and was, therefore, unnatural. Echoing Schopenhauer and Hartmann in this regard, Reich modeled his therapeutic ideal after animals (1968: 168), and therapy for him became a kind of *cogito interruptus*. In Rieff's words:

> At the moment he began to philosophize, man became the sick animal, thinking his disease. The first great anti-philosopher, Hegel, had foreseen the end of philosophy and its transformation into history. The anti-historian, Marx, had foreseen the end of history and its transformation into political economy. The Freudo-Marxist, Reich, had foreseen the end of all defensive, abstract thinking, including psychology, as the analysis of defensive thinking. (154)

Like all prophets, Reich was what Rieff calls "the scientist of the revolution meant to end all revolutions" (167).

Reich's brand of Marxism included certain "feminist" ideals about the origin of society in matriarchy—an idea he lifted from anthropologist Bronislaw Malinowski's *Sex and Repression in Savage Society* (1927)[63]—according to which naturally sociable man long ago fell into patriarchy, and then into totalitarianism. Following Sir James Frazer's work on totemism, Freud had rather fantasized in *Totem and Taboo* (1913) that "the problems of social psychology . . . should prove soluble on the basis of one single concrete point—man's relation to his father" (1913b: 157). Against Freud, then, Reich (1931) attacked the "compulsory family" of patriarchy (see also 1952: 58), along with the kind of character formation that sustained the patriarch's capitalism. In the 1920's Reich lived out his beliefs and was seriously involved in the Psychoanalytic Polyclinic in Vienna, where analysis was provided pro bono for those unable to afford the hourly fee; he also helped found "the first sex hygiene clinics for workers and employees" (I. O. Reich 1969: 17). "While Freud developed his death-instinct theory which said 'the misery comes from the inside,' " Reich states with pride, "I went out where the people were.... *I had drawn the social consequences of the [early] libido theory. To Freud's mind, this was the worst thing I did*" (1952: 51; his emphasis). Or, again, "I took the responsibility for Freud, that is, for the things Freud did not want" (116, n. 191). Despite some of Reich's later qualifications, he was avidly committed to the ideal of communism in the early thirties, and had willingly put his work where his mouth was (see Sharaf 1983: 182).

It is perhaps no surprise that this socially conscious side of Reich's early work was attractive to some French thinkers, such as Gilles Deleuze and Felix Guattari, in the wake of 1968 and its disappointments. According to analysts Janine Chasseguet-Smirgel and Bela Grunberger, Deleuze and Guattari's *Anti-Oedipus* of 1972 was a "revamped Reich, made to seem more sophisticated by being filtered through philosophy and through Lacan" (1986: 11). Things were the same but different in Reichian America. Reich's belief in the therapeutic value of a much freer sexual life was critically influential for the American "Beat Generation" and other chic radicals of the 1950's, as can be found in the works of William Burroughs, Allen Ginsberg, and Norman Mailer.[64] In both countries, though, Reich's work was rightly understood as sexual *and* political. Reich, after all, had argued that authoritarianism could be defeated only in a society that affirmed genitality against the "armoring" of neurotic character formation. As Rieff puts it, "Building character was [conceived by Reich as] a fraud which authority perpetrated on life" (1968: 169). Whereas Freud once theorized a "crust" in the "psychic apparatus" that serves as a protective wall against dangerous stimulus from outside, Reich proposed in his *Character Analysis* that "we can conceive of the character of the ego—perhaps the Freudian ego in general—as an armour protecting the id against the stimuli of the outer world" (1927–33: 171). The development of the ego character was thus, for Reich, "a progressive unfolding, splitting, and antithesis of simple vegetative functions" (318). As Robinson remarks: "Character was [for Reich] in fact the economic antithesis of the orgasm. It developed, quite literally, at the expense of the orgasm; it 'consumed' the psychic energy not discharged in sexuality" (1969: 25).

Reich believed that Oedipal dynamics—those loosely connected with Hegel's master/slave dialectic—could not only be analyzed, as in Freud's work, but prevented. Or again, neuroses and "bad" character formation would disappear once the internal contradictions of capitalism and its handmaiden, the family, made true mental health possible for the individual. To this utopic end, active genitality was a prophylaxis against the neuroses of capitalist society.

There is no doubt, though, that Reich's character analysis was seriously overoptimistic as a practical psychotherapy. But, for Reich, the psychoanalytic solutions—such as abreaction, sublimation, and the becoming conscious of a conflict—either did not always work, or did not go far enough (1927: 213); analysis was just a "preparatory" stage in an overall treatment (217). The goal of Reich's therapy, even when he was careful not to contradict Freud in the late 1920's, involved not only the ideal of genital potency but of prevention of neurosis altogether (based on a recognition of the socioeconomic context).[65] As Freud is reported to have said after a presentation by Reich, character analysis was "dictated too much by therapeutic ambition" (in Sterba 1982: 111). Understandably, while Reich felt that character armoring could be removed by a more interventionist therapy, some analysts felt that this aspect of his work was quite simply "sadistic" (Sterba 1982: 87).[66] And once again, Freud himself stated that pregenital drive components were not amenable to an orgasmic release, and that many neurotics had perfectly satisfactory orgasms with no good effect.[67] Freud more simply felt that Reich's attention to the social causes of unhappiness and to prophylaxis "had nothing to do with the middle road [*Mittelweg*] of psychoanalysis" (in Reich 1952: 58)—a sentiment he repeated in the 1930's to Joseph Wortis.

In a letter of February 27, 1932, to Oscar Pfister, Freud thus states of Reich: "One can spare oneself the refutation [of Reich's ideas] . . . if one knows how abnormal they are themselves" (in Falzeder 1996). According to historian Ronald Clark, it was ultimately Reich's zealous advocacy of Marxism that killed his relationship with Freud in the late 1920's, and not so much the extreme orgasm theory that he erected against Freud's late dualism (1980: 407). But it is more profoundly true to say that the political and the biological are of one piece in Reich's work (Rieff 1968: 168–69). Reich himself certainly felt that "a red thread of logic led him from one step to the next" throughout his career (I. O. Reich 1969: 9). This thread was the theme of energy which began with the libido theory of a psychoanalytic biology and ended with the orgone theory of "vegetotherapy" and "orgonomy." Indeed, at the end of the day Reich's orgone theory reworked a theory that had made psychoanalysis possible: Mesmer's idea that the universe is flooded with magnetic fluid.

Reich's wife, Ilse Ollendorff Reich, offers the four most common explanations given for Freud's break with Reich: political differences, disagreement about the sexual basis of neurosis, Freud's refusal to analyze Reich, and disagreement over the social implications of psychoanalysis (I. O. Reich 1969: 14). Interestingly enough, both Ilse and Reich's first wife, Annie Pink (a former patient of Reich's and later an analyst), leaned toward the third explanation: Freud's refusal to analyze Reich. Although Reich didn't commit suicide after this rejection, as Tausk had done when rejected by Freud eight years before, he did fall into a "deep depression" that landed him in a sanitarium in Davos, Switzerland, for three and a half months—apparently for tuberculosis (a disease from which his brother and father had died).

Reich's final period in America is an interesting, if bizarre, chapter in intellectual history that brings him full circle concerning Freud's death-drive theory. In the early 1930's, both the International Psychoanalytic Association and the German Communist Party repudiated his work. As a result, Reich focused more exclusively upon his own characterological studies. In 1942, a few years after he moved to the United States, he founded an orgone research facility called Orgonon, on farm land near Rangeley, Maine (I. O. Reich 1969: 68). Like Freud, he became the leader of a movement complete with disciples, publishing house, and journals; and like institutional psychoanalysis, he founded a child clinic, conducted conferences, workshops, and so on. To his "discovery" of the blue libido energy that surrounds the living, Reich eventually added "DOR," or Deadly Orgone Energy (or radiation), which, he claimed, is measurable with a Geiger counter. Ironically, this new "dualistic cosmology" took him back to the Freud of *BPP* and, more especially, to *Civilization and Its Discontents*. In what was to be his last theoretical essay, "Re-emergence of the Death Instinct as 'DOR' Energy" (1956), Reich effectively repeats Freud's dualism of life and death drives in the new opposition of orgone energy versus the DOR of atomic or nuclear energy (Robinson 1969: 68).[68] Indeed, the older Reich came to agree with Freud's pessimism about political and social intervention, citing Freud's comment that "it is not our purpose, or the purpose of our existence, to save the world." As Reich put it, "I am just where Freud was in 1930" (1952: 58). And thus he states of his old views: "I believed that capitalism was bad, but I don't believe, today, that the misery stems from capitalism. The misery is older than capitalism" (104).

As Reich's career "faded imperceptibly into farce" (Robinson 1969: 73), paranoia merged with his considerable megalomania in the idea that Cosmic Orgone Engineers (CORE) from other planets, dismayed by human disregard for life, were engineering DOR on earth as a way of ridding a polluting, destructive species. Among his other activities, he invented an orgone energy accumulator (a box), a new orgone-energy motor, and an orgone enhancing "cloud busting" device. He also began to believe that DOR was in part the exhaust fumes of flying saucers. Meanwhile, while Reich made rain and worried about aliens and communist spies, the Food and Drug Administration sued him in 1954 for claiming that his orgone accumulators could cure cancer. Tragically, Reich refused to attend his own trial and was slapped with a contempt-of-court charge and sentenced to (an overly severe and cruel) two years in a federal penitentiary in Danbury, Connecticut. Ten days into his sentence he was transferred to the prison in Lewisburg, Pennsylvania, apparently because they had psychiatric treatment facilities (which he refused). On November 3, 1957, eight months into his sentence, he died in his sleep from a heart attack (cf. I. O. Reich 1969; Robinson 1969: 72–73; Mann 1973: 24–25).

Fromm Versus Marcuse. Erich Fromm shared Reich's early interest in Marxism and also his distaste for Freud's death-drive theory. An analyst, sociologist, and one-time member of the Institute of Social Research in Frankfurt, Fromm attempted to synthesize Freud and Marx as early as *The Development and Dogma of Christ* (1931). The Institute of Social Research was at this time under the directorship of Max Horkheimer, who promoted both philosophical and psychological studies. On this last score Horkheimer was especially interested in Freud's work, and effected loose ties between his institute and the newly founded (February 1929) Frankfurt Psychoanalytic Institute; apparently Freud wrote two letters of appreciation to Horkheimer (see Jay 1973: 88). Fromm's involvement with the institute thus gave him the institutional space to explore his interest in Freud and Marx.

Put very briefly, both Fromm and Reich disagreed with Freud's tragic view that human nature was naturally bad; agreed that an authentic self lay buried under the baneful influence of society; agreed that the patriarchal family repeated the structure of capitalism; sought refuge in matriarchal theory,[69] although Fromm focused not on libido but on ego instincts; and agreed that genital satisfaction was important for normal mental health, although Reich took this to far greater lengths than Fromm (see Burston 1991: 59–60). Reich, however, was unfriendly toward Fromm, who was crowding his intellectual turf. Consequently they kept their distance in person and in print.[70]

The Fromm of the 1930's tried to relate Freud's focus on the individual with the historically contingent class position of the family (see Fromm 1970). Like Reich, he rejected Freud's death-drive theory but understood that it at least constituted some sort of recognition, albeit belated, of aggressivity in human behavior (1973: 439). During this time Horkheimer sympathized with Fromm and was similarly critical about the limitations that the death-drive theory placed on the possibility of historical change (Jay 1973: 101). In his classic text *Escape from Freedom*, Fromm writes:

> The assumption of the death-instinct is satisfactory inasmuch as it takes into consideration the full weight of destructive tendencies, which had been neglected in Freud's earlier theories. But it is not satisfactory inasmuch as it resorts

to a biological explanation that fails to take into account sufficiently of the fact that the amount of destructiveness varies enormously among individuals and social groups. (1941: 182)

Just the same, for Fromm the death drive marked a positive turn in Freud's work away from the mechanistic philosophy of the nineteenth century.

Whereas Freud under the influence of his late dualism locates the source of human misery within the organism as masochism or sadism, Fromm argues that "the key problem of psychology is that of the specific kind of relatedness of the individual towards the world" (1941: 12). Like Reich, Fromm recognized that Freud's focus on the instincts or drives was paid for by a withdrawal of concern for the object world. The death drive in particular precludes a close analysis of difference between social groups across cultures and history, since the base-line measure is always individual biology and psychology. And as Fromm argues, "Every society has its own distinctive *libidinal structure*, even as it has its own economic, social, political, and cultural structure. This libidinal structure is the product of the influence of socioeconomic conditions on human drives" (1970: 132).

"Man is primarily a social being," Fromm argues, and consequently is best understood on the basis of the "libidinal structure of society," that is, upon relatedness and "social character" (1941: 290). Fromm's work is at times prescient of the later British school of object relations, who share with him a humanistic and interpersonal approach toward questions of human authenticity, as well as a distaste for the old *Instinkt* or *Trieb* theories. Consider in this respect "The Application of Psychoanalysis to Marx's Theory" in which Fromm recounts his own Freudo-Marxist efforts:

> I have tried to show . . . that the various strivings of man, who is primarily a social being, develop as a result of his need for "assimilation" (of things) and "socialization" (with people), and that the forms of assimilation and socialization that constitute his main passions depend on the social structure in which he exists. Man in this concept is seen as characterized by his passionate strivings towards objects—men and nature—and his need of relating himself to the world. (1981: 29)

Fromm rejected the idea that human nature was comprised of a competitive, aggressive, or egotistical core as a fancy of nineteenth-century speculation in the areas of biology, economics, and (finally with Freud) psychology (1955: 343). For Fromm, such attitudes reflect an essentially conservative bias that favors stasis rather than dynamism and change. As his disenchantment with Freudian analysis grew in the thirties, Fromm attempted to breathe some hope and love into an overworn, romantic, pessimistic psychology. Eventually, he championed the integration of ethics and psychology (see Jay 1973: 100).

Given their clinical-sociological outlook, it is understandable that Fromm and the other "neo-Freudians"—a group that includes Karen Horney, Harry Stack Sullivan, and Clara Thompson, but also, on occasion, Franz Alexander and Abram Kardiner—would discard the untenable biologism of the death-drive theory. It is certainly true that Freud's descriptive work, based as it was (in principle, at least) on his clinical approach, gave the neo-Freudians the justification with which to refashion psychoanalytic theory. From the clinical perspective they obviously had good reasons for dropping Freud's death-drive theory, which, in retrospect, was only a few shades less ridiculous than Reich's obsessive ranting about Deadly Orgone Energy.

Despite this, Fromm's neo-Freudian orientation managed to prick up the ears of some more radical, less clinically minded thinkers. Fromm's 1935 defense of, and rapprochement with, the more interventionist analytic techniques of Sandor Ferenczi and Georg Groddeck effectively marked the beginning of his movement away from orthodox analysis (Burston 1991: 211–12). But his changing views also came into conflict with the darker philosophies of his Frankfurt colleagues, Horkheimer and Adorno, with whom he also broke ranks. In fact, by the forties Horkheimer openly rejected Fromm's therapeutic views about socialization and even reversed his earlier position on the death drive; it may have been bad biology, he recanted, but Freud at least had his heart in the right place (Jay 1973: 103). Similarly, in a lecture in Los Angeles in April 1946, Theodor Adorno attacked Fromm and the revisionist reading of Freud. As he put it, the revisionist (or neo-Freudian) advocacy of integrated character was "an ideological cloak for the psychological status quo of each individual" (in Jay 1973: 104; cf. 103–105). Elsewhere Adorno spoke bitingly about the "business-like revisionists" (1951: 60), who followed a "straight line of development between the gospel of happiness and the construction of camps of extermination" (63).

Although similar views were expressed in an essay of 1945 by Paul Goodman, it was another former Frankfurt Institute colleague, the philosopher Herbert Marcuse, who most famously took Fromm to task for what he argued was essentially a psychology of adaptation. While Marcuse had little direct interest in Freud during the thirties (while in Frankfurt), he became increasingly interested in Freud by the 1950's. Fromm had optimistically argued that individual authenticity—nonalienated subjectivity, that is—was rare under the repressive conditions of capitalism but not impossible (1955: 348–49; cf. Jay 1973: 100). Marcuse, however, insisted that Fromm had dropped the Marxist ball by giving up the true condition for happiness in civilization, namely, revolution leading to a nonrepressive stage of history. In effect, Marcuse accused Fromm and the neo-Freudians of being dupes of the capitalist system, which they invariably mistook as their point of measure as practice-bound, psychoanalytic therapists (cf. Marcuse 1956: 81; 1955a: 256).[71] "Therapy is faced," Marcuse writes, "with a situation in which it seems to help the Establishment rather than the individual" (1970: 44); or again, "The analyst acts as the spokesman (silent spokesman!) of *reason*" (45; his emphasis). Effectively, Marcuse echoed Adorno by blasting the revisionists for turning psychoanalytic theory into an "ideology" (1955a: 240) and, moreover, for peddling what he called a "pre-Freudian consciousness psychology" that was a regrettable and gross "mutilation" of Freud's views (1956: 80).

Just as Marcuse had tried in his *Reason and Revolution* (1941) to salvage the radicalness of Hegel against the positivists of the nineteenth century, he tried with his *Eros and Civilization* (1955) to salvage the radicalness of Freud against the clinically minded revisionists of the twentieth (Robinson 1969: 155–70). To this ambitious and sometimes curious end, Marcuse outlined the deficiencies of neo-Freudian theorizing, especially its tendency to flatten the hard edge of Freud's most uncomfortable theoretical insights—including his views on sexuality and the death drive. At the same time, Marcuse embraced the more metaphysical Freud the better to dialectically resolve the fatalistic philosophy of psychoanalysis with his own brand of Marxian optimism (200–201). In this way Marcuse not only tried to outmaneuver Fromm and the neo-Freudians by reinterpreting the spirit of Freud's own theory—which, he claimed, "is in its very substance sociological" (1955a: 5; cf. 1970: 1)—but to synthesize in good dialectical fashion the ahistorical, dualistic, and psychological Freud with the historical, dialectical, and political Marx.

Marcuse's appropriation of Freud is, in this respect, less peculiar than it seems at first. Marcuse demands a return to a state before history was arrested in its fateful development—in effect, he calls for a return to the dynamism (or dialectic) of progressive sociohistorical change. In this way he uses Freud's dualistic ontology as an instrument of social critique, one with which we might recharge dialectics and put history back on its proper path. Of course, his entire approach provides the perfect rationale for ignoring analytic therapy. Why is that? Because for Marcuse the sheer instrumentality of psychoanalytic theory is *itself* therapeutic and historically revolutionary.

Bouncing off certain hints in Freud's work, Marcuse claims that society represses its citizens more than what is necessary or "basic," an abuse he translates into the economic language of "surplus repression" (1955a: 35). "The extent of this surplus-repression provides the standard of measurement: the smaller it is, the less repressive is the stage of civilization" (88). Marcuse thus *quantifies* suffering with an economic calculus borrowed from the later works of Freud but more or less owing to Marx. For similar reasons, he theorizes a disjunction between Freud's reality principle and a less ideal, expedient, and historically relative "performance principle" (35). Having set in place a juncture between Marxist ideal and capitalist ideology, Marcuse is then able to condemn modern Western civilization for failing to rise to its socioeconomic potential. Happiness, according to Marcuse, has been replaced by labor as a "goal of civilization" (1970: 9). In a lecture originally delivered in 1956 on the one hundredth anniversary of Freud's birth, later published as the first of his *Five Lectures*, Marcuse thus states: "Contemporary civilization has developed social wealth to a point where the renunciations and burdens placed on individuals seem more and more unnecessary and irrational" (1970: 3; cf. 1955a: 87). Capitalists, he similarly charges, restrict the share in wealth even as they restrict the share in happiness: the "need for toil" under capitalism is "only 'artificially' perpetuated—in the interest of preserving the system of domination" (1955a [2d ed.]: xi). Worse yet, the preservation of the status quo undercuts the power of the negative, erasing opposition and conflict in the creation of a unified, but essentially false, ideology. Having thus been "hammered into a unity as never before," Marcuse enjoins, society has succumbed to the rule of a perverted reality principle, an "oppression of a particular kind: it is rational unfreedom, rational domination" (1970: 4, 12). According to Marcuse, then, the human "organism" becomes "free for unpleasurable labor as the content of life" (34).

The stage of capitalism had become for Marcuse not just an unmoving, static moment in history that restricts the dialectically transformative power of world spirit, but a *regressive* force in this regard (1955a: 101). This is effectively what he means by the "fatal dialectic of civilization": every bit of capitalist progress releases only more social destructiveness (54; cf. 1970: 18), a self-defeating catch-22 or "vicious circle of progress" (1970: 36) only imperfectly reflected in Freud's own work *Civilization and Its Discontents*. Marcuse writes: "Culture demands continuous sublimation; it thereby weakens Eros, the builder of culture. And desexualization, by weakening Eros, unbinds the destructive impulse" (1955a: 83; cf. 1970: 5). "This would mean," Marcuse further contends, "that progress remains committed to a regressive trend in the instinctual structure" (1955a: 108).

Freud, however, had tied the hopes of civilization precisely to our capacity for repression through sublimated sexuality; to be sure, his "solution" to the problem of unhappiness in civilization was not along the path of *unrestricted* libido. Marcuse quite knowingly rejects Freud's tragic and ahistorical portrait, proposing instead that sexuality and freedom are not essentially cut off from civilization and sexuality and that the capitalist version of reality can change and doesn't represent the end of history; in short, "the wheel of progress [can turn] in another direction" (1955a [2d ed.]: xvii)."We must," he therefore suggests, "undertake a decisive correction of Freudian theory" (1970: 39). To this end he argues that if work and sublimation lead to the desexualization and desublimation (see Marcuse 1964: 78–79; 1970: 4, 9) of Eros under the ego-driven performance principle, such inherently pleasurable activities as play (1955a: 187), polymorphous perversity (49), fantasy and imagination (141) can lead to a resexualization of Eros and a desublimation of repressive labor under the id-driven pleasure principle. "Their unrepressed development," Marcuse argues, "would eroticize the organism to such an extent that it would counteract the desexualization of the organism required by its social utilization as an instrument of labor" (1955a: 39). Critical of Reich's localization of pleasure in the genitals, Marcuse rather advocates a *generalized sexuality* (1970: 9; cf. 1955a: 239) that reflects the aims of communism vis-à-vis labor: generalized sexuality as the well-rounded worker.

If Marcuse (1955b; 1956), initially in the pages of the radical socialist journal *Dissent*, jockeyed with Fromm for a position as both the most Freudian and Marxist of Freudo-Marxists, it is nonetheless true that he reversed the usual analytic and Marxist lines on Freud's biological drive theory. Unlike Reich, Fromm, or nearly any other Freudo-Marxist, Marcuse argued that the hydraulic metaphors of Freud's drive theory, while untenable from a scientifically coherent biological perspective, were essential from a Marxist-philosophical one; for, as we have seen, they provide a means for *quantifying* human misery. To his credit, Marcuse understood that Freud's radical critique of society was conditioned on the old drive theory; jettison the one and the other had no foundation, let alone any teeth. In the early days of Freudian-Marxism, Reich was almost alone in recognizing this fundamental fact; Reich's denial of the late dualism and his revisions of analytic theory, for example his theory of masochism, is based on this recognition. Others though, including Fromm and the Frankfurt Institute, typically relied upon and cited Freud's later works even as they disparaged *BPP* (Slater 1977: 104, 109–112). Consequently they made a mess of their theories.

"The truth of psychoanalysis lies," Marcuse thus asserts, "in its loyalty to its most provocative hypothesis" (1970: 61). Adorno had already said as much with his witty remark, from *Minima Moralia*, "In psycho-analysis nothing is true except the exaggerations" (1951: 49). In a review article for the *Nation*, "Theory and Therapy in Freud," Marcuse writes that the

> scientific purification [of Freud's metapsychology] is perhaps intended to adjust the theory to the requirements of therapy and technique, but the development has had quite a different effect. The hypotheses and exaggerations which are being eliminated are precisely those which oppose the smooth incorporation of

psychoanalysis into the established system of culture and its smooth functioning as a socially rewarded activity. (1957: 200)

Marcuse rejected the Enlightenment Freud, what he called the "rationalist program of psychoanalysis" (1970: 45), which so attracted the neo-Freudians and ego psychologists. In this sense and more he was not unlike French analyst Jacques Lacan." 'Where the id was, ego shall develop,'" Marcuse complains, "is perhaps the most rational formulation I can imagine finding in psychology" (33).

Like Lacan, in fact, Marcuse wanted to radically recondition the metapsychological "hypotheses and exaggerations"—the primary processes, the pleasure principle, the death drive—because he thought they gave him the means to describe how it is that an individual can oppose the rules of ego, society, and the performance principle. For according to this conceptual toolbox, the raw materials of personality were in essence anticonformist. In turn, Marcuse advocated a *really real* reality principle against which he measured the evils of capitalist ideology. Thus, whereas someone like Reich, according to Marcuse, neglected "the historical dynamic of the sex instincts and of their fusion with the destructive impulses" (1955a: 239), Marcuse was inclined to embrace Freud's (by then unpopular) notion of primary masochism or death drive.[72] According to Marcuse's version, with the "traumatic transformation" (1970: 6) of reality into performance, basic into surplus repression—the fusion, in other words, of civilization to death rather than to Eros—capitalism shortened the detour on the path toward death when it could have, for the first time in history, lengthened it (see 1955a [2d ed.]: xxv). A life-denying mode of production was making existence ever more deadly. It is important to note that the prophetic optimism of Marcuse's work here goes well beyond the dour views that Horkheimer and Adorno espoused during the thirties; as Martin Jay puts it, they "maintained a tactful silence" after *Eros and Civilization* was published (1973: 111; cf. 109–112).

Marcuse's willingness to deal in abstractions is most clearly reflected in his unusual advocacy of Freud's death-drive theory. Paul Robinson shares this interest, plausibly suggesting that Marcuse's acceptance of the death drive—like that of so many others—was based on his sensitivity to the horrors of this century. "I sense," Robinson surmises, "that Marcuse felt the need for some conceptual means with which to come to terms with twentieth-century violence, and Freud's death instinct fulfilled that need ideally. The notion suited Marcuse's propensity for ambitious abstraction—his residual Hegelianism—and his sense of outrage and horror at the historical events he saw unfolding before him" (1969: 212; cf. also Geoghegan 1981: 47–48). In fact, Marcuse says as much in numerous places, even claiming that Freud's views were "corroborated" by world events (1970: 61).

Given such extreme formulations, it is understandable that Fromm thought that Marcuse's philosophical "position is an example of human nihilism disguised as radicalism" (1955: 349). Yet Fromm's criticism is ultimately misplaced, since at bottom Marcuse's reading *resolves* the problem of Freud's pessimism with Marx's optimistic vision of a new social order. His goal of a nonrepressive society is not nihilistic, at least not in the usual sense of that word, because the dark Freudian means (i.e., the late dualism) were only used to justify a bright Marxist end; once again, the Marcuse of *Eros and Civilization* exuded an optimism, a "sanguine confidence," that other critical theorists did not share (Jay 1973: 112). Consequently, it was necessary for Marcuse to demonstrate that Freud's "theory contains elements that break through this rationalization [for repressive civilization]; they shatter the predominant tradition of Western thought and even suggest its reversal" (1955a: 17). Of course, Marcuse was ironically willing to accept Fromm's designation that he was a nihilist if, by that word, Fromm meant to say that Marcuse was "part of the Great Refusal[73] to play the game" of capitalism (1956: 81). Obviously Marcuse envisaged himself, not Fromm, as the true humanist.

Marcuse's acceptance of Freud's phylogenetic imagination is, on the other hand, somewhat less easy to rationalize. In *Eros and Civilization* Marcuse adopts Freud's recapitulation thesis "for its symbolic value" (1955a: 60), for what Robinson rightly calls a "capitalist allegory" (1969: 208): with it Marcuse recounts the battle between sons (horde, proletariat) and father (patriarch, capitalist), the father's murder at the hands of the sons (revolution), and the resumption of the father's laws by the chastened, guilty sons (failed revolution and resumption of repressive order). Symbolic though this story may be, it is not at all incidental to Marcuse's larger story of liberation and utopia denied. First of all, Marcuse needed a theory of ontogeny to bridge the distance between the individual and the collective, psychology and materialism, the ahistorical Freud and the historical Marx. And he did this, just as Freud himself had done, by invoking an outdated biology: "The ontogenetic case history repeats," he asserts, "the phylogenetic history of mankind" (1970: 45). Marcuse pushed this fiction even further in later years by asserting that "civilization arises in pleasure" (19), and that labor was "*originally libidinous*" (20; his emphasis). If one takes this view seriously, a peculiar conclusion can be drawn: dialectical change is the sublation of an ideal state that underwrites the entire venture from the beginning, from the origin. Actually,

Marcuse simply echoes Hegel's own view in this regard, namely, that civilization and reason will become natural over history. Or more exactly still, and as Marcuse himself puts it, the "repressive solution" to the problems of sociality is "not a natural ... but rather a socio-historical process which became part of nature" (20). This story thereby becomes the ultimate justification for Marcuse's view that while psychoanalysis may appear "to be purely biological, [it] is fundamentally social and historical" (1). Of course, whatever heuristic value Marcuse managed to squeeze from his anthropobiological imagination, it is clear that it undermines the status of the materialist view of history, which is based on the assumption of a real, eventful history of struggle (see MacIntyre 1970: 51).

While Marcuse's reinterpretation of Freud is attractive in its broad sweep, at least among intellectuals who share his "residual Hegelianism," it is problematic in some more basic ways. As suggested, Marcuse is insensitive to clinical and empirical detail just as he is too impressed with unprovable abstraction imported, perhaps too hastily, from Hegel, Marx, Freud, Adorno, and others. Arguably, however, the direction of this critique should be shifted slightly: Marcuse's apparent disinterest in clinical matters is in fact conditioned upon his quite uncritical acceptance of Freud's so-called "findings." He piled his bits and pieces of philosophy on top of the bits and pieces of Freud's own creation, which he more or less *took for granted*. As one commentator correctly remarks, Marcuse "not only made highly dubious claims concerning [Freud's] work but somewhat uncritically imported certain of the latter's equally dubious concepts ... into his social theory" (Geoghegan 1981: 103). Without question, then, Marcuse's *motivated disinterest* (a will to ignorance, as Nietzsche might say) in clinical issues and, for that matter, in the very real conditions of psychoanalytic politics—like Adorno and Horkheimer before him (see Burston 1991: 212)—compromise his theoretical edifice. One can see in Marcuse's theory (and in the theory of his Frankfurt colleagues) an idealization of Freud and, for that matter, a naivete that is unfortunately not so rare among philosophers.[74]

Marcuse's critics are also quite right to emphasize that Freud would never have recognized himself in this work; Marcuse bent Freudian concepts, such as repression, well out of shape to fit his own brand of revisionism. As Fromm reminds us in his reply to Marcuse's stinging attack, Freud was conservative in his personal life, liberal in his politics, and unmoved by social reform of any kind. "Freud was a critic of society," Fromm states, "*but his criticism was not that of contemporary capitalistic society, but of civilization as such*" (1955: 342; his emphasis). On the other hand, it is worth recalling once again that the strength of Marcuse's appropriation of psychoanalysis can be positively measured according to how much it *differs* from Freud's work. Marcuse sought to liberate Freud from his own limitations and from the conformism implicit in neo-Freudian theory—once again, an attitude that Lacan echoes in his own "return to Freud." Indeed, it was Marcuse's task to uncover "the hidden trend in psychoanalysis" (1955a: 11–20), to tease out "the deepest and most revolutionary nucleus of Freudian thought" (1970: 6), despite—or even in contrast to—Freud's own predilections and beliefs. In this sense he proceeded almost hermeneutically, an approach he would have learned from his one-time mentor in Freiburg, the philosopher Martin Heidegger. As Marcuse says in good Heideggerian fashion, "The true spirit of psychoanalytic theory lives in the uncompromising efforts to reveal the antihumanistic forces behind the philosophy of productiveness [i.e., capitalism]" (221). Or again, and more pointedly: "The liberation from this state [of capitalism] seems to require, not the arrest of alienation, but its consummation" (105). Marcuse tried to think through the contradictions of Freud's psychology and capitalism to their logical end or consummation, *die Vollendung*—a word Heidegger liked to employ on occasion. Yet Marcuse substantiated his own thought through a process of dialectics borrowed from Hegel and Marx.[75] From this perspective, then, the criticism that Marcuse is not a good Freudian hardly disturbs the thrust of his philosophical attempt to *synthesize* Freud and Marx: to preserve and overcome the partial truths of a biological psychology and a materialistic politics. In other words, if the name of the game is indeed freeing Freud from his own limitations, then Marcuse was probably better off without Fromm's historically accurate but theoretically unusable Freud. After all, accurate description rarely makes for a timely prescription—and Marcuse certainly thought he had the cure for what ails us.

Obviously, though, Marcuse's revision of psychoanalysis pushes and pulls Freud in hitherto unknown directions and is essentially *additive*. It does not really partake in a destruction or dismantling, *Destruktion* or *Abbau*, of Freudianism, nor does it envisage a clearing, *die Lichtung*, wherein something truly new might be imagined. It is certainly not Heideggerian in this sense. It is on the contrary as fantastical as anything Freud wrote—perhaps more so, if that's possible. With this in mind, the most devastating rejection of Marcuse's thinking comes from the philosopher Alasdair MacIntyre (1970), who bluntly rejects the questionable content of his Freudian-Marxism. Railing against the "comic pomposity of his discussion of sex" (47), MacIntyre points out that Marcuse never really defines what his vision of a polymorphously perverse society is supposed to look like, based as it is on the most speculative hypotheses available. As Robinson puts it, Marcuse "was no Lenin" and tended to ignore the crucial question of "tactics" (1969: 223). And thus Marcuse's utopia—one in which "life would consist of free time" (Marcuse 1970: 39)—is "in fact empty" (MacIntyre 1970: 53). In short, Marcuse's philosophy is full of hot air. In this way MacIntyre wickedly deflated the Modern Master of "Marcusemania," what the French called "*la drugstorisation de Marcuse*" (in Geoghagen 1981: 1), effectively anticipating Marcuse's decline amongst theorists from either psychoanalytic or Marxist camps.

It should be noted that Marcuse himself was ambivalent about the commodification of his name during the sixties. On the one hand, and despite his long disenchantment with the radical potential of the "proletariat" (about which he was nearly as silent as death), Marcuse flattered the students by eventually handing them that very role (1955a [2d ed.]: xxi). Some have claimed that a slogan of the Columbia University student uprising of 1968, "The riot is the social extension of the orgasm," derives from a poor reading of Marcuse's *Eros and Civilization* (Torrey 1992: 179). For his part, Marcuse was an uncomfortable guru and took steps to distance himself from the cultural experimentation of the students (see Marcuse 1970: 69). He also began, no doubt with the students in mind, to downplay the role of psychoanalysis and sexuality in his political theory; at one point, for instance, he went out of his way to reject the "pansexualism" of the time (1970: 40).[76] In the end, though, Marcuse seems decidedly nostalgic for the dark lines that once marked the immutable difference between friend and foe, and which made any political fight at least a good clean one. In this last respect, ironically, he is not unlike some of his conservative enemies, such as Allan Bloom. In any case, and despite his retreat from things Freudian, Marcuse always remained faithful to one aspect of Freudianism: the death-drive theory (Robinson 1969: 242).

Dialectical Coda. Two other gurus of nonrepressive society at this time in America are regularly cited alongside Marcuse: one is the anarchist Paul Goodman, author of *Growing Up Absurd: Problems of Youth in the Organized Society* (1960); the other is the liberal Norman O. Brown, author of *Life Against Death: The Psychoanalytical Meaning of History* (1959). One can begin to measure their influence in sheer number of books sold. Goodman's book sold over one hundred thousand copies in its first few years, while Brown's sold over fifty thousand by 1966 (Torrey 1992: 182–83). Goodman had published articles about repressive society as early as the forties and became one of the early exponents of Gestalt therapy, which, by the sixties, became a key feature of the "personal growth movement" in America. Brown was on the other hand a doubtful guru, having devoted his intellectual life to classical studies. It was not until Marcuse suggested that he read Freud in 1953 that Brown even considered psychoanalysis; in the next years Brown even attended Marcuse's class lectures at Brandeis University. "Freud had the effect," Brown was later to reflect, "of destroying my universe" (in Morgan 1963: 100–135; also cited in Torrey 1992: 182).

As one commentator puts it, Marcuse's and Brown's works "play much the same tune to the fat and complacent Eisenhower fifties" (Shepherd 1976: 11). Brown, like Marcuse, challenged the pessimistic conclusions that Freud had drawn, and argued that the death-drive theory of the late dualism had to go. "The psychoanalytical practitioners," Brown writes, "have good reason to draw back from Freud's final instinct theory. The theory, as he left it, results in complete therapeutic pessimism, and is therefore worse than useless for therapists" (1959: 79). Brown proposed in its place a dialectical psychoanalysis, a "metaphysics of hope rather than despair" (82) that allowed for the possibility of personal transformation based on a return to the original unity of opposites that supposedly characterizes childhood (83). This reunification of life and death, according to Brown, "can be envisioned only as the end of the historical process" (87)—an end not, as Hegel would have it, of Absolute Spirit, but of "Absolute Body" (89). One can already see that Brown takes his analytic insights in idiosyncratic directions—variously cerebral and entertaining, but more or less questionable. In the final chapter of *Life Against Death*, "The Resurrection of the Body," there is a glimpse of Brown's Christian beliefs that in later years would increasingly determine the character of his interest in psychoanalysis.

Just how much the critique of repressive society was actually understood by the readers of Reich, Marcuse, Goodman, and Brown is an open question. One wonders how many student activists, reflecting upon their zealous appropriation of such psychoanalytically inspired radicalism, would share Morris Dickstein's circumspect views about his time at Columbia University. Speaking of Marcuse's and Brown's work, he frankly admits, "To me they meant not some ontological breakthrough for human nature, but probably just plain fucking, lots of it. . . . These men seemed to promise that good times were just around the corner" (in Torrey 1992: 184). Another prophet to the students, Jacques Lacan, rose to prominence in the France of the late sixties, and we can legitimately wonder how much of his message the student radicals in France understood. Like Marcuse, Lacan was heavily influenced by Hegelianism as it was filtered through Marx. Yet Lacan was far more interested in the role of language in psychoanalysis than Marcuse ever was. In the next section I want to turn to Lacan's work on Freud's *Beyond the Pleasure Principle*, which is structured by his view of the ego and ego psychology.

Interestingly enough, Lacan's "return to Freud" may have been the sort of interpretation of psychoanalysis that Marcuse would have liked to see in Fromm and the other American neo-Freudians. For as I mentioned earlier, it is an interpretation that is essentially anti-American and, to that extent at least, perfectly Freudian.

LACAN AND THE DECENTERING 'BEYOND'

> Self-consciousness exists in and for itself when, and by the fact that, it exists for another; that is, it exists only in being acknowledged.
> —G. W. F. Hegel, *The Phenomenology of Spirit*[77]

In his seminar *The Ego in Freud's Theory and in the Technique of Psychoanalysis, 1954–1955*, Lacan outlines the importance of Freud's *BPP* for his own "return to Freud." According to Lacan, Freud wrote *BPP* as a decisive response to a growing crisis over analytic technique (1954–55: 11). By this crisis, Lacan as always means the lamentable rise of ego psychology: "the second topography," he states of Freud's work of the twenties, "was undertaken in order to put back in its place an ego which had begun to slide back to its old position" (44). Remaking Freud in his own image, Lacan in other words found it "necessary to maintain the principle of the decentring of the subject" (11). Accordingly, Lacan declares in the third lecture:

> In man, there's already a crack, a profound perturbation of the regulation of life. That's the importance of the notion introduced by Freud of the death instinct. Not that the death instinct is such an enlightened notion in itself. What has to be comprehended is that he was forced to introduce it so as to remind us of a salient fact of his experience, just when it was beginning to get lost. (37)

"Everything Freud wrote," Lacan says, "aimed at reestablishing the exact perspective of the excentricity of the subject in relation to the ego" (44; cf. 208–209). For Lacan, then, *BPP* is "[not] simply Freudian metaphysics" (24), but a calculated attempt to return psychoanalysis to its origins as a radical technique for eliciting and interpreting the patient's unconscious. Consequently, Freud's later work only makes sense when sufficient attention is paid to his pronouncements on the ego (21), around which, as he says, "everything must be organised" (45).

In spite of the abstractions of analytic theory, what is at stake for Lacan's rereading of Freud is the *practice*—or, more exactly, the institutionalization—of psychoanalysis. That the true meaning of Freud's so-called experience was "beginning to get lost" appeared to him as a failure of reading, if not of nerve, in the face of Freud's basic discovery of the fractured subject. It reflected, in short, the questionable restitution of "the good old ego" (59)—its "entification" (12) and "camouflage" (14) for what is basic and true in psychoanalysis—and, therefore, a reification of what Lacan calls the Imaginary register. As Lacan repeatedly insists, "The core of our being does not coincide with the ego" (44; cf. 326). "What corresponds to the ego," he rather contends, "is what I sometimes call the sum of the prejudices which any knowledge comprises" (41); or again, the ego is the "systematic refusal to acknowledge reality" (Lacan 1953: 12).

According to Lacan, Freud wanted to "remind us of the fact that not only is there an absolute dissymmetry between the subject of the unconscious and the organisation of the ego, but also a radical difference" (1954–55: 59). Such dissymmetry is precisely what eludes the ego psychologists who claim that the analysis of resistance and defense is just the flip side of the analysis of the raw materials of everyday life—as though these two realms correspond, Lacan says, "as right side out to inside out" (120). By analyzing the one side, ego analysts automatically thought they had analyzed the other. Lacan argues, and rather convincingly, that Freud never made this assumption (209) since, among other things, he never reduced the secondary processes of consciousness to the primary processes of the unconscious. Lacan furthermore believes that Freud recognized a tendency among analysts to conflate these realms, and wrote *BPP* so that they "would not lose sight of the cutting edge" of his more basic id psychology (65; cf. 59).

In 1936 Lacan introduced his most famous idea, "the mirror stage," around which his critique of ego psychology revolves; he significantly revised this early attempt in "The Mirror Stage as Formative of the Function of the I" (1949), which was later collected in his *Écrits* (1966). Interestingly enough, a mirror plays a small role in *Beyond the Pleasure Principle*, where Freud describes in a footnote how little Ernst made himself "disappear," like the spool, *fort*, in a full-length mirror (1920a: 15, n. 1). Lacan, though, lifted the idea from psychologist Henri Wallon (1931), who anticipated some aspects of Lacan's version of the mirror stage (see Borch-Jacobsen 1991: 46–47). Lacan was primarily interested in the idea that the child's attachment to his or her own mirror image is the prototype of our imaginary fascination, and inevitable identification, with something we are not: namely, an "ideal unity, a salutary *imago*" (1966: 19). The human animal, Lacan reminds us, is born premature and, thus, is uniquely inclined to identify itself with the stable body image found in the mirror. In a paper read to The British Psycho-Analytical Society in 1951, Lacan states: "We cannot fail to appreciate the affective value which the gestalt of the vision of the whole body-image may assume [for the child] when we consider the fact that it appears against a background of organic disturbance and discord, in which all the indications are that we should seek the origins of the image of the 'body in bits and pieces' " (1953: 15). Lacan qualifies that such narcissistic self-appraisal is a visual image "given to him [i.e., the child] only as a *Gestalt*, that is to say, in an exteriority" (1966: 2). It is an image, Lacan translates, that "alienates him from himself" (19); an image, in effect, of the *statue* (Lacan 1953: 15). In his seminar on the ego Lacan basically repeats the idea, fashionable in Kojèvian France, that this ideal of the mirror image is "an alienated, virtual reality" (1954–55: 50). As Kojève himself taught, "It is in this other that the meaning of his life is condensed. Therefore, he [his identity] is 'outside of himself' " (1939: 13; cf. Hegel 1807: 112). So, hanging "over the abyss of a dizzying Assent," Lacan argues that this subject is always "in constant danger of sliding back again into the chaos from which he started" (1953: 15). Lacan had thereby devised his own tragic story of human existence to buttress Freud's Oedipal saga: "The libidinal tension that shackles the subject to the constant pursuit of an illusory unity which is always luring him away from himself, is surely related to that agony of dereliction which is Man's particular and tragic destiny. Here we see how Freud was led to his deviant concept of a death instinct" (16). This brooding conclusion, which is, again, typical of French philosophy in the wake of Kojève's lectures at the École des Hautes Études (1933–39), was invariably anti-Cartesian and antihumanistic. "The subject is no one," Lacan writes. "It is decomposed, in pieces. And it is jammed, sucked in by the image, the deceiving and realised image, of the other, or equally by its own specular image" (1954–55: 54). In short, the *imago du corps morcelé* is the image of the *castrated* subject (see Lacan 1953: 13).

Far from following the path of developmental psychology, Lacan's mirror stage is really an ontological thesis about subjectivity (1966: 2). Indeed, large tracts of Lacan's seminar *Freud's Papers on Technique, 1953–1954* were intended as a refutation of the developmental interpretation of the mirror stage assumed by some members of his audience (Forrester 1990: 118–19); characteristically, Lacan was always reinstructing and outpacing those who risked identifying themselves as Lacanians. It is important to note, however, that Lacan's interest in the mirror was itself a reflection of the romantic view of the double as *unheimlich*. As suggested earlier, Freud connected the uncanny with his theory of primary (or "absolute") narcissism, according to which the double is fearful because it underscores our essential mortality; the double is seen as our inevitable fate, a corpse-in-waiting. As Borch-Jacobsen (1991: 46) argues, Lacan rejected Freud's somewhat confused theory of primary narcissism, and proposed in its place his own theory of the mirror stage. This theory is tied up with Lacan's consuming interest in the role of desire in mental life. According to Lacan, at some point after eight months the child seeks recognition in the other or, more literally, in an idealized mirror image. This is a prototypical relation that Lacan rubs up against "the iron law of our time" (1966: 26): namely, the master/slave dialectic of Hegel's *Phenomenology of Spirit*. More exactly, Lacan adopts a certain version of Hegel filtered through Heidegger's early existential work (e.g., *Being and Time*) on the finitude (or mortality) of the subject, and through the Marxist reinterpretation of Hegel popularized by Kojève (through his seminars, later gathered as an *Introduction to the Reading of Hegel*). "Desire is human only if the one desires," Kojève states, "not the body, but the Desire of the other" (1939: 6). Or as Lacan writes in "Some Reflections on the Ego," "The object of man's desire, and we are not the first to say this, is essentially an object desired by someone else" (1953: 12). Reading Marx reading Hegel, Kojève teaches that human Desire (a word he often capitalizes) exceeds animal Desire because it "transcend[s] the given that is given to it" (1939: 5) and risks life itself in a "fight to the death for pure prestige" (7)—what Hegel called a "trial by death" (1807: 114). Lacan more or less repeats this lesson, according to which human desire is beyond mere need just as language is beyond mere biology (Borch-Jacobsen 1991: 11; cf. Lacan 1978: 115). As Lacan puts it in the *Écrits*: "The satisfaction of human desire is possible only when mediated by the desire and the labour of the other" (1966: 26).

For Lacan, then, the philosophically bankrupt magicians called ego psychologists were duped by the specularity of the unified self-image; by the apparent domination (and exemplarity) of the ego in psychic life; by believing in (or admiring) their own self-image reflected in the eyes of their loving patients; and by the fantasy of their own technical prowess as increasingly better clinicians than Freud. The therapeutic alliance forged between the egos of doctor and patient was, he thus felt, an enormous technical blunder (1954–55: 68; 1953: 16), if not an instance of clinical and intellectual grandiosity. Of the ego and its exponents, he therefore complains: "Far from being understood as it should have been, there was a general rush, exactly like the kids getting out of school—*Ah! Our nice little ego is back again! It all makes sense now! We're now back on the well-beaten paths of general psychology*" (1954–55: 11; his emphasis). In short, the first and second generation of analysts, those naughty children, "reverted to a confused, unitary, naturalistic conception of man, of the ego, and by the same token the instincts" (37). Against this psychology of the "everyman" (11), this "refusion of psychoanalysis with general psychology" (13), Lacan reads Freud as having returned psychoanalysis to a dualistic conception of psychic life, a return by which he intended to save psychoanalysis from becoming just another "philosophy of nature." And this operation, Lacan twice repeats in his seminar of 1954–55, was taken by Freud "at all costs" (37, 39).

Of course, the cost of doing business in this way is heavy indeed. Freud flirted with certain questionable metabiological and metaphysical ideas in *BPP* and, as a result, risked his creation on an investment in thinking without ground, that is to say, without capital. A kind of unmanageable inflation has, in turn, necessitated all kinds of cost-saving—or face-saving—measures among worried psychoanalysts. While American ego psychologists simply dropped—or, more exactly, thought they dropped—the more speculative parts of Freud's metapsychology, Lacan proved a far more creative bookkeeper. With recourse to "another domain of experience," he boldly advised that his audience turn Freud's later work "to your own profit" (41).

It is certainly true that Lacan's "return to Freud" emphasized a side of psychoanalysis that was unjustifiably minimized by ego psychologists. Yet Lacan had a way of making the master a precursor of his own enlightened views about psychoanalysis. In this way Lacan's view of psychoanalysis is a cracked mirror held up against a coopted, stale, establishment image of Freud—but an image, just the same, that Freud himself shared to some extent. To take one example, Lacan steadfastly refused to accept the biologist in Freud, stating rather incredulously that "Freudian biology has nothing to do with biology. It is a matter of manipulating symbols with the aim of resolving energy questions" (75). That this metaphorical Freud is not supported by Freud's own work—which, incidentally, Lacan rarely cites—or by the complicated intellectual context out of which *BPP* was fashioned, is a bold yet troubling claim. To the extent that it saves Freud from himself, this view simply whitewashes the history of psychoanalysis just as assuredly as the ego psychological view of Freud; in fact, both groups tend to overestimate Freud's mysterious control over the evolution of his own creation, and both have tried to minimize his lifelong biologism. For his part, Lacan polemicized that Freud's recourse to a theory of psychic energy—to the economic and mechanistic theories of the nineteenth century—only disguised his more interesting, more essential, views about symbolization and language. The upshot: a discourse of biological "instinct" was replaced by one of symbolical "drive." To this often peculiar end Lacan traces a movement from the *Project for a Scientific Psychology* (1895) to *The Interpretation of Dreams* (1900) to *Beyond the Pleasure Principle* (1920), according to which Freud finally understood what he had truly created, and what had to be done to safeguard the essence of that creation. "It is said," Lacan declares, that Freud abandons a physiologising perspective [ca. 1895] for a psychologising perspective [ca. 1900]. That's not the point. He discovers the operation of the symbol as such, the manifestation of the symbol . . . in its displacements, puns, plays on words, jokes working all on their own in the dream machine. . . . It took him another twenty years . . . to be able to look back to his premises and to try to recover what it means in terms of energy. That is what required him to produce the new elaboration of the beyond of the pleasure principle and of the death instinct. (76)

Just as Freud quite literally burned some of his early efforts or consigned them to the trash can in his effort to control history in advance, Lacan effectively remakes the sputtering machine of Freud's early mechanistic efforts into the efficient "dream machine" of his own structural psychoanalysis; a machine he duly translates into the language of cybernetic and information theories that were fashionable in the fifties. All of which is to say, at the end of the day, that Freud managed to discover that the unconscious is structured something like a language.

In this respect, Lacan at times proceeds by way of hermeneutic interpretation, finding in a thread or two of Freudian text (or allusion) a rope upon which to hang the truth of an entire corpus. And so his conclusions are rationalized by his procedure, according to which "the full significance of meaning far surpasses the signs manipulated by the individual. Man is always cultivating a great many more signs than he thinks. That's what the Freudian discovery is about—a new attitude to man. That's what man after Freud is" (122). For Lacan, the full significance of Freud's own work surpassed his finite understanding. To the extent that Freud invariably wrote an unthought into his corpus, he was all along waiting for an other, some Lacan, to read the signs of his texts and reveal the hidden meanings that surpassed his partial understanding and perspective. To put a more generous spin on things, the situation with Lacan is similar to Marcuse: both were trying to save Freud from his greatest problems, from his own limitations as a theorist, even as they piled their own pet theories onto his own. Lacan only made his point a bit more aggressively than Marcuse.

Lacan's view of the death drive is a case in point. He mentions, only to dismiss, those who equate Freud's principle of constancy with the actual death of the organism. For Lacan, this equation "confuse[s] the pleasure principle with what we think Freud designated under the name of the death instinct. I say *what we think*, because, when Freud speaks of the death instinct, he is, thank God, designating something less absurd, less anti-biological, antiscientific" (82). Lacan, in short, refuses to take Freud at his word—for Freud does, as noted above many times, very clearly equate constancy with organic death. Instead, "thank God," Lacan's Freud is "obliged" to think the great thought of the death drive because the detour called "human experience, human interchanges, intersubjectivity" is what truly interests him (80–81). For Lacan, we know, "all analytic experience is an experience of signification" (325). And thus, to the extent that "the human being goes beyond the real which is biologically natural to it" (322), he or she must struggle with the language of the other. As Lacan put it at the end of his seminar on the ego:

> This is the point where we open into the symbolic order, which isn't the libidinal order in which the ego is inscribed, along with all the drives. It tends beyond the pleasure principle, beyond the limits of life, and that is why Freud identifies it with the death instinct. . . . The death instinct is only the mask of the symbolic order, in so far—this is what Freud writes—in so far as it hasn't been realised. As long as the symbolic recognition hasn't been instituted, by definition, the symbolic order is dumb.
>
> The symbolic order is simultaneously non-being and insisting to be, this is what Freud has in mind when he talks about the death instinct as being what is most fundamental—a symbolic order in travail, in the process of coming, insisting on being realised. (326)

Through the dialectic with the other one becomes a human being, which is to say, once again, that one is recognized (or "realized") in the eyes of at least one person. As Kojève states, "The human being can be formed only if at least two of these Desires confront one another" (1939: 7).

Consequently, Lacan more or less makes of repetition a desire, a compulsion or *Zwang*, for *communion* with at least one other being (1954–55: 88–89). Repetition is, in effect, the basic condition of the dialectic of desire leading to recognition. Kojève put it this way years before: "It is only by being 'recognized' by another, by many others, or—in the extreme—by all others, that a human being is really human" (1939: 9). Such is the "herd" within which Kojève explicitly locates *human* reality as *recognized* reality (8). Lacan understood Kojève's meaning perfectly, saying flatly that "this discourse [with the other] produces a small circuit in which an entire family, an entire coterie, an entire camp, an entire nation or half the world will be caught" (1954–55: 90). Such repetition is guaranteed by the fact that the subject of language, so unlike the fictitious mirror-ideal, is always "caught up in the symbolic piece-meal, decomposed." Or to put it differently, the subject is caught, and rather perversely so, by a form of representation understood through, and called by the name of, psychoanalysis—"the analytic relation, which can only be understood as a communication" (115). The death drive is, as a result, meaningful as a reflection of the negation and alienation of the subject living in the "world of the symbol" (210). The central phenomenon of repetition is, then, the royal road to an understanding that my subjectivity is always elsewhere, in sum, that "*I is an other*"—*Je est un autre* (7; his emphasis).

The detour of life, of endless miscommunication and *méconnaissance*, is thereupon brought into relation with the endless dialectic that is life and death. As suggested, this dialectic is what Lacan will call—as always, following Kojève following Marx following Hegel—a struggle for "pure prestige," for recognition in the eyes of the other, in a fight to the death without, for all of that, actually killing or being killed. For obviously, as Kojève reminds us, recognition demands that the adversary remain alive—albeit reduced to the position of the Slave (1939: 8–9)—and overcome dialectically (15). Desire, Lacan repeats, "is caught from end to end in the dialect of alienation and no longer has any other means of expression than through the desire for recognition and the recognition of desire" (1954–55: 212). Such desire is intimately connected, by way of a circle, to death: "The object of desire," Lacan states in *The Four Fundamental Concepts of Psycho-Analysis*, "is the cause of desire, and this object that is the cause of desire is the object of the drive" (1978: 243).

To what end, then, does Lacanian psychoanalysis aim? As Colette Audry suggests to Lacan, who nods his approval:

> Prior to analysis, it [the ego] is only a pure, imaginary mirage. From then on, analysis amounts to being a demystification of what was previously imaginary. So we get to the final point—once demystification has been accomplished, we find ourselves in the presence of death. All that is left is to wait and contemplate death. (in Lacan 1954–55: 214)

Or as Lacan more vividly suggests, analysis is over when, as with Oedipus, the analysand "tears his face apart" (1954–55: 214). Death, Borch-Jacobsen (1991) reminds us, is the Absolute Master, *des absoluten Herrn*, for a life governed by this tragic dialectic, a limit that structures existence until, at least, it is actually crossed (see Hegel 1807: 117). Death "as such," Lacan of course admits, "doesn't mean anything" (1954–55: 206). Indeed, Lacan always directs his attention to the "essential part of human experience": namely, "that which causes the subject to exist ... on the level of the emergence of the symbolic" (219). In good dialectical fashion, Lacan's subject may be decomposed and cadaverized but is not, for all of that, dead.

But things are not so complicated, I dare say, with Freud. Lacan thoroughly obscures the metapsychological meaning of *Beyond the Pleasure*

Principle, first of all, because he overextends the range of what he repeatedly calls "the Freudian experience" (see 222–23) and, second, because he fails to appreciate the actual limits of Freud's imagination. For, quite literally, *life* is for Freud in *BPP* a regrettable detour away from death and from the pleasures of the id. Life itself is alienated from death, just as the ego is alienated from the id, an assumption that allows Freud—all self-congratulatory "thank Gods" notwithstanding—to make of the body (organic *and* social) a ghostly apparition of the truest state: nonexistence. According to Lacan, though, "The Freudian experience" is (paradoxically, it seems) grounded upon a desire that is "prior to any kind of experience, prior to any considerations concerning the world of appearances and the world of essences" (222). "It is desire," Lacan states, "which achieves the primitive structuration of the human world, desire as unconscious" (224); and again, "the desire in question is prior to any kind of conceptualisation" (225) and "emerges just as it becomes embodied in speech" (234). As usual, Lacan echoes Kojève, who states: "To understand man by understanding his 'origin' is, therefore, to understand the origin of the I revealed by speech" (1939: 3). But for the Freud of *BPP* what is *prior* to speech is a *before* of existence that is unrepresentable, literally unspeakable, because *nonexistent*. This before is the "beyond of the pleasure principle" of an entirely different order than that of "analytic experience" and its (full or empty) speech acts. Freud states rather clearly that this order, which he calls *meta*psychologic, is "independent" of the orders of experience governed by the laws of psychoanalysis (i.e., by the pleasure principle). Suffice to say, at this juncture, that this extreme view of life and death is not at all "symbolic" in Lacan's sense. On the contrary, the deepest meaning in *BPP* is essentially literal, sitting right there on the surface, tied up as it is with his rather strange discussion of primary (or "absolute") narcissism; a discussion, as suggested, that Lacan carefully sidesteps with his theories of the mirror stage and of desire. (I will get back to this theory of primary narcissism a bit later.) Nor is Freud's logic, as we have seen, simply dialectical in the way that Lacan claims; in its most radical formulation, the beyond is not "alienated life, ex-sisting, this life in the other" (1954–55: 233). Rather, the beyond Freud introduces is radically *outside* the "dialectic" of the life and death drives. Like some demoniacal unmoved mover, Freud's death-drive theory is an ideal (of sorts) that complicates both his old theories and the "experiences" upon which they are purportedly based. And this, I think, is precisely why Lacan takes the linguistic route with Freud: the symbolic saves Freud from the extremity, also the absurdity, of his inflated speculations introduced in *BPP*. Quite simply, Lacan couldn't accept what Freud had to say any more than the ego psychologists could and so he made of *BPP* a dream symbolizing something else, something more, in a word, something *French*. As we will see, this is a familiar story.

> To begin with, the man who wants to be recognized by another in no sense wants to recognize him in turn. If he succeeds, then, the recognition will not be mutual and reciprocal: he will be the recognized but will not recognize the one who recognizes him.
> —Alexandre Kojève, *Introduction to the Reading of Hegel*[78]

For Lacan in 1965 the "hermeneutic *Beyond*" was also a "stolen *Beyond*." That at least is what he thought—or pretended to think (Roudinesco 1990: 390–91)—when the philosopher Paul Ricoeur published his *De l'interprétation: Essai sur Freud* (1965), later translated into English as *Freud and Philosophy* (1970). Lacan had already seen something of himself in Ricoeur's interpretation of Freud a few years earlier, at the Bonneval Colloquium in 1960. Yet Lacan's initial reaction to his apparent double was not by any means an uncanny one. On the contrary, Lacan courted the well-respected philosopher and invited him to his seminars at Sainte-Anne. One could even say that Lacan loved himself in this new image. In response, Ricoeur politely attended Lacan's seminars during the next three years, but quietly admitted to friends that he didn't understand a word of Lacan's elaborate discourse. As he would later concede, he found the seminars "uselessly difficult and perverse in its proclivity to suspension" (in Roudinesco 1990: 392).

Lacan's claim that Ricoeur lifted his ideas from the public seminars doesn't hold much water, and most commentators are careful to draw a line between their different views of Freud. As Roudinesco puts it, Ricoeur was influenced by a tradition of post-Hegelian phenomenology that "yoked a Christian tradition of deciphering texts to a modern philosophy of existence—it being understood that hermeneutics was not a 'reading' or a 'return' to texts, but an attempt to 'interpret' them" (1990: 391; cf. 396). It is certainly true that Ricoeur, a hermeneut with an interest in phenomenology, was not just another proponent of the structuralism that characterized French thought in the sixties, and which Lacan adopted in his return to Freud (392). Instead, Ricoeur (1965: 395) paid close attention to the economic side of Freud's thought, a tactic that was meant as a passing criticism of Lacan's idea that the unconscious is structured like a language (see Boothby 1991: 131–37). "The linguistic interpretation," he writes, "does not constitute an alternative to the economic explanation; it simply prevents the latter from being reified by showing that the mechanisms that come under the economics are accessible only in their relation to hermeneutics" (1965: 396). Thus, while Ricoeur admits that his and Lacan's critique of behaviorism are similar, he states, "We diverge . . . when I go on to criticize a conception that eliminates energy concepts in favor of linguistics" (367, n. 37).[79]

Against a perceived linguistic bias in Lacan's work, Ricoeur tried to *mediate* what he considered the two basic tensions of Freud's epistemology: between the neurologic and hermeneutic, materialist and interpretive, biologically instinctual and psychologically driven, strategies for reading the unconscious. According to Ricoeur, Freud both assumed and ignored these distinctions (66), since he advocated what was essentially a "mixed or even ambiguous discourse" (65). As Ricoeur qualifies in a later essay, "A Philosophical Interpretation of Freud," this mixed discourse "intermingles questions of meaning (the meaning of dreams, symptoms, culture, etc.) and questions of force (cathexis, economic accounting, conflict, repression, etc.)" (1974b: 160). As a consequence, the Ricoeur of the 1960's set as his task the following: "to overcome the gap between the two orders of discourse and to reach the point where one sees that the energetics implies a hermeneutics and the hermeneutics discloses an energetics. That point is where the positing or emergence of desire manifests itself in and through a process of symbolization" (1965: 65; see also 1974b: 167–68). It is important to recognize that Ricoeur saw his interpretive task as consonant with the aims of Freud's own discourse, which was justifiably mixed because it "is appropriate to the reality which it wishes to take into account, namely, the binding force and meaning in a semantics of desire" (1974b: 160). The mixed discourse of Freud is, in other words, a realistically *dialectical* discourse: "This dialectic is that of the very situation explored by psychoanalysis, namely, the interlacing of desire and culture" (164). And so Freud's discourse is quite irreducible to biology or semantics (169).

At the heart of *Freud and Philosophy* lies Ricoeur's examination of Freud's *Beyond the Pleasure Principle*, what he calls the "least hermeneutic and most speculative of Freud's essays" (1965: 281). As a hermeneut of some distinction, Ricoeur provides an unusually evenhanded *explication de texte*, attending to the messy details that rarely get the attention they deserve in the literature—philosophic or otherwise. Basically his explication pivots around a nuanced interpretation of the death drive, which he connects with Hegel's view of negation. Ricoeur, though, is careful to take aim at those who uncritically toss Hegel and Freud together (317). As he states succinctly in his essay "Consciousness and the Unconscious":

> We cannot simply add up Hegel and Freud and give to each half a man.... We must enter into the most complete opposition between consciousness as history [i.e., Hegel] and the unconscious as fate [i.e., Freud] if we wish to acquire the right to overcome this opposition and understand the identity of the two opposed systematics, one of which is a synthesis of consciousness, the other an analysis of the unconscious. But neither their opposition nor their identity gives us the right of eclecticism. Three cups of the unconscious, and a pinch of consciousness is not our recipe at any price. Eclecticism is always the enemy of the dialectic. (1974a: 118–19)

If Ricoeur's criticism is generally true of the literature on *BPP*, it also seems to be a pointed remark at Lacan, who never hesitated to add a cup of Hegel to a pinch of Heidegger, and so on. It is an entirely valid criticism, one that Derrida would repeat in the early seventies. It is no surprise, then, that Ricoeur ignored Lacan in *Freud and Philosophy*, whom he viewed as an enemy of the kind of dialectical work he himself championed.

Without question a more thoughtful synthesis of Freud and Hegel is at the forefront of Ricoeur's integration of phenomenology and hermeneutics, teleology and archaeology (see 1974b: 161, 173–74). As Don Ihde suggests, "Ricoeur sees in both Freud and Hegel a hermeneutics which deliberately displaces the immediacy of consciousness," albeit from an inverse perspective: while Freud the archeologist looked to the past and to fate, Hegel the teleologist looked to the future and to history (1974a: xvi; see Whitebook 1995: 230–31).

Ricoeur argues that the link between Freud and Hegel is critically made along the path opened by Freud's death drive, on the one hand, and by what Hegel called "the work of the negative" (1965: 318) on the other. In his 1925 essay "Negation," Freud introduced what Ricoeur calls an " 'economics' of negation," according to which consciousness always proceeds by way of negation (1925b: 239). Although, according to Freud, negation "belongs to the instinct for destruction" (239), Ricoeur carefully notes that Freud does not simply say that negation is "another representative of the death instinct"—such as aggressivity—"but only says that negation is genetically derived from it by 'substitution' " (1965: 317). Such a substitution is, just the same, seemingly fundamental to the normal functioning of consciousness as described by Freud. The relation Freud posits between the death drive and negation—and, indirectly, to Hegel—is therefore a complex and surprising one:

> It is not surprising that negation is derived from the death instinct by way of substitution. On the contrary, what is surprising is that the death instinct is rep-

resented by such an important function which has nothing to do with destructiveness, but rather with the symbolization of play [e.g., the *fort/da* game], with aesthetic creation [e.g., Freud's Leonardo], and with reality-testing itself. This discovery is enough to throw into flux the whole analysis of the representatives of instincts. The death instinct is not closed in upon destructiveness, which is, we said, its clamour; perhaps it opens out onto other aspects of the "work of the negative," which remain "silent" like itself. (317–18)

Freud's discussion of negation allows Ricoeur to see, not just the destructive side of the death drive, but also the nonpathological and creative side (cf. 1965: 286) associated with Freud's (rather slippery) concept of *sublimation*. The role of sublimation, Ricoeur tells us, is best witnessed through the work of conscience (or guilt, the superego) on the big stage of culture: "Culture comes on the scene," he writes, "making life prevail against death: its supreme weapon is to employ internalized violence against externalized violence; its supreme ruse is to make death work against death" (309). It is not simply the case, then, that Freud counterposes life against death, but that death is an integral part of life. Such is the paradox of Freud's notion of culture, where the "excess" of meaning attributed to the death drive suggests "that the death instinct . . . may conceal another possible meaning" (313)—one that is positive.

And so Ricoeur reserves a special place for the death-drive theory within what he calls the "architecture of Freudianism" (1974b: 164–65). According to this schema, Freud's thought can be divided into "three great masses" or, more rigorously, into a "continuum which goes from a mechanistic representation of the psychic mechanism to a romantic dramaturgy of life and death." Basically, Ricoeur thinks that there is a kind of "development" from Freud's early neurological work to his later dualistic theory, all of which, nonetheless, is structured by "a homogeneous milieu, namely, the desire's effect on meaning" (165). What he calls the "third theoretical network" is necessitated by the "alterations imposed by the introduction of the death instinct" into the old psychoanalytic "edifice." Of this new network, Freud's late dualism, he writes:

> This alteration reaches the very foundations of existence, for it involves a redistribution of forces in terms of the polarity Eros-Thanatos. As the relation between instinct and culture remains the principal leading thread, however, this basic alteration also affects every aspect of culture. Indeed, the entry of the death instinct implies the most important reinterpretation of culture, that which is expressed in *Civilization and Its Discontents*. It is in guilt, in the discontent of the civilized individual, and in the clamor of war that the mute instinct begins to cry out. (165)

Again, grounded in a semantics of desire, Ricoeur's dialectic repeats on a philosophical level the dialectic that Freud implies with his "mixed," but nonetheless developing, discourse.

Where does this leave us? By taking the subject as a kind of text, as an object of interpretation, Ricoeur believes that the hermeneut in Freud challenges the traditional philosophy of the cogito. Like Marx and Nietzsche before him, Freud engaged in a "hermeneutics of suspicion," through which he tried to interpret the reality behind mere appearance and consciousness. In many ways, this interpretation is far more attractive than Lacan's, since he sticks close to the relevant texts and refrains from reading himself into Freud's work and intentions. On the other hand, his overall attempt to oppose and then synthesize the relative positions of Freud and Hegel, hermeneutics and phenomenology, seems hopelessly dated today. Actually, this project was *already* dated when Ricoeur first published *Freud and Philosophy* in 1965. Obviously the faddish Lacan had nothing to worry about from Ricoeur. The very old-fashioned Ricoeur could never compete with a discourse that was irreducible to any one method or theorist, that would abruptly change shape to suit the intellectual cause *du jour*, that—in a word—was radically *other*, passing as it did through the stations of Hegel, Heidegger, Kojève, and so on. Ricoeur, perhaps, was not thief enough to make that much difference in Lacanian France. After their first meeting in 1960, Lacan had wanted Ricoeur to recognize his special contribution to psychoanalytic interpretation in the pages of the work in progress, *Freud and Philosophy*. Instead, with its publication in 1965 Lacan not only found that Ricoeur's position had not budged an inch but that Ricoeur had even criticized him in passing. Indeed, to be referred to in passing was probably the hardest part of Ricoeur's treatment of Lacan; at bottom Lacan was probably less angered by the apparent theft of his ideas than by the insult of being ignored and turned into a slave. For although Lacan was all too willing to recognize his own return in Ricoeur's masterful interpretation, Ricoeur was hardly able to recognize himself in Lacan's free-associational, disjointed, unsystematized seminars. Lacan's outrage about the apparent theft of ideas merely masked an embarrassing *méconnaisance* according to which Ricoeur, the master-who-knows, had become the embodiment of everything Lacan wished his ego could be. Lacan got the message as early as the end of 1963. After one of his lectures, he gave Ricoeur a call: " 'What do you think, *mon cher*, of what I enunciated today?' Ricoeur answered abruptly, 'I was just in the process of telling myself that I find what you say impenetrable.' In a fury Lacan hung up" (in Roudinesco 1990: 393). Ricoeur was left hanging on the other end of a line, the bewildered analyst of a patient he didn't know he had. For his part, Lacan seemed to understand just how he had failed to implement the crux of his own teaching—at least as it was gleaned from Kojève, Marx, and Hegel. Having made Ricoeur his master he inadvertently made himself into a slave unworthy of recognition. In this respect, the Protestant Ricoeur was a poor priest and an even poorer analyst for the lapsed Catholic in Lacan: Ricoeur's silence was nearly absolute, his mirror inviolable, his forgiveness unforthcoming.

In his dealings with another French philosopher, Jacques Derrida, Lacan seemed to recall that mutual recognition is an ideal, probably an impossibility, and he adjusted his strategy accordingly. Instead of making the other into the One Who Knows, instead of completing himself in the other's (seemingly perfect) imago, he more carefully, if audaciously, reserved the right to know, the right to priority, for himself alone. Just as he had accused Ricoeur of intellectual theft in the mid-sixties, a few years later Lacan informed Derrida that he was not very original either. The incident occurred over a salad bar at a now famous conference in Baltimore in 1966, an event that loosely coincides with the coming-out of French poststructuralism in America. According to Roudinesco, Derrida met Lacan for the first time at the conference dinner.

> Derrida raised the questions which concerned him about the Cartesian subject, substance, and the signifier. Standing as he sampled a plate of cole slaw, Lacan replied that *his* subject was the same as the one his interlocutor had opposed to the theory of the subject. In itself, the remark was not false. But Lacan then added, "You can't bear my having already said what you want to say."
> (1990: 410)

Derrida wasn't amused, and apparently responded: "*That* is not my problem." At their next encounter Derrida made the mistake of confiding to Lacan a personal anecdote about his own family that Lacan later incorporated into a public lecture (411; cf. Derrida 1995–96). Lacan closed his interpretation of this family scene with a provocation to Derrida: "It's up to the father, who told it to me, to hear me from where I speak or not."

Naturally, Derrida was insulted. While he refused to accept Lacan's authority as the master analyst, at least while he was alive, he kept fairly quiet about Lacan's popular "return to Freud." It was only in an interview of 1971 that Derrida turned the tables on Lacan, stating that Lacan's work on the Symbolic, Imaginary, and Real was in fact caught "within the system that I put into question" (1972a: 84). In a long footnote appended to the interview, Derrida attacks in uncharacteristically clear language Lacan's contribution to psychoanalysis: Lacan's discourse of "full speech" repeats a Western bias that connects presence and truth (108); his importation of Hegel, Husserl, and Heidegger into a new configuration with Freud is facile (108–109); his resurrection of Saussurian linguistics is phonologistic (109); and his interpretation of Freud does not address the problematic concept of writing. In effect, Derrida accuses Lacan of inventing a kind of "new metaphysics"—complete with reference to authenticity, Being, and so on—that he himself had spent his time deconstructing. Rather less convincing are Derrida's hypocritical statements about Lacan's "style," remarks that could just as easily be made about Derrida's own efforts—especially those of the last fifteen years or so. "In relation to the difficulties that interested me," Derrida writes, "I read this style, above all, as an art of evasion" (110).

Derrida also comments upon Lacan's "Seminar on 'The Purloined Letter,'" which Lacan first delivered in 1955—a text that Derrida takes to task in his "The Purveyor [Facteur] of Truth" of 1975. Whereas Lacan argues that the letter of truth, like the unconscious, always finds its destination, Derrida offers a theory of misdirection that upsets Lacan's simplistic "postal" system: for Derrida, the letter does not necessarily reach its destination except as a theoretical or metaphysical ideal of correspondence without loss, error, misappropriation, and so on.

As I will discuss momentarily, Derrida's deconstruction is not so much interested in the fact that communication happens, which it obviously does on a certain mundane level, but that it always fails in certain ways at the limits of intelligibility. Misinterpretation or misdirection is always the risk and condition of any attempt to speak of, for, or as the truth. This interest in the failures of communication is of course reflected in Freud's own discourse. But Freud and Derrida approach the margins (and marginalia) from a different, though not exactly opposite, direction; to stretch it a little, one could say that Freud is to Derrida what Hegel is to Marx. For while Freud expands meaning to *contract the marginal*, leading some to complain that he is a deterministic pessimist, Derrida expands the marginal to *contract the meaningful*, leading some to complain that he is an indeterministic nihilist; Freud forces reason into the margin as a self-styled "conquistador," while Derrida forces the margin into reason as a guerrilla fighter (or terrorist, as Michel Foucault once complained). Or for Freud, once again, it is the margin that explodes, while for Derrida it is the meaning that implodes. Despite their different orientations, however, both locate the joke effect in a similar slippage of meaning, of semiotic fixity, in the confusion generated between an uncertain inside and outside, center and margin, reason and accident.

In the next section I will examine Derrida's work on psychoanalysis a bit more carefully, especially his work on *BPP*, which suffers from some of the same problems that we find in Lacan. While there are a small handful of deconstructive works on Freud and psychoanalysis, including those by

Rodolphe Gasché (1974) and Samuel Weber (1982, 1988), I have limited my remarks in what follows to Derrida alone.[80]

Derrida and the Deconstructive 'Beyond'; or, How One Philosophizes with a (Jacques-) Hammer

Derrida's Freud has everything and nothing to do with the different traditions of Freud interpretation that I have sketched so far, from biography to philosophy. First of all, Derrida is not an intellectual historian and doesn't always bother to track, or carefully consider, the various interpretative strategies that have been adopted for reading Freud. Secondly, and more important from his perspective, he doesn't have to because deconstruction is a response to a tradition which is so obviously *constructive*—a tradition that is, as Derrida might put it, logocentric, or theo-logocentric, or onto-theologocentric, or phono-logocentric, and so on. In other words, the tradition is -centric or centered, always organized and structured one way or another around a guiding thought, whether it be biographical, biological, clinical, or philosophical. By contrast, Derrida's reading of Freud is decentering of Western metaphysics, an aspect of his perspective that needs to be unpacked if one is to understand his work on Freud.

In this chapter I want to outline what is at stake in Derrida's deconstruction of Freud's *Beyond the Pleasure Principle*, first of all, as it appeared in "Freud and the Scene of Writing" of 1967, and then again in his long essay of 1980 "To Speculate—On 'Freud,'" from *The Post Card: From Socrates to Freud and Beyond*. Derrida's central themes: a general theory of writing, Freud's participation in the history of metaphysics, the radicalness of Freud's efforts, the autobiographical institutionalization of psychoanalysis, and, as always, the "crypt" that problematizes psychoanalytic conceptualizations in advance.

THE ARCHI-ÉCRITURE OF 'BEYOND'

> It is with a graphematics still to come, rather than with a linguistics dominated by an ancient phonologism, that psychoanalysis sees itself as destined to collaborate.
> —Jacques Derrida, "Freud and the Scene of Writing"[81]

Like Lacan, Ricoeur, and some other French commentators, Derrida's interpretive efforts are located between the lines of Freud's text, typically those metapsychological texts wherein Freud propounds his most speculative, dualistic theories: the primary and secondary systems, the unconscious and consciousness, pleasure and reality principles, death and life drives. But what sets Derrida apart from his contemporaries is an additional effort to locate meaning (albeit of a deconstructive explosive kind) along the fault lines of Freud's argumentation. Unlike the piecemeal theories of Lacan, Derrida's deconstruction is grounded in the Continental tradition (see Gasché 1986); unlike the hermeneutic philosophy of Ricoeur, Derrida's deconstruction is not driven by the need to complete or correct Freud's thought.

In Derrida's "grammatological" work of the 1960's, he audaciously mapped his own interest in *writing* onto Freud's theories—the better, it would seem, to establish Freud, not only as a late figure in the history of Western metaphysics, but as an important precursor, like Nietzsche and Heidegger, of Derrida's own brand of radicalism. Among other things, this means we should not forget that Derrida's earliest encounter with Freud is intimately tied up with his concurrent deconstructions of Rousseau, Lévi-Strauss, and Saussure as found in *Of Grammatology* (1967b). During this productive period, Derrida was consumed by the problematic of speech and writing in the history of Western thought. According to Derrida, speech has been consistently privileged at the expense of writing, which is routinely excluded from Western ideals of representation as a poison or dangerous supplement. For this reason writing is often considered a mere memory aid, a guarantee of memory that must not be confused with memory itself. As Freud himself put this commonplace idea: "If I distrust my memory . . . I am able to supplement and guarantee its working by making a note in writing" (1925c: 227). Speech, on the other hand, has always been considered the privileged vehicle of authenticity and presence, including that form of presence known as consciousness.

Derrida contends that Freud repeats the norms of such "phonologism" even as he ventures beyond those norms at key moments in his work. Indeed, not unlike Rousseau and Lévi-Strauss, Derrida's Freud flirts with a sort of "writing" that is inimical to the "metaphysics of presence," of transparency-to-self. To demonstrate this claim, Derrida invokes a familiar story that sees Freud caught between the demands of a discourse at times scientific and metaphorical, an unresolved ambivalence played out through his view of the unconscious as, on the one hand, a quantity of energy and, on the other, as poetic and unrepresentable. And so, just as Ricoeur unpacks the meaning of Freud's "mixed or even ambiguous discourse" in 1960, Derrida in 1967 traces such ambiguity from the *Project for a Scientific Psychology* of 1895 to "A Note Upon the 'Mystic Writing-Pad' " of January 1925. Whereas Freud in the *Project* proposed a neurological theory of breaching or facilitation, *Bahnung*, (Derrida's *frayage*), according to which memory and psyche are developed as resistance to external forces—ultimately as a consequence of the difference created between permeable and nonpermeable membranes—in the "Note" he offers a revised theory with the help of the *Wunderblock*, or mystic writing pad (1925c: 225–32). Derrida marvels at this five-page "Note," in which Freud offers a fresh description of the conscious, preconscious, and perceptual systems that was first introduced in the *Project*. Only now, significantly for Derrida, the permeable and nonpermeable membranes have been replaced by a non-neurological metaphor, a metaphor of *writing* borrowed from a simple technology. The writing pad, like modern derivatives still used by children, is a device that allows writing on a surface to be continually erased, and thus continually renewed (like the work of perception and memory), even as it registers that writing as impressions upon the wax below. Freud describes the device in some detail:

> The Mystic Pad is a slab of dark brown resin or wax with paper edging; over the slab is laid a thin transparent sheet, the top end of which is firmly secured to the slab while its bottom end rests on it without being fixed to it. This transparent sheet is the more interesting part of the little device. It itself consists of two layers, which can be detached from each other except at their two ends. The upper layer is a transparent piece of celluloid; the lower layer is made of thin translucent waxed paper. When the apparatus is not in use, the lower surface of the waxed paper adheres lightly to the upper surface of the wax slab. (1925c: 228–9)

Freud's theory of the psyche as a kind of writing that is constantly effaced, but nonetheless present—deep in the wax, that is, repressed in the unconscious (231)—is certainly an interesting rendering of the old neurological theory. Freud says as much, claiming that the model of the writing pad "shows remarkable agreement with my hypothetical structure of our perceptual apparatus" (228). He continues:

> If, while the Mystic Pad has writing on it, we cautiously raise the celluloid from the waxed paper, we can see the writing just as clearly on the surface of the latter, and the question may arise why there should be any necessity for the celluloid portion of the cover. Experiment will then show that the thin paper would be easily crumpled or torn if one were to write directly upon it with the stylus. The layer of celluloid thus acts as a protective sheath for the waxed paper, to keep off injurious effects from without. The celluloid is a "protective shield against stimuli" [as first discussed in the *Project*]; the layer which actually receives the stimuli is the paper. I may at this point recall that in *Beyond the Pleasure Principle* I showed that the perceptual apparatus of our mind consists of two layers, of an external protective shield against stimuli whose task it is to diminish the strength of excitations coming in, and of a surface behind it which

receives stimuli, namely the system *Pcpt.-Cs.* [perceptual-conscious system]. (230)

Characteristically, Derrida is not inclined to view the writing pad as just the latest disguise, a metaphor, for the biological bedrock of psychoanalysis. And in a way he doesn't care; Freud's vacillations are taken in and of themselves, sans judgment, with only a perfunctory acknowledgment of the historical context of Freud's arguments. Derrida appropriates Freud's model of the psyche as a kind of writing, making it function as what one commentator rightly calls "yet another parable of deconstruction" (Norris 1982: 122).[82] As Christopher Johnson therefore suggests, Derrida's interpretation of Freud in "Freud and the Scene of Writing" is not entirely innocent: "Freud's use of the scriptural metaphor at different stages of his intellectual itinerary is not necessarily immediately and obviously assimilable to Derrida's general theory of writing" (1993: 68).

For Derrida, though, it is not a question of whether or not Freud's theories are correct, but of how far beyond logocentric discourse they tread—intentionally or not. Or, less charitably, it is a question of how far they can be *pushed* in that direction. "Our aim is limited," Derrida writes, "to locate in Freud's text several points of reference, and to isolate ... those elements of psychoanalysis which can only uneasily be contained within logocentric closure" (1967a: 198). Freud's recourse to a metaphor of the writing machine—already loaded with significance for Derrida—is just such a point of reference, one that in deconstructive hands has little or nothing to do with psychoanalytic concepts as they are normally conceived and which, Derrida insists, must be bracketed in quotation marks (197). In this respect Derrida is careful to emphasize that "the deconstruction of logocentricism is not a psychoanalysis of philosophy" (196), and as such is not concerned, for example, with the historical "repression" of writing in psychoanalytic terms. As Johnson therefore puts it, Derrida is not trying to rehabilitate a forgotten or repressed form of writing, but to pinpoint in Freud a movement "beyond the everyday understanding of writing in order to postulate a 'writing' more fundamental to signifying practices in general, a 'writing' that is the condition of all forms of expression, whether scriptural, vocal, or otherwise" (1993: 66; see Derrida 1967a: 197).

Derrida's conclusions in this regard would be stunning if they were not so wildly overdetermined by his attempt to outline, again and again, the structure of what he calls archi-*écriture*: an original kind of writing, based on his explication of *différance* (a neologism for the differing and deferring undecidability that undoes conceptual purity[83]), that crosses out in advance any metaphysical concept of an origin. To this end he continually makes Freud's writing machine work for the aims of deconstruction. For example, Derrida claims the following of Freud's *Project*:

> Beneath an indicial neurology ... we repeatedly find a persistent attempt to account for the psyche in terms of spacing, a topography of traces, a map of breaches; and we repeatedly find an attempt to locate consciousness or quality in a space whose structure and possibility must be rethought, along with the attempt to describe the "functioning of the apparatus" in terms of pure differences and locations.... And when he [Freud] renounces neurology and anatomical localizations, it will be not in order to abandon his topographical preoccupations, but to transform them. Trace will become *gramme*; and the region of breaching a ciphered spacing. (1967a: 205)

Derrida's Freud will have confronted the limits of thought, not, say, as an existential confrontation with death, but as an epistemological break with his early neurological work and, more generally, with the history of metaphysics. Or again, Freud's scientist faith in neurobiology gives way to a metaphorics of writing, of *gramme*, just as assuredly as psychoanalysis gives way to the pressures of a Derridian grammatology;[84] or, at least, it gives way to the extent that it has "an historical originality" (199).

Derrida's originality is to have challenged the basic assumptions of metaphysics, including the privilege accorded to originality, with a tool of interpretation called deconstruction. Freud's "originality" is that he was *almost* deconstructive in his thinking. Derrida certainly makes the most out of clues he finds scattered across the Freudian corpus. In "The Claims of Psycho-Analysis to Scientific Interest," for instance, Freud remarks, "It is even more appropriate to compare dreams with a system of writing than with a language" (in 1913a: 177). To this admission Derrida states that he has "nothing to add, interpret, alter" (1967a: 220), taking it as *literal* evidence that Freud himself has invoked in his work a "graphematics still to come." Other examples are less literal-minded, naturally, and certainly do require creative additions, interpretations, and alterations. Take for example Freud's concept of "breaching," in which Derrida finds a hint, really an excuse, for thinking the thought of an originary violence at the heart of Western metaphysics, a thought, as Johnson (1993: 71–72) brilliantly exposes, that Derrida has Freud share with Lévi-Strauss, and in nearly identical language.[85] For Derrida this originary violence is represented, literally re-presented, by a theory of repetition and deferral that can be, or must be, mapped onto Freud's theories of the death drive and the repetition compulsion. For having drawn a line between breaching and the origin of memory (1967a: 200–201), Derrida makes of life itself the time of a repetition that is also a deferral. A deferral of what? Death. And it is here, precisely, that *BPP* plays an important role in the deconstructive "scene of writing": "No doubt life protects itself by repetition, trace, *différance* (deferral)" (203). Consider, in this context, Derrida's remarks about the life and death drives:

> Life must be thought of as a trace before Being may be determined as presence. This is the only condition on which we can say that life *is* death, that repetition and the beyond of the pleasure principle are native and congenital to that which they transgress. When Freud writes in the *Project* that "facilitations [breachings] serve the primary function," he is forbidding us to be surprised by *Beyond the Pleasure Principle*. He complies with a dual necessity: that of recognizing *différance* [difference and deferral] at the origin, and at the same time of crossing out the concept of *primariness*. . . . It is thus the delay which is in the beginning . . . a non-origin which is originary. . . .
> The irreducibility of the "effect of deferral" [*Nachträglichkeit*]—such, no doubt, is Freud's discovery. (203)

And, really, there is no doubt. Freud's discovery is the inevitable *rediscovery*, the repetition, of the deconstructive condition of all human existence: ultimately, that the unconscious is structured not like a language, as the woefully logocentric Lacan would have it, but like a *writing* or, more loosely, like a text (see Derrida 1967b: 68).

> The unconscious text is already a weave of pure traces, differences in which meaning and force are united—a text nowhere present, consisting of archives which are *always already* transcriptions. Originary prints. Everything begins with reproduction. Always already: repositories of a meaning which was never present, whose signified presence is always reconstituted by deferral, *nachträglich*, belatedly [*après coup*], supplementarily: for the *nachträglich* also means *supplementary*. (Ibid.: 211)

Of course, by *Nachträglichkeit* Freud means to account for the baffling fact that memories of trauma sometimes appear, like magic, only years after the incipient event. How can we explain, Freud asks, the deferred action (literally the aftereffect) of such a trauma? And what role does repetition play in this action?

Now, *why* Freud posed these questions, and to what end (be it clinical, theoretical, political, or whatever), is not asked by Derrida. It is enough, simply, that Freud adopted a rich and evocative language, or that Freud's words, and to some extent his concepts, fit (or can be jammed) into the agenda of deconstruction. Judgment doesn't play a significant part in this agenda and this is, I think, a very serious shortcoming of Derrida's overall interpretation of Freud. In this respect Derrida is the big bang theorist of poststructuralism: judgment belongs to the secondary (supplemental, poisonous) effects of the human endeavor to discover the truth by a process that always already effaces its own efforts; deconstruction is not judgmental, that is, because it is concerned precisely with this originary process of self-erasure.

For example, Freud (heroically) tried to represent the workings of the unconscious, by definition an impossible task, a task that produces in its wake the troubled history of psychoanalysis. Better yet, and to his (apparent) credit, Freud recognized the inherent difficulty of representing the unrepresentable, and offered the writing pad not as the thing-in-itself, but as "a *concrete representation* of the way in which I tried to *picture* the functioning of the psychic apparatus of our mind" (1925c: 232; my emphasis). In short, the writing pad is what Freud explicitly calls "an auxiliary apparatus" (228, 230), which, like "the pocket-book or sheet of paper, is as it were a materialized portion of my mnemic apparatus, which I otherwise carry about with me invisible" (227). And so Derrida's Freud is and is not metaphysical; he devises his concepts only to self-consciously erase them (i.e., like the magic pad he describes). So while the model of the psyche, for Freud, should not be confused with the invisible "real thing," Derrida reminds us that the model, the supplement, is all we have and, moreover, is the best that Freud could offer. None of us can, as it were, *speak* the unconscious. Re-presentation, the repetition of a model without an original, thus structures Freud's defeat in advance and makes of any scientific psychology an elaborate pretension—if not a theoretical fiction, as Freud sometimes admitted (Derrida 1967a: 219). And so a certain kind of "writing" will always haunt Freud's metapsychology as that which can never be fully repressed or forgotten; an *original writing* that upsets concept-building even before it begins.

Although Derrida's early interest in speech and writing is a fundamental part of deconstruction, his focus has shifted over the years. Arguably this shift is a reflection of fashion and contingency: while poststructuralists made their respective stands on the question of language during the 1960's, it was the question of discipleship and authoritarianism that increasingly dominated the intellectual landscape of France during the 1970's. In both decades Lacan played the determining role, continually influencing the agenda of French intellectuals with his theories and institutional battles. In "To Speculate—On 'Freud,'" Derrida continues his examination of the myth of an origin, among much else, only now in the more accessible language of the myth of the founding father and his band of disciples. To this end Derrida provides a close textual interpretation of an essay that structures, sometimes behind the scene, much of his deconstructive imagination: *Beyond the Pleasure Principle*.

AUTOBIOGRAPHICAL 'BEYOND'

> Let us beware of saying that death is opposed to life. The living is merely a type of what is dead, and a very rare type.
> —Friedrich Nietzsche, *The Gay Science*[86]

In "Envois," the first long section of Derrida's *The Post Card*, we are presented with a collection of postcard messages and letters from Derrida to an unidentified addressee—possibly his wife, Marguerite, who happens to be an analyst, but effectively to anyone who stumbles upon them. "You might consider them," Derrida says of the letters, "as the remainders of a recently destroyed correspondence" (1980: 3). With this one-sided, selective, and fictionalized correspondence Derrida means to mimic or parody Freud's correspondence with Wilhelm Fliess (Ulmer 1985: 126). Derrida, though, does not explicate the theory of transference any more than he delves into Freud's actual dependence upon or "love" of Fliess. Instead he deconstructs the idealism of correspondence itself, first, as a medium of exchange across a distance and, second, as a philosophical theory of truth (as distinct, say, from the coherence theory of truth). Postcards, Derrida reminds us, are specially designed to convey surface meanings without betraying any depth; such depth is encoded as a private language. A number of questions therefore arise: Who has access to this secret depth or private language? By what means or method do we procure such access? And what are the inherent limitations of access when one side of the equation (literally one side, as in the case of Freud's letters to Fliess, and generally one side, as in the case of subjectivity) is always missing?

The limits of interpretation, combined with the overflowing of authorial intention, are at the heart of the deconstructive enterprise, which is often reflected in Derrida's work by a meandering, digressive, nonlinear style of exposition.[87] Naturally, it is this (sometimes frustrating) quality that Derrida values most in Freud's work, especially in *Beyond the Pleasure Principle*. In "To Speculate—On 'Freud,'" Derrida is more candid about his interpretative aims than in the early essay. "I will propose a selective, filtrating, discriminating reading," Derrida now advises, one that will "make legible the nonpositional structure of *Beyond*" (1980: 261). To this end Derrida concedes from the start that he "corrupts" Freud's meaning of "speculation," finding in that word another opportunity for thinking the fundamental truths of deconstruction. As he says, "A certain reading of his text, the one I am attempting here, cannot fail to come across" the work of this speculation (277). Derrida thus adopts (as a caution, but also as a rhetorical device) the fictional language of the "as if":

> I am acting as if the very thing he [Freud] appears to analyze, for example the relation between the two principles [pleasure and reality], were already an element of speculative structure in general. . . . I am alleging that speculation is not only a mode of research named by Freud, not only the oblique object of his discourse, but also the operation of his writing, the scene (of that) which he makes by writing what he writes here, that which makes him do it, and that which he makes to do, that which makes him write and that which he makes—or lets—write. (283–84; see also 303, 322, 328)

Having laid his cards on the table, Derrida proceeds to turn biographical details to deconstructive ends that have little to do with the norms of historical scholarship, repeating in this respect his earlier appropriation of psychoanalysis to the work of archi-*écriture*. More exactly, Derrida has biography play second fiddle to the unpacking of a certain kind of "autobiography." As he puts it, *BPP* "is autobiographical, but in a completely different way than has been believed up to now" (322). Derrida's notion of autobiography, like speculation, is unabashedly deconstructive: "The passage we are seeking is otherwise [than empirico-biographical], and more labyrinthine, of another labyrinth and another crypt" (328). Staring into this other crypt,[88] Derrida undertakes to "overlap what Freud says with what he does, or rather what happens (without happening) in *Beyond*" (397). This rejigging of autobiography, already a pointed critique of subjectivity and the cult of documentation, is thus ventured along the lines of the *performative* structure of Freud's text (see 391). "Freud does with (without) the object of his text," Derrida argues, "exactly what Ernst does with (without) his spool" (320). Consequently, and perhaps ironically, Freud is his own best (or only?) example of the compulsive repetition that he describes in *BPP*, and imputes to others (e.g., children, soldiers, patients). That is, Freud is "a more or less living description of his own writing" (303); "he does what he is describing" (320), inscribing within his text "an autobiography that instructs" (322). Freud's *BPP* is, in still other words, a *reflection* about and through death, what Derrida calls an unprecedented "auto-bio-thanato-hetero-graphical scene of writing" (336).

This *mise-en-abyme*, or game within a game, reveals a speculative playfulness in Freud's text that Derrida himself adopts throughout the essay—and to some good effect. Derrida, for instance, throws out the clever idea that Freud *is* the pleasure principle, the *PP*—in French the *pépé* or "grandpa"—not just of little Ernst, but of, in, and for psychoanalysis (see 287, n. 18). Or again, Freud is the self-sufficient ground of psychoanalysis, in debt to no one and no philosophy. This, indeed, is the crux of Freud's inherently contradictory demand for a psychoanalytic science: that it be independent of, yet entirely dependent upon, his name and authority. As such, Derrida's Freud writes letters to himself, "as if someone were sending himself a message informing himself by certified letter, on an official document, of the attested existence of a theoretical history to which he himself . . . gave the send-off" (274; cf. 332). Freud, in other words, submits to the "postal principle": the (post-) master sends his authority off in order to establish a safe distance from himself, from psychoanalysis, for the purpose of instituting the transference to and with himself (339). And for others, including the slaves of psychoanalysis. It is this elaborate send-off that intrigues the letter carrier in Derrida. For as he insists, every letter sent is a letter risked; one that may or may not reach its destination, including (perhaps most especially) the circular return to sender (e.g., see 23). Passing from hand to hand, it may even wind up purloined, as yet another figure in the crypt of deconstruction. (Of course it does.)

Attending to the self-implicating rhetoric of *BPP*, Derrida convincingly demonstrates that Freud casts out pieces of speculation and, as though operating a yo-yo, reels them back in again. Risking himself to establish himself (psychoanalysis), Derrida argues that Freud's psychoanalytic speculation "advances without advancing" (293), "repeats itself in place" (296), and never takes a conclusive step toward a scientific or philosophical conclusion (288). As Christopher Norris explains it: "Like little Ernst, he [Freud] wants to venture on to dangerous ground, experience the provisional loss of mastery, so long as he can pull on the string, so to speak, and recover his powers of theoretical command" (1987: 209; cf. Derrida 1980: 321). The return of authority to the father *is* the game, the scene of writing, the stakes of which are obviously very high. On the one hand, Freud risks the authority of psychoanalysis in the search for a force that goes beyond the pleasure principle and its papa. On the other hand, he limits this risk through a strategy of deferral that leaves the narrative of *BPP* limping interminably to and fro (389). Derrida makes a fair observation: although Freud speaks of taking "steps" forward a total of ten times (336), "not an inch of ground is gained" (294). The limitation of the pleasure principle, of psychoanalysis "it(him)self" (as the translator puts it), is never seriously entertained; nothing outstrips or overflows the PP, the papa and his science. Not for long, anyway. The insatiable desire of and for interpretation is therefore revealed by Derrida as a legacy that has Freud, step by alogical step, running on the spot. Such is the redoubtable *legacy*, in French the *legs*, of Derrida's Freud (see 52). And such is the "rhythm" of pleasure, as foretold by Nietzsche and seconded by Derrida (405–409).

Derrida thus pursues in Freud's *Beyond the Pleasure Principle* what he calls elsewhere the "borderline between the 'work' and the 'life' . . . [that] is neither active nor passive, neither outside nor inside" (1985: 5). By following the steps of speculation that go nowhere, a game of "repetition of repetition" (1980: 302), Derrida exposes the *Freudian* borderline that performs a subtle displacement of (the promise of) ultimate synthesis: speculation, like life, is all detour. "The speculation which is in question," Derrida repeatedly states of *BPP*, "cannot purely and simply· refer to the speculative of the Hegelian type" (277; cf. 395; 401). More generally, just as Derrida's "Freud," carefully erased in quotation marks in the title, cannot be reduced to any one biographical event or subject identity, it also "*can no longer be read solely* as a theoretical argument" (303; his emphasis). Of the "structure of this text," Derrida thus insists that it does "not correspond to any genre, to any philosophical or scientific model" (278). Instead, the structure of *BPP*, based upon Freud's alogical speculation, corresponds to what Derrida (inevitably, predictably) calls the "athesis": the suspension of relation between thesis and antithesis (the *pas de thèse*), as well as the possibility of *Aufhebung* (sublation, Derrida's *relève*), the movement of lifting up and preserving loosely associated with synthesis (260–71). Conclusion: the psychoanalysis is a "paralysis."

Derrida provides concrete examples of this non-Hegelian, deconstructive paralysis at work in *BPP*. Freud, for instance, maintains that the reality principle is not opposed to the pleasure principle, but is merely its representative (or delegate); the reality principle functions as a deferral of pleasure, not as its opposite. The difference between the two principles is therefore an internal matter; that is, "it is the same *différant*, in *différance* with itself" (283; 400–401). Similarly, Freud is careful to introduce a death drive that is not so much in contradiction with the pleasure principle—with psychoanalysis and its founder—but that is independent of and older than that principle (1920a: 32; Derrida 1980: 349–50). In this respect the silent death drive "produces effects of ventriloquism without origin, without emission, and without addressee" (Derrida 1980: 341). In effect, the death drive precedes the law of pleasure but does not contradict it. "There is something older than the law," Derrida argues, "within the law" (350). As always, it is not a question of contradiction but of overlapping: the unbound primary processes (*pp*), such as the repetition compulsion and death drive, are ultimately bound (or cathected) under the authority of the pleasure principle (394). As Freud puts it, the transformation of unconscious primary processes to conscious secondary processes "occurs on *behalf* of the pleasure principle; the binding is a preparatory act which introduces and assures the dominance of the pleasure principle" (1920a: 62; Derrida 1980: 395). In the end everything comes back to papa, the small-case "pp" being (literally and figuratively) just an instance of the large-case PP. Moreover, like the two principles, the life drive is not the opposite of the death drive, as thesis is to antithesis; rather life is the detour, the deferral, of death. With the help of what Freud called the "component drives," *Partialtriebe*, we fashion our own deaths (Freud 1920a: 39); according to this "autothanatography" (Derrida 1980: 393), we send ourselves off, deferring an improper or untimely death in order to find a death proper to ourselves. In Derrida's words: "One must send away the non-proper, reappropriate oneself, make oneself come back (*da!*) until death. Send oneself the message of one's own death" (355; 359–61).[89] Derrida therefore argues that "If death is not opposable it is, already, *life death*" (285; his emphasis; cf. 355). "Beyond all oppositions," Derrida remarks of the life and death drives, "without any possible identification of synthesis, it is indeed a question of an *economy* of death, of a law of the proper which governs and indefatigably seeks the proper event, its own" (359; cf. 394; see also Derrida 1968: 150).

Like the pleasure and reality principles, and like the life and death drives, repetition is also split in two by the dualistic Freud. As that which enables communication between the primary and secondary processes, repetition carries within itself the dual qualities of drive and of demonic haunting (1980: 352). Such repetition follows the same alogic as the other pairings at work in Freud's metapsychology. But here Derrida is also invoking a familiar theme, that of the origin that is not originary, in order to establish "a general deconstruction" or "generalized *fort:da*" (377), one that is supposedly at the bottom of Freud's theorizing in *BPP*. Such repetition is the logical condition of difference, and thus of binding; and as Freud insists, the immoderate pleasures of the primary processes are moderated by this original work of binding (396; 400–402). "Every being-together," Derrida thus writes, "begins by *binding-itself*, by a binding-itself in a differential relation. It thereby sends and posts itself. Destines itself. Which does not mean: it arrives" (402). Binding is assumed by Freud, for himself and for his science, and for Derrida it is a binding on the order of *différance*. According to Derrida, and not surprisingly, it is this self-divided foundation based upon repetition that Freud invoked when he gestured toward a "beyond" of the pleasure principle (353). "Henceforth," Derrida claims, "we must no longer say, and we know why, that he [the child, patient, Freud, etc.] *goes beyond*, but that he *comes back within*" (353). Apparently one is always within the fold (or folds) of psychoanalysis—just as one is always already within the circle of representation. Or again, one is bound to write oneself into a bind.

And, indeed, if the theory implies the father, so too does the rhetoric imply the network of proponents and opponents of psychoanalysis, the outside and inside of the fold. The PP sends away the opponents of psychoanalysis, cuts them off from the fold, which is to say that it/he retains control of "the scene of writing or inheritance"; or again, it/he is in control of all the string/sons, the *fils*. The true heirs of psychoanalysis always return to papa, the pleasure principle, and thus differ with the doctrine without actually opposing it. Dissidents like Adler and Jung, on the other hand, oppose the papa's doctrine because they are truly other, *fort*, that is, outside the reach or transference of the papa.

In sum: while Freud does open *BPP* to "often far-fetched speculation," specifically that of the death drive and the repetition compulsion, he controls in advance the trauma he inflicts upon himself-psychoanalysis—the better, presumably, to establish his own uncontested authority in the field of the living, that is, in the life of psychoanalysis. Everything comes back to Freud, who in his cool indifference to the hypotheses of *BPP* becomes the living space of death (that is, of *différance*) for psychoanalysis and who in his compulsive repetition of hypotheses becomes the repetition compulsion both older than and independent of psychoanalysis. Always and already it is Freud, a self-described devil's advocate, who holds all the cards, including the ace of spades, the death card.

Or is it Derrida? A natural question, not the least because Derrida makes a point of underlining the confusion of proper names in *BPP*, "from Socrates to Freud and Beyond," finding in each name a relay in a network of couriers. It is certainly easy to find Derrida himself haunting the pages of his interpretation of Freud. For example, when Derrida translates Freud's cool indifference to the speculations of *BPP* as follows, he seems to be speaking of (or to, or for) himself: "Go look for yourself, as for me I like it, the beyond of the PP is my rightful pleasure. The hypothesis of the death drive: for myself I like it, and above all it interests me, I find, and thus I take my interest there" (385). According to Derrida's Heideggerianized Freud, the speculation in question is not a matter of belief but of *Being*, of finding oneself—one's own interest in life, one's own way of trodding the path toward death. Derrida takes up this challenge, being just as interested in the death-drive theory as Freud, although for his own reasons—a self-interest that Freud wrote into the theory itself. The "scene of writing" is therefore an elaborate staging of Derrida-writing-Derrida. Or, more exactly, it is a scene in which Derrida writes "Freud" in order to find him(it)self; he sends himself on the detour called Freud-psychoanalysis in order to establish himself, deconstruction, as the latest courier in a vast (freely associated) network of couriers. Like Freud, Derrida is an authentic papa, the da-da of a movement. Or again, Derrida *is* deconstruction.

On the one hand, Derrida's self-involvement in Freud's discourse *sous rature* is not a problem. We too are free to take him, *da*, or leave him, *fort*—assuming, of course, that our interest really is our own, which is a problem of suggestion (all the more so when it is a question of staring at the endless vacillations of a text, structured, for example, like a watch dangling to and fro in front of the mesmerized reader). On the other hand, the extreme self-involvement of Derrida in his interpretation may be a strategy but it is also a problem,[90] at least for readers willing to take his work as seriously as he takes himself. And this is very serious indeed. For it is in the philosophic mode, rather than the poetic, that Derrida insists that the deconstruction of Freud is an *essential* reading—perhaps the most essential of all readings. "By all rights," Derrida claims, "these [deconstructive] questions have precedence over any possible debate on the subject of the alleged theses of this book [i.e., *BPP*], the theses too precipitously believed in. Prior questions which, to my knowledge, have never been asked" (377). Before belief there is, or should be, deconstruction; one must suspend solutions, including debates about the "alleged theses" of *BPP*, by invoking the undecidable elements within concepts. Or as Derrida explicitly states elsewhere, there is a "duty in deconstruction": "And if I speak so often of the incalculable or undecidable it's not out of a simple predilection for play nor in order to neutralize decision: on the contrary, I believe there is no responsibility, no ethico-political decision, that does not pass through the proofs of the incalculable or undecidable" (1991: 108). Far from being a just-so, as-if, fairy-tale treatment of psychoanalysis, and far from being an exercise of play for its own sake, Derrida's deconstruction is duty-bound to unconceal the ultimate foundations of Western metaphysics. For if all knowledge is representation, and if all representation is founded upon an abyss, then it is to this abyss that we thinkers have a duty to attend.

Of course, the dutiful work of deconstruction suspends in advance not just the "alleged theses" about *BPP*, but also the history of psychoanalysis altogether—a self-serving piece of suspension that conveniently rationalizes Derrida's enlightened disinterest, or ignorance, of said perspectives. In addition, Derrida's motivated disinterest in the aftereffects of the deconstructive big bang has the not incidental benefit that only deconstruction is safely situated beyond (that is, *deep within*) criticism, the only interpretation that matters—a fine example of having one's cake and eating it too.

And then there is Derrida's typically French disregard of Freud's biologism. Although Derrida is right to reject as naive those interpretations that dismiss Freud's *BPP* as a frivolous or neurotic exercise, he is very wrong to ignore Freud's use and abuse of biology, which is certainly not just another detour or trope among tropes in *BPP* (Derrida 1980: 363–65). It is, on the contrary, the original detour, the master trope which structures the logic of *BPP*. Any reading that fails to come to grips with this unfashionable and even depressing fact is a *bad* reading. It is really as simple as that. And thus, while Derrida is insightful about Freud's self-involvement in his own "artificial hypotheses" and is a master at teasing out the twists and turns of Freud's alogic, his reading is fatally flawed by its over-indulgent preoccupation with itself, that is, with deconstruction. Instead of tossing another spool into the crypt—a game or practice that has lost its initial charm—Derrida might have addressed the role of ontogenesis, phylogenesis, recapitulation, and acquired characteristics in Freud's theory of repetition; he might have paid as much attention to Haeckel and Lamarck as he paid to Plato and Heidegger. Yet, significantly, their names don't even appear in his work.

Of course, critics will reply that my argument is just as self-serving, and therefore flawed, as anything Derrida offers; that Derrida's failure, on my reading, is merely that he is too little like Frank Sulloway and, in turn, like me. But it is more to the point to say that *Derrida is too little like Freud*, whom he ignores and subjects to often startling interpretive violence. Let me be blunt about this: the appropriation of Freud to the ends of deconstruction is far from innocent, but is obviously very calculated (with all the resonance this has to a "duty," or lack thereof, in deconstruction). Moreover, Derrida is *not* Freud and deconstruction is *not* psychoanalysis. Stanley Fish is among the few critics both candid and sophisticated enough to draw the proper conclusion:

> This is not to say that Freud's text cannot be opened, only that it is not his intention to open it. This is certainly the intention of Lacan, [Peter] Brooks, Jacques Derrida, Ned Lukacher, Neil Hertz, and all the other "oppositional" readers who have been recently so busy. It is their project to interrogate the text from an angle that brings to the surface what its operation necessarily excludes [e.g., ambiguity], but the undoubted success of that project says nothing of the Freudian text; it says only that if one submits the text to an interpretive pressure different from the interpretive pressure that produced it in the first place, it will become a different text. There is no natural bar to such an exercise (no text in and of itself) which can be repeated ad infinitum, but to repeat it is to prove nothing except that it can be done; once it is done in the service of a thesis *about* the text it becomes a form of closure itself. (1988: 203–204, n. 11)

That's it in a nutshell: the discourses of ambiguity (in their many guises) are anything but ambiguous or open. And so, while Derrida's interpretations may be good Derrida, they are more often than not bad Freud (see Dufresne 1997b)—the cryptic surd of deconstructive *différance* too frequently being just another ab-surd piece of calculated indifference, for example, to the *history* of differences.[91]

Clearly Derrida is not alone in these regards, having repeated, for example, some of the same problems we found in Lacan. In fact, I can think of three rather unfortunate features that Derrida and Lacan share in common, and which have come to infect the works of their followers everywhere: first, *ignorance* about the history of psychoanalysis (an ahistoricism inherited from structuralism); second, *faith* in the plasticity of Freud's doctrines (inherited partly from French surrealism); and third, *prejudice* that such plasticity reveals the true essence of Freud's discovery (inherited partly from hermeneutics). In short, psychoanalysis à la française is willfully, and sometimes dogmatically, interpretive. Although fashionability is its short-term strength, irrelevance is its long-term weakness.

And, so, where are we today? For those with ears big enough to hear, the poststructuralist revolution is over. The time of deconstruction, once the cutting edge of this movement, has passed away almost as assuredly as psychoanalysis. I say *almost*—for nothing can be as dead as psychoanalysis, which, having survived its own passing, still enjoys a zombie's afterlife. I doubt deconstruction will be so (un)lucky.

In the next and final section of this book, I will suspend the ahistoricism of French interpretations of Freud and engage the text on an issue that has yet to be confronted very carefully in the literature: Freud's avoidance of (the critique of) suggestion in psychoanalysis, which is bound up with his rejection of sociality and his concordant penchant for a mechanistic and biologistic view of psychic development. In the end, the Freud of *BPP* would rather consign the individual to death than face the mob, mass, horde, or even, and I think most especially, his annoying *critics*.

CHAPTER 3

The Other 'Beyond'

A.K.A. 'GROUP PSYCHOLOGY AND THE ANALYSIS OF THE EGO'

A number of porcupines huddled together for warmth on a cold day in winter; but, as they began to prick one another with their quills, they were obliged to disperse. However the cold drove them together again, when just the same thing happened. At last, after many turns of huddling and dispersing, they discovered that they would be best off by remaining at a little distance from one another. In the same way the need of society drives the human porcupines together, only to be mutually repelled by the many prickly and disagreeable qualities of their nature. The moderate distance which they at last discover to be the only tolerable condition of intercourse is the code of politeness and fine manners; and those who transgress it are roughly told—in the English phrase—*to keep their distance*. By this arrangement the mutual need of warmth is only very moderately satisfied; but then people do not get pricked. A man who has some heat in himself prefers to remain outside, where he will neither prick other people nor get pricked himself.
—Arthur Schopenhauer, *Studies in Pessimism*

One has, I think, to reckon with the fact that there are present in all men destructive, and therefore anti-social and anti-cultural, trends and that in a great number of people these are strong enough to determine their behaviour in human society.
—Sigmund Freud, "The Future of an Illusion"

It is a significant though mostly ignored fact that Freud began thinking about group psychology, *Massenpsychologie*, during the same period (1919–20) that he wrote *Beyond the Pleasure Principle*. To his principle partner-in-speculation, Sandor Ferenczi, Freud wrote on March 23, 1919, that he had formulated a "simple idea that will serve as a psychoanalytic foundation for group psychology" (in Jones 1957: 42; cf. Freud and Ferenczi 1996: 354). As Jones surmised, "When he [Freud] was being held up over the difficulties inherent in the earlier book [i.e., *BPP*], he turned to the second." During fits and starts, what was conceived as an essay became the draft for a small book sometime in August or September of 1920. Freud then rewrote *Massenpsychologie und Ich-Analyse* at the beginning of the new year, sending it to the printers on March 28, 1921 (Jones 1957: 43). It appeared in the *International Psychoanalytic Press* less than five months later.

James Strachey, the general editor of the *Standard Edition*, nonetheless claims that "there is little direct connection" between *BPP* and *Group Psychology and the Analysis of the Ego* (in Freud 1921: 67). While this is a fairly common assumption, evidence suggests otherwise. On a very simple, even "direct" level, *Group Psychology* examines in greater detail the life drive, Eros, that Freud introduced in *Beyond the Pleasure Principle*; put a bit loosely, the subject of death belongs to the first book just as life, love, sexuality, and Eros belong to the second. As Max Schur suggests, Freud "translated the 'sober' psychoanalytic theory of the conflict between the life and death instincts into language which revealed its applicability to all mankind" (1972: 349). There are, in addition, less direct but arguably more important connections between the two works. *Group Psychology* exposes some rich themes that are at times only silently at work in *BPP*—themes such as totemism, narcissism, guilt, mourning and, more provocatively, seduction, hypnosis, and suggestion—even as it foreshadows the brooding conclusions about *Kultur* that are found in Freud's late "cultural" works, such as *Civilization and Its Discontents* (1930).

Sustained by what is at once old and new in psychoanalysis, *BPP* and *Group Psychology* thus function together like hinges upon which Freud's metapsychology swings, as in a breeze, one way and then another. Of course, this very fact renders any attempt to differentiate old from new an artificial and unjustifiable prejudice. For, as we will see, in *BPP* and *Group Psychology* the old *is* the new, the pre-psychoanalytic *is* the psychoanalytic, and vice versa.

In the first section of what follows I explore the psycho-physicalist context within which Freud devised not just the death-drive theory, but an implicit theory about the Others of group psychology. Central to my thesis is the claim that metapsychology works at times against, and at times for, the theory of psychoanalysis. Next, I examine more closely the role of the Other in Freud's *Beyond the Pleasure Principle*, in particular following Freud's treatment of a problem that continued to haunt his work his entire life: suggestion. In both sections I expose Freud's essential biologism, which was, just the same, a scientized reflection of his own philosophic impulse and narcissistic psychology.

Becoming Dead

DEFENSE, GROWTH, AND GROUP IDENTIFICATION

> Restriction of the individual's aggressiveness is the first and perhaps the severest sacrifice which society requires of him.
> —Sigmund Freud,
> *New Introductory Lectures on Psycho-Analysis*[1]

Economically speaking, it is simplest to begin with the speculative extremes that Freud,"out of curiosity" (1920a: 24, 59), outlines in chapter five of *BPP*. "Let us suppose," Freud writes,"that all organic instincts are conservative, are acquired historically [i.e., ontogenetically] and tend towards the restoration of an earlier state of things. It follows that the phenomena of organic development must be attributed to external disturbing and diverting influences" (37–38). Leaning heavily upon Fechner's "principle of constancy,"[2] Freud proceeds to push the logic of instinctual conservatism over the edge with the claim that "*the aim of all life is death*" (38; his emphasis). As he put it in *The Ego and the Id* of 1923, life "consists of a continuous descent towards death" (1923a: 47). While this peculiar notion of progress, this *obiter dicta* of *Beyond the Pleasure Principle*, is familiar territory for most historians of psychoanalysis, not enough has been made of Freud's claim—lifted, as suggested earlier, from the pages of Ferenczi's essay of 1913,"Stages in the Development of the Sense of Reality" (Freud 1920a: 41, n. 3)—that "organic development" is something "imposed" upon the organism from outside (38). As Freud put it, death itself "is a manifestation of adaptation to the external conditions of life" (46).[3] That this view of growth has more or less been ignored is unfortunate, since this strict mechanistic theory more or less structures Freud's metapsychological imagination here and in the texts that follow.

In fact, the key to understanding the connection between *BPP* and *Group Psychology* lies in a general theory of defense and growth—in that order—that Freud proposed in *BPP* but which is already present in his *Project for a Scientific Psychology* of 1895. Rebuilding much of the fallen wall of the psycho-physicalistic *Project*, wherein he was primarily concerned with the problem of defense, Freud in *BPP* argues that an organism grows only to the extent that some external force, energy, stimuli, or excitation threatens its existence. This threat compels the organism to defend itself and thus, by reaction formation, to grow. Freud variously calls this defensive structure a "screen," "sieve" (1895a: 309–10), "crust," "shield," "envelope," "membrane," or "barrier" (1920a: 26–29), but with his background in neurology he quite literally means to invoke the image of the "receptive cortical layer" (27) of the cerebral cortex.

This outermost layer of the psychic or "mental apparatus" is for Freud the limit and condition of all further development, including consciousness (26). As he suggests in 1923, "consciousness is the *surface* of the mental apparatus" from both a "functional" and "anatomical" perspective (1923a: 19). Speaking of the entire organism, the "living vesicle," Freud writes in *BPP*:

> This little fragment of living substance is suspended in the middle of the external world charged with the most powerful energies; it would be killed by the stimulation emanating from these if it were not provided with a protective shield against stimuli. It acquires the shield in this way: its outermost surface ceases to have the structure proper to living matter, becomes to some degree inorganic and thenceforward functions as a special envelope or membrane resistant to stimuli. . . . By its death, the outer layer has saved all the deeper ones from a similar fate. (1920a: 27)

Typically the "powerful energies" from the external world test, and thus indirectly help reinforce, the outermost layer of psychic crust. But sometimes energy overwhelms the crust as a "flooding" (29), *Überschwemmung*, of the organism. In these cases the psychic apparatus is traumatized accordingly: "We describe as 'traumatic,'" Freud states, "a breach in an otherwise efficacious barrier against stimuli" (29; cf. 1900, 5: 600). It is important to note that Freud distinguishes between two kinds of trauma—those that originate in the external world, and those that originate within the organism. Built as a defensive response to external stimuli, the crust is not designed to shield itself from "endogenous" (1895a: 297) or "internal" stimuli (1920a: 29) or, what is the same thing, from instinctual energy (34). Instinctual energy is rather conceived as a traitor operating covertly within the walled city of the mind. Freud proposes that the psychic apparatus is forced to treat internal excitations "as though they were acting, not from the inside, but from the outside"—a defensive strategy better known by the term "projection" (29).

Evidently, then, extended exposure to stimuli gives the psychic apparatus a hard exterior, a shell with which to protect the soft, delicate interior of the psyche. Since the presence of hostile energy is nothing short of a continuous test of the mind's constitutional strengths and weaknesses, energy is always, in its most extreme formulation, traumatic: one must be pinched, so to speak, in order to stay awake and grow. Barring this, one falls asleep and dreams, perchance to die. And here indeed is the rub, for Freud, like Ferenczi, thought of sleep and the accompanying dream state as a withdrawal from the external world (see 1917a: 234) and, thus, as a momentary victory of the death drive and the primary processes (see 1895a: 336).[4] Consequently, from the perspective of the energy (putting aside, for the moment, that energy does not have a perspective) trauma is both necessary and good. Energy is life, life is energy. Or as Freud states in *The Ego and the Id*: "The emergence of life would thus be the cause of the continuance of life and also at the same time the striving towards death" (1923a: 40–41).

Freud's earliest belief that life is a series of incremental accumulations is also, and perhaps not surprisingly, reflected in his later theory of psychosexual development. More exactly, it is tied up with his view of the infant's innate narcissism. As the analyst Herman Nunberg put it, "The infant during the first weeks of his extrauterine life is completely narcissistic. He takes but little notice of the outer world" (1955: 212). Or as Freud and William C. Bullitt argue in their pathography of Woodrow Wilson:

> The libido first stores itself in love of self: Narcissism. This phase is clearly visible in an infant. His interests are confined to the acts and products of his own body. He finds all his courses of pleasure in himself. To be sure, even an unweaned child has a love-object; the breast of his mother. He can, however, do nothing but to introject this object into himself and treat it as a part of himself. (Freud and Bullitt 1966: 37)

Freud had originally thought of narcissism as a chronological "phase" in the child's development, but eventually began to abstract that phase from the time of life and sexuality altogether; it became, in a word, "fundamental" (Borch-Jacobsen 1988: 95). This change of tone and concurrent raising of the stakes—the very stakes of metapsychology—is reflected in Freud's essay "On Narcissism: An Introduction" (1914), but also in the late pronouncements he appends to some of his old essays, including *Three Essays on the Theory of Sexuality* (1905). For example, in the *Three Essays* Freud states that "the narcissistic libidinal cathexis of the ego is the original state of things, realized in earliest childhood, and is merely covered by the later extrusions of libido, but in essentials persists behind them" (1905b: 218).

Just like the physical growth of the organism, which for Freud is determined by Lamarckian inheritance, the more complicated psychosexual development is conditioned by the child's earliest object relations. In this respect Freud paved the way for analysts of the object-relations school to speculate that the mother (or, more simply, her breast) is for the infant an object that mediates the external world; from the infant's narcissistic perspective, such objects are not just of the world, two things among others, but are the world altogether.[5] As Freud himself put it in his posthumously published "Findings, Ideas, Problems" (1941), children at first identify with an object completely, essentially believing that " 'the breast is a part of me, I am the breast' " (1940: 299; cf. Ibid.: 188–89). At the same time, this infant narcissist—whom Freud had already dubbed "His Majesty the Ego" (1908a: 150) and "His Majesty the Baby" (1914b: 91)—demands satisfaction, for instance, sustenance.

But just what the infant *really* wants is complicated by the time Freud writes *BPP*, since he implies that the infant, like all of us, is driven by death. Freud's unwillingness to confront this aspect of the infant's desire directly is already evidenced in "On Narcissism," wherein he puts the train of thought carefully aside: "The disturbances to which a child's original narcissism is exposed, the reactions with which he seeks to protect himself from them and the paths into which he is forced in doing so—these are themes which I propose to leave on one side, as an important field of work which still awaits exploration" (1914b: 92). Now, if Freud did not want to speak about these "disturbances," "reactions," and "paths" in 1914, the new dualism of 1920 made it nearly impossible for him to ignore what the mother actually does when she *protects* the infant from harm. Common sense suggests that the mother defends the delicate organism from the hostile world and from its Others; for example, from too great a stimulus, such as a traumatic seduction or beating. But insofar as the mother is a part of that world, a part of the stimulus around her, she is also a cog in the wheel of Freud's mechanistic view of physical and mental growth. A piece of the analytic machinery, the mother's "protection" of the infant suggests two competing interpretations: in the first, the good-enough mother (as Winnicott put it) protects the premature infant *from Others*; in the second, the mother protects the infant *from itself*, that is, from its drive for death and nonexistence. From the first perspective the mother is seen as the infant's ally against the dangerous impress of culture, while from the second perspective she is seen as society's ally against the dangerous impress of biology.

Strangely enough, it was the second perspective that caught Freud's fancy and determined his antisociological metapsychology. According to this view, if only implicitly, by working *against* the child's innate death drive, the mother acts as a protective crust on behalf of her infant—the defenseless little narcissist. An agent of society, of the mass, the mother is therefore driven—*as though by instinct*, it might be said—to betray the infant's biologically innate drive for death. She is always a bad-enough Other who interferes in the biological order on behalf of the mass. For she is the first to compel, repress, seduce, and pervert the biological organism to grow along the ontogenetic lines prescribed by society, in effect, to help "transform narcissistic libido into object-libido" (1940: 150). No one is spared this trauma, and for a very good reason: "In the space of a few years the little primitive creature must turn into a civilized human being" (185). This tragic figure appears for the first time during Freud's discussion "Female Sexuality" in 1931:

> It is noteworthy that girls regularly accuse their mothers of seducing them. This is because they necessarily received their first, or at any rate their strongest, genital sensations when they were being cleaned and having their toilet attended to by their mother. . . . The fact that the mother thus unavoidably initiates the child into the phallic phase is, I think, the reason why, in phantasies of later years, the father so regularly appears as the sexual seducer. When the girl turns away from the mother, she also makes over to her father her introduction into sexual life. (1931: 238; cf. 1940: 188)

Insofar as the mother plays a traditional role in the family, she is, in short, the earliest force of and for culture against the biological death drive; mother and Eros alike are what Freud calls "breakers of the peace," *Störenfried* (1920a: 63).

And actually mother and Eros have a lot in common—so much so that, from a certain perspective, the mother's presence is virtually indistinguishable from the traumatic energy of the external world in general. After all, she generates, regulates, and channels stimuli but does not and cannot deny it altogether.[6] This reduction of the mother to an abstract force of Eros and culture—or to its filter—is in fact an essential assumption of Freud's metapsychology. For it is according to this peculiar logic that the mother becomes an invisible, unremarkable, and even disposable part of Freud's overall theory. Why is that? First of all, because her role could just as easily be played by any number of forces in the external world—including, for example, a father or a child psychologist. As Freud states in "An Outline of Psycho-Analysis" (1940), despite the importance of the mother-child bond, the path of sociality is historically predetermined: "The phylogenetic foundation has so much the upper hand over personal accidental experience that it makes no difference whether a child has really sucked at the breast or has been brought up on the bottle and never enjoyed the tenderness of a mother's care. In both cases the child's development take the same path" (1940: 188–89). For this reason Freud had already rejected Rank's mother-centered, pre-Oedipal theory: "Being a completely narcissistic creature, [the infant] is totally unaware of her [i.e., mother's] existence as an object" (1926: 130; see Kramer 1996).

Once someone (or, more simply, some *force*) gives the developing infant the thick skin that was once provided as an artificial protection, the infant becomes a group subject—by which Freud, after 1920, means a socialized, encrusted, and finally sadistic mass individual. As he suggests in *Group*

Psychology, "Features which were characteristic of the individual" are "extinguished in him by the formation of the group" (1921: 86). Overturning the values of our traditional moralists, Freud basically concludes that it is a repressive, hypnotic, and even homosexualized (altruistic) society that interferes with narcissism; a society or external world that enforces the rule of Eros over and above the individual's drive for death. Ultimately, in other words, the group forces the id-driven narcissist (the infant, *infans*) to *speak* the ego-driven language of sociality. From that point onward the socialized child converts the uncivilized pleasure of dying from sources within (i.e., the death drive) into the civilized pain of dying from sources without (e.g., bad luck, other people; bad luck *as* other people). Sociality thereby teaches everyone, by hook or by crook, the inauthentic language of victimhood—of circumstance, fate, god, devil, or whatever—where everyone blames the Other and abstains from responsibility for one's singular fate, ultimately for one's own death, in the grand illusion of an environment that singly determines behavior. All action is thereby reduced to masochism, sadism, or some perverted mixture therein: "This concurrent and mutually opposing action of the two basic instincts," as Freud put it, "gives rise to the whole variegation of the phenomena of life" (1940: 149). Or as he more pointedly suggests in his *New Introductory Lectures* of 1933, we are left with the choice of killing ourselves or killing Others: "A sad disclosure indeed for the moralist!" (1933a: 105).

Despite appearances, it is worth emphasizing at this juncture that the Freud of *BPP* is not advocating something along the lines of an existential recognition of one's fundamental finitude, of human being-for-death. Rather, existentialism is a possibility that remains within but not *beyond* the limits of psychoanalysis; in short, existentialism is not *meta*-psychological. For obviously existentialism is predicated upon existence, *ex-tendre*, that is, upon life. Consequently, although Freud the clinician was always on the side of the individual, he insisted, metapsychologically speaking, that the individual be *dead* first. This is the mortified object that Freud meant to invoke, in his most extreme formulations, by the "individual."

CAUSATION AND EXISTENCE

> August 22 [1938].—Space may be the projection of the extension of the psychical apparatus. No other derivation possible. Instead of Kant's *a priori* determinants of our psychical apparatus. Psyche is extended; knows nothing about it.
> —Sigmund Freud, "Findings, Ideas, Problems"[7]

It appears that Freud both did and did not allow a place for the external world in his theory of mental functioning. On the one hand, he accepted the psycho-Lamarckian idea that our direct experience of the external world shapes our subsequent physical and psychical evolution. On the other hand, he rejected all social (and socialist) explanations for the onset of neuroses, claiming that sickness was individually (biologically) determined. These two aspects of Freud's approach may be less a contradiction than a paradox. First of all, it is not just that the course of life is affected by the external world. Since existence is the accumulation and repetition of historic encounters with the external world, one cannot legitimately separate the psychical response, the mental growth, from the external stimulus. Rather, the inner world of affect is always a reflection of the outer world of effect. In this respect we should not forget that the inheritance of acquired characteristics is just that: an *inheritance*, a biological encoding of the past.

Freud makes of the external world the biological stuff of our ancestry, which is to say that ontogenesis repeats phylogenesis. To an extent this is an ironic conclusion, since the phylogenetic past which all humans share evokes the image of Jung's "collective unconscious." Even so, for Freud this inheritance is still mediated on the individual level—that is to say, idiosyncratically—just as a single nighttime noise is always subject to a particular response among different dreamers. In short, although the external world can and will affect psychic reality, one can never say what form that affect will assume. Correspondence, as every Freudian knows, is always impressionistic, even surrealistic, and never naively realistic.

If, then, psychic reality (qua fantasy) remains somewhat deaf to the external world, it is because the outer world of impersonal force is a *necessary but insufficient cause* of its development. This particular formulation has important and generally unrecognized repercussions for Freud's theory of physical growth and mental development, which is, in this respect, Aristotelian. Having reduced the external world to a bevy of mechanistic forces—literally like the natural elements, such as wind, rain, sun, and so on—Freud conceived of the psychic apparatus as an *unfolding* of latent potentialities. As he states in *Beyond the Pleasure Principle*, "Almost all energy with which the [psychic] apparatus is filled arises from its innate instinctual impulses" (1920a: 10), impulses, once again, that are only projected secondarily onto the external world. Thus, at its deepest level, life unfolds in a direction given in advance or, as Aristotle put it, life is teleological, passing through material, formal, efficient, and final causes. Or again, like the acorn that becomes an oak tree, the organism's growth is *in part* caused by the external world functioning as an efficient or propelling cause. As Freud puts it at one point in *BPP*, "In the last resort, what has left its mark on the development of organisms must be the history of the earth we live in and of its relation to the sun" (38).

It is of course rather confusing that, according to Freud, the most latent of all potential "developments," the deepest of all psychic wells, is death itself. Death is both the purposeful end and meaningful beginning of existence; Freud's metapsychology is for this reason circular. As such, the *purpose* and *meaning* of existence, or—and this is really the same thing—the dream of existence, has nothing to do with the external world. Meaning is an intangible quality that is simply beyond materialism and, interestingly enough, beyond psychoanalysis. As we are beginning to see, the intangible is always metapsychological.

The secondary status Freud assigns to the external world is similarly reflected in his treatment of *Kultur* as a whole. Like the natural world, the social world is always mediated, and thus distorted, by the individual psyche. And actually Freud's treatment of the Others of society is already an epistemological conundrum about the existence of the external world in general.[8] It may not be stretching it too far to say that Freud offers a proof for the existence of the external world with his idea that a quantity of stimulus threatens the psychic apparatus from some position *outside* its borders. Apparently, that is, there is *something* out there.

While Descartes grounded his most clear and distinct first principle in his own subjectivity—*Cogito, ergo sum*—the psycho-physicalistic Freud dispensed with cogitation and more simply concluded that *I am stimulated, therefore I defend, I grow, I exist*; for Freud, consciousness is a late by-product of an elaborate mechanico-defensive process. This mechanistic description of growth is, in fact, only another way of saying that the very fact of stimulus or energy plays the role of the Other—or, more rigorously, of *Others*—in Freud's metapsychology. To these Others Freud gave a host of rather impersonal names—Eros, life, love, libido, sexuality—and made of them a *propelling* cause of existence. The organism, which is given as a material cause (as the animate born from the inanimate), is only made aware of the outside world because some force acts upon its outermost border as an efficient cause of its growth and its becoming conscious.

Aristotle's famous example of the acorn that becomes an oak tree is perhaps an appropriate, if telling, image, given Freud's mechanistic approach to growth.[9] Of course, trees do not become conscious, the very condition Freud had trouble explaining in his *Project for a Scientific Psychology* of 1895 (see Strachey, in Freud 1895a: 293). Actually, though, Freud had trouble explaining consciousness, that peculiar aspect of *human* existence, in all of his subsequent efforts. Simply put, Freud never came to grips with either natural or social realities, which were continually problematized by his lifelong commitment to a mechanistic theory of growth. For Freud the Others of his metapsychology are not necessarily subjects, as it might be supposed, but are generalized as pure energy—a collective force of Eros. Existence is thus problematized for all subjects, with the possible exception of the investigator himself. Among other things, Freud therefore opened himself up to a doubt about the external world which we already find with Descartes, who wondered aloud if he had been dreaming the world, or had been placed under the spell of an evil genius, a *malin Génie*. Only, for Freud, the evil genius is nothing but the anonymous mass of Others who compel the individual to live an illusory existence, a force of love that disturbs the intellectual and psychological perfection that is narcissism on the verge of solipsism.[10] The devil of Freud's metapsychological imagination is, quite simply, the clamor of the crowd, a *noise* above which the individual cannot hear himself think. And thus the true individual desires nothing more than *silence*. I'll return to this in a moment.

To the extent that Freud proves the existence of an external world of demonic forces, he is remarkably dismissive of its individual subjects—assuming, again, that there are any. It is true that these generalized Others of Eros, the mass or even the mob, sometimes assume in Freud's writings the apparent shape of an Other, perhaps even a subject (e.g., a mother). This possibility, just to be clear, is undermined by Freud's physicalist model of energy, but also by his lifelong belief that neurosis is largely a matter of "phylogenetic disposition." As suggested above in "Biological *Beyond*s," Freud's bizarre speculation that life is determined by "the history of the earth we live in and of its relation to the sun" is by no means an aberration in his thought. In "Instincts and Their Vicissitudes" (1915), Freud claims that "instincts themselves are, at least in part, precipitates of the effects of external stimulation, which in the course of phylogenesis have brought about modifications in the living substance" (1915a: 120). Or, in a late (1919) addition to *The Interpretation of Dreams*, Freud states that "the individual's development is in fact an abbreviated recapitulation influenced by the chance circumstances of life" (1900, 5: 548). It is abundantly clear that in the metapsychology papers of 1915 and in *BPP* Freud is very taken with Ferenczi's speculations about archaic inheritance—for example, with the deleterious effects of the Ice Age on the human psyche—believing that there is a natural correlation between the development of humankind and the different neuroses. As Freud states in an abandoned metapsychological essay on the transference neuroses, "The hitherto predominantly friendly outside world, which bestows every satisfaction, transformed itself into a mass of threatening perils" (1987: 14). This "hard school of the glacial period," as Freud privately said to Ferenczi (Freud and Ferenczi 1996: 66), not only created a disposition to anxiety that, in Lamarckian fashion, has been passed from generation to generation, but it created society in general—including the full spectrum of intellectual activities which are themselves elaborate attempts to defend one's self from a hostile environment (Freud 1987: 15).

I want to state this programmatically: it is not just that the nasty subjects of the world can be *any Other* at all, but they can be *any efficient cause* that interferes with or restricts the organism's solipsistic and narcissistic drive for death. Freud's "philosophy of the subject" is, therefore, always and already a thanatographical metaphysics of impressive and impersonal energy, a strange cauldron of fantastic speculation that is, indeed, a kind of sorcery. As Freud says, he must occasionally have recourse to the "witch Prehistory or Phylogenesis" (Freud and Andreas-Salomé 1966: 80), or again, to the "Witch Metapsychology" (1937: 225).

Freud's solipsistic rejection of the Others as a *meaningful* part of the individual's existence is, then, an essential characteristic of his metapsychological worldview. It is for example reflected in his potentially bewildering review of the biological literature on cellular reproduction and decay in chapter 6 of *BPP*. There Freud ensures us that existence is not primarily dependent on any Other whatsoever, and to this end minimizes the role of coalescence (or, more loosely put, reproduction) in the life processes:

> How is it that the coalescence of two only slightly different cells can bring about a renewal of life? The experiment which replaces the conjugation of protozoa by the application of chemical or even of mechanical stimuli, enables us to give what is no doubt a conclusive reply to this question. *The result* [i.e., the renewal of life] *is brought about by the influx of fresh amounts of stimulus.* This tallies well with the hypothesis that the life process of the individual leads for internal reasons to an abolition of chemical tensions, that is to say, to death, whereas union with the living substance of a different individual increases those tensions, introducing what may be described as fresh 'vital differences' which must be lived off. (1920a: 55; my emphasis)

Similarly, according to Freud's gloss of research conducted by the American biologist L. L. Woodruff, "The recuperative effects of conjugation can . . . be replaced by certain stimulating agents, by alterations in the composition of the fluid which provides their nourishment, by raising their temperature or by shaking them" (48). Thus, although conjugation is "no doubt the forerunner of the sexual reproduction of higher creatures," the most basic driving force of life is fresh stimulus of a chemical or mechanical nature—a shake-and-bake theory of existence. In other words, the prolongation of life is a function of a fresh influx of force that, in principle, does not need coalescence with an Other. Or more exactly, coalescence assists life, but only because it is an efficient cause like any other, such as the Ice Age.

During this technical discussion of Woodruff, Freud rather surprisingly drops a broad hint about the mysterious mechanics of the death drive that, being silent, should have eluded his grasp. Even Woodruff, Freud now qualifies, agrees that cells die without the presence of a fresh influx of stimulus. Woodruff, Freud writes, is

> able to prove conclusively that it was only the products of its own metabolism which had the fatal results for the particular kind of animalcule. For the same animalculae which inevitably perished if they were crowded together in their own nutrient fluid flourished in a solution which was over-saturated with the waste products of a distantly related species. An infusorian, therefore, if it is left to itself, dies a natural death owing to its incomplete voidance of the products of its own metabolism. (It may be that the same incapacity is the ultimate cause of the death of all higher animals as well). (48–49)

In other, more colorful, words, Freud effectively concludes that organisms choke and die on their own waste while they prosper on the waste of Others.[11] Freud thereby invokes a "beyond" of *conjugation and orgasm* (leading to life) in the more fundamental truth of *isolation and expulsion* (leading to death). The problem of solipsism thus becomes a problem of waste management.

The brief appearance of the waste metaphor cannot be accidental, since it coincides perfectly with fin-de-siècle beliefs about autointoxication by constipation. The toxic effect of constipation was a major health concern during Freud's life—a misconception fueled by the popular appetite for water cures, enemas, purgatives, and, eventually, for invasive surgical procedures on the colon, bowel, intestine, and so forth (see Shorter 1994: 47–49). There is no doubt that Freud was aware of and influenced by these theories, which were well known to physicians.[12] For instance, this theory is reflected in Freud's early toxicological view of anxiety as the consequence of "dammed up libido."[13] It is, in addition, a rather tantalizing fact that Elie Metchnikoff, the Russian doctor who indirectly influenced Freud's theory of the death drive (through Sabina Spielrein), was also "the discoverer in the 1890's of a fundamental mechanism of inflammation" (48) that affects the large intestine. Metchnikoff's research became the very rationale by which surgeons in Freud's time took hopeful stabs at curing symptoms of the bowel that were in all likelihood psychosomatic in origin.

It is therefore probable that Freud's death-drive theory reflects the sociomedical prejudices of his time, thus demonstrating how far Freud could bend his most abstract theories to accommodate traditional physiological explanations of illness. Of course, this was especially true when it was a question of explaining away his own chronic ailments.[14] We should not overlook the fact that Freud himself suffered a lifetime battle with his bowel—what he nicknamed his "Karlsbad ailment" and "poor Konrad" (Freud 1987: xvii; Jones 1955: 83)—and regularly visited the spa at Karlsbad where he indulged in the water, as opposed to the talking, cure.[15] "The emptiness of a life devoted to the care of a full bowel is becoming unbearable," Freud laments in a 1911 letter to his wife, Martha (in Jones 1955: 90). According to Jones, Freud's condition was characterized by "chronic constipation," although "It was at times diagnosed as colitis, inflammation of the gall bladder, simple indigestion or chronic appendicitis" (391). Jones was suspicious enough to add that "the disorder was also in part a psychosomatic relic" of days long past.

Biographically speaking, then, the death drive may have provided Freud with the ultimate rationalization for a symptom for which he had no psychological explanation and no physiological control. Constipation was a symptom, like the repetition compulsion, that went beyond the pleasure principle; in short, it was an affect of the death drive.[16]

SOCIALITY AND THE ABSOLUTE NARCISSIST

> Such a limitation of narcissism can, according to our theoretical views, only be produced by one factor, a libidinal tie with other people. Love for oneself knows only one barrier—love for others, love for objects.
> —Sigmund Freud, *Group Psychology and the Analysis of the Ego*[17]

It is well known that Freud, in the misnamed "cultural" or "sociological" works that follow *Beyond the Pleasure Principle*, was obsessed with the perverted and perverting, socialized and socializing Others, and with their collective psychology. This is no accident, since for Freud the social is always a function of the individual; it is only amid the group that pleasure in death becomes for the "individual" such a pain in the ass—that is, where everything natural or biological is turned on its head. Death is the essence of an authentic individuality that is denied under the compulsion or threat of a society that demands for every subject a group identity—to wit, a life. Only thereafter is the primacy of the inner world redirected or projected outward onto the screen of the external world; a stage upon which the essential war of self against self has raged since the beginning of time. Time, indeed, is the measure of this trauma called life, and Freud went out of his way to destroy its history and obliterate its baneful influence upon the mass individual. To this apocryphal end he erected a theory of the free, ahistorical, lifeless "subject," a subject that precedes time and subjectivity, a subject, silent as mum, that is already an inanimate object, "dead."

Given the extreme aims of this metapsychological fantasy, it cannot be surprising that Freud at times expressed deep pessimism about therapeutic interventions of any kind. For if death is conceived as the ultimate relief from the unhappy tensions of life, then any therapy less than euthanasia is bound to be at best partially effective and, thus, interminable. The best of all possible therapies is always the one that does the least to interfere with, or the most to promote, the patient's bid to re-member or re-cognize the *ultimate* basis of existence: silence, nonreciprocity, inanimacy, mother earth. Hence the theatrical death that characterizes the analytic encounter, where the analyst (as Lacan understood best), like the death drive, always does his best work in silence. A theatrical taste of the real thing, analytic therapy thus treads upon the existential ground that metapsychology, as suggested, can quite simply do without.

Freud's growing pessimism about psychoanalysis and society—and in the end, frankly, there is no difference between these two—is reflected in his own critical appraisal of *Civilization and Its Discontents* during a gathering of colleagues on March 20, 1930.[18] These remarks, attributed to Freud by the analyst Richard Sterba, are significant. Freud begins his self-critique by complaining that he did not deal substantially enough in this work with the subject of guilt (in Sterba 1982: 113). Freud's second criticism is indirectly connected to this concern, but is altogether more serious and more extreme:

> None of you has noted one omission in the work, and this is a gigantic disgrace. I myself only noticed it after the book was already printed. My omission is excusable, but not yours. I had good reason to forget something that I know very distinctly. If I had not forgotten it, but had written it down, it would have been unbearable. Thus, it was an opportunistic tendency that expressed itself through this forgetting. The forgotten piece belongs to the possibilities of happiness; in fact, this is the most important possibility because it is the only one that is psychologically unassailable. Thus, the book does not mention the only condition for happiness that is really sufficient. (114)

At this point Freud, with a flair for the dramatic, recites an ode from Horace in Latin, "Si fractus inlabatur [sic] orbis / impavidum ferient ruinae" (Horace *Odes* 3.3.7–8), which he apparently mistranslates for his colleagues along the lines of: "If the firmament [i.e., sky] should break to pieces over him / the fragments will bury a fearless man."[19] He continues: "This possibility of happiness is so very sad. It is the person who relies completely upon himself. A caricature of this type is Falstaff. We can tolerate him as a caricature, but otherwise he is unbearable. This is the absolute narcissist. My omission was a real defect in the presentation" (in Sterba 1982: 114).

This is a remarkable and telling criticism on Freud's part, first of all, because the limits of psychoanalysis and sociality in general are exposed by the "sad" fiction of the "absolute narcissist." And what is absolute narcissism? According to Freud in "An Outline of Psycho-Analysis" (1940), when the "whole available quota of libido is stored up" we have a state of "absolute, primary *narcissism*. It lasts till the ego begins to cathect the ideas of objects with libido, to transform narcissistic libido into object-libido" (1940: 150; his emphasis). The situation is nicely summarized by Ferenczi, who writes: "We are able to love (recognize) objects only by a sacrifice of our narcissism, which is after all but a fresh illustration of the well-known psychoanalytical fact that all object-love takes place at the expense of narcissism" (1926a: 377).

Not incidentally, it was the problem of narcissism that complicated Freud's early dualism in the first place and that encouraged him to postulate the more distinct dualism of the life and death drives. But by the time Freud wrote his metapsychology papers he was obviously intrigued with the problem of a *primary* or *fundamental* narcissism, a new and abstract foundation that, as suggested, raised considerably the stakes of his speculative ambitions. In the popular *Introductory Lectures on Psycho-Analysis* that immediately follow his metapsychological papers of 1915, Freud declares that self-love "cannot be an exceptional or trivial event. On the contrary it is probable that this narcissism is the universal and original state of things, from which object-love is only later developed, without the narcissism necessarily disappearing on that account" (1916–17, 16: 416; see also 1913b: 89). Or as Freud puts it in "Instincts and Their Vicissitudes": "Hate, as a relation to objects, is older than love. It derives from the narcissistic ego's primordial repudiation of the external world with its outpouring of stimuli" (1915a: 139). Basically Freud contends that narcissism is a form of psychosis that is antisocial and, like death, "beyond" the interventions of any Other—including the psychoanalyst.[20] It therefore follows that *absolute* narcissism is the only possibility for a type of happiness in civilization that "is psychologically unassailable." Why? Again, because absolute narcissism is quite literally beyond society, love, and the pleasure principle: untouchable, unapproachable, even unimaginable. Freud adopts similar language in *Totem and Taboo*—where he speaks of love, and self-love in particular, as "psychologically so remarkable" and "the normal prototype of the psychoses" (1913b: 89)—and again in his essay "On Narcissism," where he discusses the enviable narcissism of the child: "an unassailable libidinal position which we ourselves have since abandoned" (1914b: 89).

Yet the "so very sad" ideal of an original and absolute narcissism is, as Freud admits, a "caricature." More exactly put, it is a parody of an ideal, if not a reductio ad absurdum of a wild train of thought. All fantasy aside, Freud is careful to admit that no social being could be an absolute narcissist and, in any case, no one could bear his presence if he arrived on the scene at this late date. For if it is already difficult to tolerate the narcissistic infant, it would be all the more "unbearable" to tolerate the similarly asocial adult. His character would be "in the profoundest sense hostile to civilization" (1940: 185), essentially "unready" for and "insusceptible" to culture (see 201). Nonetheless, Freud maintains a very special role for the absolute narcissist in a place, time, or theory of splendid isolation set far apart from the energetic mass of Others, the maddening horde, society. It is no doubt for this very reason that he chastises himself and his followers especially for "forgetting" this well-established piece of the metapsychological puzzle. I am of course thinking of the primal father first introduced in *Totem and Taboo* as the original condition of guilt and, thus, of civilization. But I am also thinking of his return nine years later, *after* the publication of *BPP*, in a chapter from *Group Psychology* called "The Group and the Primal Horde." The father, Freud tells us in this later work, was "free," that is, "he loved no one but himself" (1921: 123).

> He, at the very beginning of the history of mankind, was the "superman" whom Nietzsche only expected from the future. Even to-day the members of a group stand in need of the illusion that they are equally and justly loved by their leader; *but the leader himself need love no one else, he may be of a masterful nature, absolutely narcissistic, self-confident and independent.* We know that love puts a check upon narcissism, and it would be possible to show how, operating this way, it became a factor of civilization. (123–24; my emphasis)

Since things are not spelled out in *Civilization and Its Discontents*, about which Freud modestly claims to have "discovered afresh the most banal truths" (Freud and Andreas-Salomé 1966: 181), it may be helpful to put this entire paradox of *Kultur* (society or civilization) another way. According to Freud, the absolute narcissist is the sole condition of the possibility of happiness in civilization and yet his is an untenable and impossible condition. For just as the father's death at the hands of his parricidal sons brings about, retrospectively, guilt and renunciation and, thus, repressive civilization, it simultaneously brings about the death of true happiness: absolute narcissism. Or, more precisely, his death brings about homosexual group love as a "check on narcissism," an expression of guilt that plagues the sons and becomes "a factor of civilization"—and, thus, an enemy of the most pure or absolute expression of happiness: death. In any case, Freud insists that the father's narcissism lingers in society as a latent principle of destruction among the unhappy band of brothers. "Some portion of self-destructiveness remains within," as Freud put it in 1938, "till at last it succeeds in killing the individual" (1940: 150).

At the risk of being pedantic, I should emphasize that everything metapsychological boils down to the difference between the dead but authentic individual and the alive but inauthentic group. In point of fact, the drives of death and life are basically drives of radical individualism and mass individualism (i.e., group identity), the second derivative upon and contaminated by the first. Against our traditionally inverted perspectives, "freedom" in this view is always a freedom *from* a group identity based on life, love, libido, sexuality, and Eros: biologically speaking, that is, the mass individual is driven away from sociality and toward the freedom of true individuality qua death. Such freedom is reflected in the simple facts of sleep, parapraxis, and similar failures of ego functioning that are the meat and potatoes of analytic interpretation. Psychic determinism in this view is nothing but the inevitable and finally total failure of the individual to maintain an illusory identity with the group. The psychopathology of everyday life is thus found in the many cracks along the seams of group relations; or, if you prefer, it is destruction that wins the day, every day, because death, not love, conquers all.

It is certainly true that Freud, in the very first paragraph of *Group Psychology*, admits that "only rarely and under exceptional conditions is individual psychology in a position to disregard the relations of this individual to others" (1921: 68). Yet as rare and exceptional as this condition may be, it becomes for Freud nothing less than the rule—the so very sad ideal—by which he measures all social relations in his *Massenpsychologie*. Freud matter-of-factly rejects the possibility of a "*social* instinct," by which he means the popular "herd instinct" as developed by the English surgeon Wilfred Trotter, and directs his attention, as usual, "towards two other possibilities: that the social instinct may not be a primitive one and insusceptible of dissection, and that it may be possible to discover the beginnings of its development in a narrower circle, such as that of the family" (70). As Freud suggests, this "narrower circle" coincides with the "narrow dimension of this little book" on group psychology, by which he means the truth of individual psychology understood via the privileged tools of psychoanalysis.

As complicated a picture as this is, it requires one final clarification. If life is but a "detour" on the path leading toward death, and if it is a path determined on some level by one's own choice, as Freud argues in BPP (see 1920a: 38–39), then the act of parricide which is supposed to form the backbone of society is obviously an illusion. Indeed, it is the greatest illusion of all: namely, the illusion that the environment (in this case a murderous one) really matters, first, for the group (or horde) and its psychology and, second, for the individual and his psychology upon which the group is logically dependent. In other words, the primal father's death cannot in principle be a case of bloody murder. Following the dictates of primary masochism, the father must have on the contrary *chosen* (on some level) the means for his own execution at the hands of the Others; for he alone is responsible for pursuing a path toward death that is singularly appropriate to him. In this respect I am impressed by the relatively banal fact that the choice of *being* dead is not available to the primal father who is *already alive* in Freud's fiction, already born the child of some Other(s)—some God(s), mother(s), earth, epidermis, or who knows what. In short, Freud begins his tale of the origin of civilization not with death—which, in any case, *cannot explain life*—but with the next best thing: the absolute narcissism of the fully grown super man-child.

Such, then, is the limited extent of Freud's pragmatism: like philosophers determined to prove the existence of the external world, the "getting started" problem is "solved" with a leap of faith from no-thing to something, in this case, from death to narcissistic life, from metapsychological speculation to psychoanalytic observation, from instinct to society. Or as Lamarck held, if evolution is always forward moving, that which was inanimate must somehow become animate—thus filling in all the evolutionary positions that were left behind during the course of evolution. Life, like flies on dung, thus appears out of nothingness, as though by magic.

The bridge between the world beyond and the material world is therefore effected by the inner world of Freud's metapsychological fiction: the superman of absolute narcissism. It is through his example that one understands life as a becoming-death. It is worth noting, though, that this "superman at the very beginning of the history of mankind," whom Freud openly contrasts with Nietzsche's *Übermensch* "from the future" (see also Freud 1920a: 42), is already found on the pages of Nietzsche's first book, *The Birth of Tragedy*. It appears there as the terrible pairing of "truth and its terror" that erupt the moment one recognizes that existence is everywhere an *absurdity* (1872: 51). Indeed, I would go so far as to say that Freud merely mouths the words (while purifying them in scientistic jargon) that Nietzsche gave to the demon and wood sprite Silenus who, when caught by King Midas, is compelled to speak about "man's greatest good." To the king, yet another questing Oedipus, Silenus laughs and finally utters the now famous words: "Ephemeral wretch, begotten by accident and toil, why do you force me to tell you what it would be your greatest boon to hear? What would be best for you is quite beyond your reach: not to have been born, not to *be*, to be *nothing*. But the second best is to die soon" (29; original emphasis).[21]

True to form, Freud paid for this tragic truth with the "nausea"

Nietzsche described in this book (52), and which Sartre popularized in his existential novel *La nausée* (1938). Freud only added a few wrinkles to the basic program: What is best is beyond our reach, or organic death. What is good is the superman of absolute narcissism, or social death. And finally, what is worst of all is life itself, which is only a virtual or living death. It is only fitting that this lowest of the low include Freud's own psychoanalytic practice, wherein he was forced (presumably by an inner compulsion) to contend with the worst when he knew very well what is best.[22] Accordingly, Freud made of therapy a modest, somber practice of converting the patient's "[uncommon] misery into common unhappiness."[23] True happiness, Freud teaches us, is not meant for this world, which can only dream, narcissistically, of oblivion.

In effect, Freud made of psychoanalysis nothing more than an elaborate detour on the way to what is truly meaningful: a metapsychology on the scent of death. Psychoanalysis thus becomes one way among others for coping with the world, itself a regrettable piece of sociality that plays at death even as it forestalls that end according to an inscrutable logic of conservation. In the end, in other words, psychoanalysis is just like life: terminable upon completion—which is to say, whenever one gets around to it.[24]

IN FREUD WE TRUST

> A crust of indifference is slowly creeping up around me; a fact I state without complaining. It is a natural development, a way of beginning to grow inorganic. The "detachment of old age," I think it is called.
> —Sigmund Freud to Lou Andreas-Salomé, May 10, 1925[25]

Throughout his metapsychological writings Freud was caught between the rock of instinct and the hard place of sociality. Similarly, his treatment was caught within the strictures of society and an ideal theory that aimed beyond that society to death. Freud, I think, tried to resolve this tension with the creation of a politically expedient hybrid: the society of psychoanalysts, the core of which was the "Secret Committee" (see Grosskurth 1991).

It is precisely on the level of the politics of knowledge that Freud's motivation for advancing metapsychology at the apparent expense of psychoanalysis makes the most sense. For if metapsychology is anything, as I will argue more carefully in the next section, it is an elaborate rationalization for dismissing the hoary mass of Others also known as the *critics* of psychoanalysis. This is because, first of all, these Others are quite simply traitors to the cause of psychoanalysis, which, in the last analysis, must be identified with Freud alone (i.e., with the primal father and absolute narcissist). And second, because these Others, by their very presence, coerce the absolute narcissist into sociality, which is to say they enable or, better yet, *influence* his development in inauthentic ways. In short, metapsychology is the name of a politico-epistemological strategy whereby all Others are reduced in mechanistic terms to a secondary or even tertiary order—to an abstract force of energy, to a mere efficient cause of development—that Freud can bind and discharge from the republic of psychoanalysis.

In this way Freud indirectly dispensed with the most serious threat to his personal and professional existence: namely, those critics like Richard von Krafft-Ebing, Albert Moll, Leopold Löwenfeld, Eugen Bleuler, Adolf von Strümpel, J. Michell Clarke, Oskar Vogt, and no doubt many others as well (Borch-Jacobsen 1996a: 15–43), who charged Freud with *suggesting* his patient's memories with his botched therapeutic technique. Freud's famous response to this criticism is brilliant. Seemingly taking his cue from King Midas, Freud not only rejected the entire world of influential or suggesting Others, but made of these annoying critics the gold with which to mint the psychoanalytic coin of fantasy and wish fulfillment: namely, the seduction theory. Of course, the fact that this currency doesn't have any stake in social reality should make thoughtful investors pause. Guaranteed in Freud's name alone, the metapsychological economy has, indeed, always been a fairy tale told from the crypt, for the crypt, and about the crypt, its gold reserve a gaping chasm that exposes psychoanalytic theory and practice as a hopelessly bankrupt venture.

On the other hand, if psychoanalysis has yet, so to speak, to choke on its own waste, it is only because some force of resistance from the outside always comes along to shake and bake its foundation. This is a wicked irony for critics who thereby become the greatest propelling force in an ever-expanding economy of psychoanalytic desires. Their "resistance," however justifiable, promotes only more and more growth, a reaction formation called the psychoanalytic Cause. Of course, this is also an irony for the metapsychologist in Freud who—at the beginning or, perhaps, the end of the day—wanted nothing to do with life and sociality. And it is here precisely that we stumble upon the great tragedy of Freud's existence, the existential cost of *being* metapsychological. It is simply this: The Midas touch was never a blessing, but a curse.

In the following section I will explore a bit more carefully how Freud put his metapsychology to work for his theory of psychoanalysis, noting especially how his treatment of suggestion in *BPP* is related to his treatment of the mass of Others described in *Group Psychology and the Analysis of the Ego*.

The Hypnotic 'Beyond'

> Suggestion is a process which can be wholly ignored by psychologists so long as they are not concerned with social life.
> —William McDougall, *Psycho-Analysis and Social Psychology*[26]

Armed with a psycho-physicalistic theory of energy, defense, and growth, Freud conveniently located the *meaningful* cause of sickness within rather than outside the organism. As noted above, he made of this outside a necessary but insufficient cause of the organism's growth. Thus Freud sidestepped the problem of outside influence or suggestion; in other words, sociality is not the key to understanding the basic psycho-physicalistic nature of the organism that unfolds over the course of a lifetime. Life is rather like the trees that bend to the favorable or unfavorable winds of change around them, which, for better or for worse, may "precipitate" growth or "hold them back" (Freud 1920a: 45) but will never determine the genus, let alone the fate, of any individual tree. In this respect Freud not only reduced sickness to a question of formative constitutional strengths and weaknesses—to inheritance—but he also reduced all sociality to a simple matter of *deformation* and *chance*. Pleasure, as he says in *BPP*, is not so much opposed by other people but is "opposed by certain other *forces or circumstances*" (9; my emphasis). Or as he says elsewhere, development is "influenced by the chance circumstances of life" (1900, 5: 548; see also 1910a: 137). From this perspective outside suggestion is merely a breeze, or even a downpour, that may impact upon the organism but cannot determine anything essential. An oak is an oak, whether it be healthy or not.

As Mikkel Borch-Jacobsen (1996) has argued, the charge of undue influence has long been made against Freud and psychoanalysis. According to his earliest critics, Freud never "recovered" repressed memories at all, but suggested them over the course of analytic treatment. In 1909 Albert Moll wrote of Freud's work, "These clinical case histories . . . produce the impression that much of the alleged histories have been introduced by the suggestive technique of the examiner" (in Borch-Jacobsen 1996: 24). At issue for Moll was not so much the content of these memories, but the analytic methodology itself (23).

Borch-Jacobsen points out that Freud was careful to defend both his findings and his reputation from the fatal charge of suggestion. To this end Freud devised an alternative explanation to account for the (supposed) presence of false memories during his early practice.[27] Basically Freud had two options: (1) admit that he had suggested the false memories of sexual abuse to his patients, or again, that he had mistaken his own visualizations of abuse as patients' memories, which would be a disaster for him personally and professionally (see Borch-Jacobsen 1997); or (2) find a way to blame the patients themselves for the false memories or false imputation of memories. Freud of course fatefully pursued the second strategy, more or less concluding that while his patients may not have been abused *in fact*, or in therapy, they nonetheless wished they had been *in fantasy*. This dubious interpretive strategy thereupon became the cornerstone of Freud's so-called "discoveries" of infantile sexuality.

As Borch-Jacobsen argues, Freud's early technical blunders were only compounded by the defensive strategy he thereafter dubbed *psychoanalysis*. It is worth remarking that his abandonment of the seduction theory in 1897 had little or nothing to do with his supposed lack of courage and moral conviction in the face of the ugly facts of child sexual abuse that we find argued by Jeffrey Masson (1984) and some feminists. On the contrary, the fundamental role of fantasy in mental life was invoked by Freud to "*rationalize* the seduction theory" (Borch-Jacobsen 1996: 22; his emphasis); it was "a way to get himself out of the *cul-de-sac* he had gotten himself into" (42). It follows that Freud's use of the Oedipus complex was nothing but "an ad hoc explanation for his patients' constant stories of paternal seduction" (43; cf. Cioffi 1998). Obviously this conclusion is, Borch-Jacobsen writes, "as disastrous for Masson as it is for the psychoanalysts: what Freud and his followers hid so carefully, or at least denied, is the *suggested* nature of those famous 'scenes'. There was a cover-up, yes, but not the one that people think" (1996: 21).

Superficially, the innovations introduced in *Beyond the Pleasure Principle* have little to do with the suggestive and strategic origins of psychoanalysis as outlined so provocatively by Borch-Jacobsen. But, as I have argued, this is a mistaken assumption—the basic reasons for which are already provided by Borch-Jacobsen. As he indicates, "the denial of the role of suggestion was constant in Freud" (27), and can be attributed to the fact that Freud always sided with his "Master," the French psychiatrist Jean-Martin Charcot, against the criticisms of Hippolyte Bernheim, according to whom Charcot's findings were the result of suggestion. Freud rather conveniently agreed with Charcot that the hypnotic "state" is separate and distinct from external influence (27–29). Borch-Jacobsen contends:

> As long as hypnosis was identified with the hysterical "state," itself understood as a modality of self-hypnosis, there was no reason to worry about the suggestive influence that Bernheim warned against, since the hypnotic treatment was supposed to do nothing more than bring an internal, autonomous psychical determinism to the surface. Such was Freud's confidence in the psychical de-

terminism that he thought it capable of "resisting" every external influence, even the therapist's most persistent pressure. (29)

I should admit that I agree with Borch-Jacobsen's basic thesis, which more or less coincides with my own view of Freud's *BPP*. As I unpack in the last section, Freud's metapsychological speculations about energy, defense, and growth structure his discussion about group psychology and the role of suggestion therein, even as they undermine what he meant by psychoanalysis as a socially embedded, even uncanny, therapeutic activity. It is not just that the Others of Freud's *Group Psychology*, that mass of energy called Eros, are present, if negatively, in *Beyond the Pleasure Principle*, but that the problem of suggestion is specifically addressed a number of times at key moments in this work. I am thinking, first of all, of the famous *"fort/da"* case that Freud introduces in chapter 2 of *BPP* and, second, of the role of repetition as it functions throughout that essay. In what follows I want to resume the analysis of the quite different aims of Freud's metapsychology and psychoanalysis, only now placing the unifying theme of suggestion at the forefront.

'FORT/DA': REPETITION USEFUL AND USELESS

Recall that the unnamed boy of this early effort at child analysis plays a game of "disappearance and return" with his toys (Freud 1920a: 15): at first he throws his toys away and plays "gone" with them; later on he supplements this one-sided game by repeatedly throwing a spool away and then pulling it back again, saying *da* or "here." When playing the first half of this game, the child says "o-o-o-o," some baby-babble that Freud translates as the German word *fort*, meaning "gone"—a translation Freud claims to verify with the child's mother (14–15). Freud speculates that the child's game reflects upon his mother's periodic presence and absence, and toys with the idea that the child is either trying to master her disappearance and return, or is actually taking "revenge" for her absence by symbolically throwing her away at will (16). Either way, the boy plays a not altogether pleasurable game with the idea of his mother. Freud begins to wonder if the child suffers from a repetition compulsion not amenable to the dictates of psychoanalysis and the pleasure principle (23)—hence the title of the work.

It is interesting, however, that Freud hides the identity of his child informant, who was in fact his own grandson Ernst, the son of his favorite daughter, Sophie. Freud states that his observations of the child were made "through a chance opportunity which presented itself," although he immediately obviates the impact of this chance with his very next breath: "It was more than a fleeting observation," he qualifies, "for I lived under the same roof as the child for some weeks, and it was some time before I discovered the meaning of the puzzling activity which he constantly repeated" (14). Luckily, Ernest Jones dates Freud's observations of Ernst as September 1915 "when he spent some weeks at his daughter's home in Hamburg" (1957: 267).[28]

At the same time, Freud is careful to establish the child's normality (see Derrida 1980: 306–309), since the playful activity is meant to demonstrate the earliest norm into which he will extend the abnormal psychology of the war neuroses. Freud looks for evidence of a repetition compulsion that is free from the effects of sociality and enculturation, an instinct that can be found at work in every nursery. "The child," Freud contends, "was not at all precocious in his intellectual development"; moreover, he was generally a "good [*anständig*] little boy" (1920a: 14). All of these textual maneuvers are made as a way of emphasizing, first, the neutrality and empirically based status of Freud's scientific observations and, second, the surprising yet universal character of Ernst's "occasional disturbing habit" of playing at *fort/da*.

Yet Freud hides his own lack of objectivity even as he hides Ernst's identity. In addition, he confuses the chance event of Ernst's play with the very fact that it was observed because it was repeated over some weeks. It is of course true that Freud had good reason for emphasizing the play's spontaneity and chancelike circumstances. For obviously a calculated or imitative play does not have a direct or even necessary relation to the instinctual matters that Freud is considering. On the other hand, and at the same time, if the playful event is spontaneous to the point of being unrepeatable (which is what we usually mean by a *chance* occurrence), then Freud would have been unable to observe the play and judge its universal applicability from the vantage of science. As always, Freud makes a point and takes it back, fort/da, a characteristic of his mode of reasoning that Derrida (1980) quite rightly locates in *BPP* as Freud's own puzzling game of nonsynthetical, literally point-less, interpretation (see also Gasché 1974: 202–205).

The problem of suggestion first appears as an allusion near the beginning of Freud's discussion of the fort/da game. Through the "chance opportunity" that lasts for weeks, Freud claims that he is able "to throw some light upon the first game played by a little boy of one and a half and *invented by himself*" (1920a: 14; my emphasis). Like all of Freud's little men, the child's normality does not preclude his status as an inventor and protoscientist. On the contrary. Yet if Freud throws some light on this puzzling and inventive game, he draws the blinds closed two and then four paragraphs later. Discussing Ernst's "great cultural achievement—the instinctual renunciation . . . which he had made in allowing his mother to go away without protesting"—Freud writes, "It is of course a matter of indifference from the point of view of judging the effective nature of the game whether the child invented it himself or took it over from some outside suggestion. Our interest is directed to another point" (15).

This is a strange admission coming on the heels of Freud's opening assertion about the child's inventiveness, with which he establishes his own neutrality as an outside observer. Everything, however, falls smoothly into place when attention is paid to "another point" that justifies Freud's "indifference" about "outside suggestion." For the point to which *BPP* is aimed, like the instinct he is introducing, is a metapsychological treatment of death. The problem of suggestion is therefore—Freud says "of course"—extraneous to the extreme direction of an examination directed *beyond* the pleasure principle. As Freud repeats many times, his metapsychological findings do not impact one way or another upon psychoanalysis and its pleasure principle; that is, metapsychology is not in contradiction to, but is *independent* of and older than psychoanalysis (Freud 1920a: 32, 35). The influential Others all around Ernst are thus incidental to this ultimate end, meaning that Freud, the scientist-grandfather, disappears just as readily from this scene of instinctual repetition as the mother already had as the (inevitable) condition of the play. Neither Freud nor the mother influence Ernst's repetition compulsion in any *meaningful* way.[29]

Even so, it is difficult to understand Freud's rather cavalier attitude toward the problem of suggestion, which, in fact, he proceeds to relate to the pleasure principle of psychoanalysis rather than to the beyond of metapsychology. Freud begins to spell out more clearly why the problem of suggestion is unimportant to the ultimate question of nonexistence that he is posing about, and against, life and sociality. Having introduced the possibility of a will to revenge over and against the will to mastery, the latter seeming to fall under the rubric of the pleasure principle, Freud writes:

> Nor shall we be helped in our hesitation between these two views by further consideration of children's play. It is clear that in their play the children repeat everything that has made a great impression on them in real life, and that in doing so they abreact the strength of the impression and, as one might put it, make themselves master of the situation. But on the other hand it is obvious that all their play is influenced by a wish that dominates them the whole time—the wish to be grown-up and to be able to do what grown-up people do. (16–17)

Just as Freud gives and takes away Ernst's inventiveness, now he gives and takes away the example of child's play altogether. How Freud is able to decide between repetition that is metapsychologic and repetition that is psychoanalytic is hard to say, although I think the answer is found in what is pragmatic, strategic, and ultimately utilitarian.

For example, Freud repeatedly draws a line between play that is *useful* and *useless* according to the extreme aims of his metapsychological examination. On the useless side sits the child who is already socialized to act (or play) like a grown-up. The mimetic abilities of children are a hallmark of social behavior and, therefore, do not reflect upon what is purely instinctual. As Freud states in chapter 5, "Children will never tire of asking an adult to repeat a game that he has shown them or played with them. . . . None of this contradicts the pleasure principle; repetition, the re-experiencing of something identical, is clearly in itself a source of pleasure" (35–36). So the fact that children often act like perfect citizens—that is, like vengeful sadists (17)—should in no way be confused with what Freud calls "a primary event" (16). That event is death.

At this point Freud previews for the first time his thoughts about group psychology, stating: "It emerges from this discussion that there is no special need to assume the existence of a special imitative instinct in order to provide a motive for play" (17). As noted earlier, Freud repeats this claim in *Group Psychology*, arguing that there is no special need to recognize, with Trotter, a "social" or "herd" instinct. For the same reasons Freud is free to dispense with the social counterpart to child's play, namely, the adult world of theater:

> The consideration of these cases and situations [found in the theatre] . . . should be undertaken by some system of aesthetics with an economic approach to its subject-matter. They are of no use for *our* purposes, since they presuppose the existence and dominance of the pleasure principle; they give no evidence of the operation of tendencies *beyond* the pleasure principle, that is, of tendencies more primitive than it and independent of it. (1920a: 17; his emphasis)

Like the socially derived play of children, theater is "of no use for *our* purposes"; it gives "no evidence" of being useful from the perspective of metapsychology. It is nonetheless true, as clinicians after Freud are often desperate to emphasize, that from the perspective of *therapy* psychoanalysis is obviously very interested in these aspects of life and living that operate according to the pleasure principle. Be that as it may, Freud himself is not really talking about therapy in *BPP*, any more than he is talking, in the extreme, about life. From the perspective of metapsychology—again, the perspective of the corpse—such details are for Freud simply "of no use."

Of course, Freud repeatedly begs the question: When is child's play *not* contaminated by the fact of sociality? His answer is implicit throughout, as when he asserts negatively, "The early efflorescence of infantile sexual life is doomed to extinction because its wishes are incompatible with reality"

(1920a: 20). To be a *useful* example for the aims of metapsychology, child's play must in other words persist in its "early efflorescence"; it must be somehow set apart from the deleterious influence of society and its reality. Why does Freud always insist upon this condition? Once again, because evidence of a repetition compulsion is not easy to isolate from a social reality that is characterized by imitative, theatrical, and inauthentic behavior.

The child's happy, almost psychotic, narcissism is unassailable from the psychoanalytic perspective; for as we have seen, such happiness is sublimely metapsychoanalytic. As Freud says in a letter to Lou Andreas-Salomé, "The inaccessibility of the child naturally corresponds exactly to its narcissism" (Freud and Andreas-Salomé 1966: 74). In its most extreme formulation, then, the most useful examples of a " 'daemonic' force at work" (1920a: 35) are those behaviors that reflect the primary processes and their natural expression as asocial, guilt-free, narcissistic wishes that are "incompatible with reality." The narcissistic child is "doomed to extinction" once "His Majesty the Baby" begins to socialize, thus becoming for Freud a coerced, untrustworthy, and useless informant from the perspective of metapsychology. More simply put, the child of society becomes a *patient*—someone of use only to Others, including of course the psychoanalysts. As Freud put it in *A Phylogenetic Fantasy*, neurosis is quite specifically "a cultural acquisition" (1987: 19) that the individual acquires over time.

Freud effectively draws a line between play that is useful and useless, guilt-free and guilty, instinctual and social, primary and secondary, on the basis of a repetition that is *not mimetic*—namely, on the basis of a primal repetition, or rather, a repetition of what is primary, instinctual. It is the case, however, that this ideal of repetition has nothing to do with society or, more exactly, with life experience. And this fact, as we will see in a moment, gets Freud into a mire of contradictions.

REPETITION PASSIONATE AND INSTINCTUAL

> We have been struck by the fact that the forgotten and repressed experiences of childhood are reproduced during the work of analysis in dreams and reactions, particularly in those occurring in the transference, although their revival runs counter to the interest of the pleasure principle; and we have explained this by supposing that in these cases a compulsion to repeat is overcoming even the pleasure principle.
> —Sigmund Freud, *New Introductory Lectures on Psycho-Analysis*[30]

While Freud's interest in repetition goes back to his earliest work in the *Project for a Scientific Psychology*, it returns most insistently as part of his papers on technique written between 1911 and 1914, especially in his essay

"Recollecting, Repeating, and Working Through" (1914).[31] In both this essay on technique and in *Beyond the Pleasure Principle*, repetition is discussed in relation to what Freud at one point calls the "essential subject of psycho-analytic study" (1920a: 52), namely, the clinical phenomenon of transference neurosis: the patient's tendency to abreact or repeat forgotten episodes from his or her past in the presence of the observing analyst.

Freud's argument begins with the claim that the method of "inducing" the patient "by human influence," by "suggestion operating as transference," does not always make conscious what is unconscious (18). Part of the problem, Freud says in *BPP*, is that suggestion does not produce in the patient a "sense of conviction" as to the "construction that has been communicated to him." "He is obliged," Freud therefore asserts, "to *repeat* the repressed material as a contemporary experience instead of, as the physician would prefer to see, *remembering* it as something belonging to the past" (18). In this way the analyst's (in principle, hypothetical) construction coincides with the patient's "contemporary experience" of that construction: the patient unconsciously acts out an experience from the past while the analyst consciously interprets the scene and judges its correspondence to the construction.

The patient's conviction about the reality of the analyst's constructions is (at least theoretically) facilitated by a fresh experience that is *recognized* in the present as a fragment of the past: "The earlier neurosis has now been replaced by a fresh, 'transference neurosis' " (18). Freud is obliged to assume a connection between earlier and "fresh" experience, between what is forgotten and then reexperienced, since re-presentation and interpretation are obviously at the heart of Freud's therapeutic practice. But to help him bridge the gap between past and present, Freud has to convert the "independent" instinct of metapsychology into an experience governed by his psychology of the pleasure principle. In effect, Freud has to *socialize* his metapsychology. To this end he speaks of the "intimate partnership" (23) that characterizes the supposedly independent realms of metapsychology and psychoanalysis, instinct and manifestation. As he says, "The compulsion to repeat, which the treatment tries to bring into its service is, as it were, drawn over by the ego to its side (clinging as the ego does to the pleasure principle)" (23). Once again, to the extent that the metapsychological compulsion to repeat is re-presented, it is invariably tamed according to the rules of psychoanalysis. In fact this is always the case, since what is properly "meta" is always beyond representation.

Yet the transference neurosis—precisely because it is the "essential subject of *psychoanalysis*" (my emphasis)—is quite clearly irreducible to Freud's *metapsychological* speculations about the compulsion to repeat. If Freud was at all faithful to the extremity of his own speculations, his discussion of the emotional repetition called transference should literally be *of no use* to his speculations about an instinct that goes beyond the pleasure principle. To begin with, as Freud himself realized (see 1926: 129), one cannot really repeat an *experience* of death. On the contrary, since one can only playfully repeat this "pale reflection of a forgotten past," such play is always already mimetic (or social) rather than instinctual play. Recall again that theater is a useless example from the perspective of metapsychology; it is mere sociality and does not impinge upon the instinctual question of nonexistence. But surely the transference neurosis is a repetition or reflection of one's dysfunction within society, for example, within one's own family. This claim is repeated again in chapter 5 of *BPP*: "The repressed instinct never ceases to strive for complete satisfaction, which would consist in the repetition of a primary experience of satisfaction. *No substitutive or reactive formations and no sublimations will suffice to remove the repressed instinct's persisting tension*" (42; my emphasis).

With his view of the transference neurosis, however, Freud takes back the very theater he already gave away as an example of no use or interest. For reasons yet unknown, Freud is driven to reserve for theater, this pale reflection of the real thing, the privileged function that child's play *sometimes* does: it is *sometimes* able to represent as repetition a portion of instinctual energy uncontaminated by sociality and, most especially, by the problems of mimesis. In short, it can produce a theater for primal, nonmimetic repetitions.

The problem here is elementary: the transference repeats socially-derived scenes from the past on the basis of an *emotional* rather than an *instinctual* tie. The only way Freud can salvage his argument is by assuming, against expectations, that transference tells the story of an even earlier time than that of existence. Transference must recreate the asocial conditions that characterize, for example, Ernst's privileged play with the spool. This indeed is more or less what Freud says in a 1919 addition (later made into a footnote) to *The Interpretation of Dreams*, probably under the influence of his case study of the Wolf Man in 1918:

> Dreams which occur in the earliest years of childhood and are retained in memory for dozens of years, often with complete sensory vividness, are almost always of great importance in enabling us to understand the history of the subject's mental development and of his neurosis. Analysis of such dreams protects the physician from errors and uncertainties which may lead, among other things, to theoretical confusion. (1900, 5: 522)

Freud doesn't say it, but by "theoretical confusion" he means the problem of suggestion. Similarly, in another passage added to *The Interpretation of Dreams* in 1919, Freud boldly asserts that "dreaming is on the whole an example of regression to the dreamer's earliest condition, a revival of his childhood, of the instinctual impulses which dominated it and of the methods of expression which were then available to him" (548). Dreaming, then, like the transference neurosis, reactivates "man's archaic heritage," that is, "what is psychically innate in him."

In case there is any doubt as to what is going on here, let me pose a question: Why does Freud bother to tie the social to the instinctual and "psychically innate" (or to what is the next best thing, the "earliest years of childhood") in this unlikely and cumbersome way? As suggested at the outset, the answer is tied up with Freud's strategy for protecting psychoanalysis from the charge of suggestion. For by claiming that there is a repetition compulsion grounded in an instinctual, innate, or uncontaminated source, the production of transference *as repetition* insulates the re-production of "memory" from the charge that it was merely suggested after the fact from some position outside biology, during or after socialization—for example, during psychoanalytic therapy. Memory as the repetition of a primal or archaic instinct within the transference is, therefore, an *unimpeachable* memory—even if it is not, in a literal sense, true. And thus the analyst is neatly protected from the sorts of "errors and uncertainties" that are suspected by his astute critics. Apparently the patient's fantasy is just that—the *patient's* fantasy, an encoded message written at the level of biology and ontogenetically triggered to repeat itself at the proper (that is, predetermined) time. And so the charge of suggestion is not a problem for Freud.

Metapsychology and psychoanalysis thus justify and reinforce each other on the basis of their mutual recourse to repetition. Ironically, then, Freud's mechanistic philosophy provides a fail-safe mechanism for protecting his psychology of fantasy life from any "outside" criticism. That Freud elides the difference between meta-analysis and psycho-analysis, between primal and mimetic forms of repetition, is a straightforward indication of how far he was willing to stretch his own assumptions whenever it suited a higher purpose: namely, the almost hermeneutic defense of his creation from outsiders.

It is, therefore, only with extreme bad faith and hypocrisy that Freud claims that he would "prefer" the patient to simply remember the repressed past without, or before, the accompanying repetition (or abreaction) and its psychoanalysis.[32] For it is by placing repetition in the gap between psychoanalysis and metapsychology that he tries to outwit those critics that make of therapeutic "acting out" a form of imitation and suggestion. Obviously Freud could not do without repetition. As he says, the "physician cannot as a rule spare his patient this phase in the treatment" (1920a: 19).

USES AND ABUSES OF SUGGESTION FOR PSYCHOANALYSIS

Having "ascribed," as he must, the compulsion to repeat "to the unconscious repressed" (20), Freud once again writes suggestion into the picture. In fact, he states very clearly that suggestion plays a decisive role in analytic therapy. He begins with the claim that "It seems probable that the compulsion [to repeat] can only express itself after the work of treatment has gone halfway to meet it and has loosened the repression." To this statement Freud appends the following footnote: "I have argued elsewhere that what thus comes to the help of the compulsion to repeat is the factor of 'suggestion' in the treatment—that is, the patient's submissiveness to the physician, which has its roots deep in his unconscious parental complex" (n. 2).

The argument from "elsewhere" mentioned in this important footnote of 1923 is an essay called "Remarks on the Theory and Practice of Dream-Interpretation" (1923b).[33] In this essay Freud cites his own remark from *Beyond the Pleasure Principle*—that "the work of treatment has gone half-way to meet it [i.e., the compulsion] and has loosened the repression"—but adds a new twist:

> It is the positive transference that gives this assistance to the compulsion to repeat. Thus an alliance has been made between the treatment and the compulsion to repeat, an alliance which is directed in the first instance against the pleasure principle but of which the ultimate purpose is the establishment of the dominion of the reality principle. (1923b: 118)

In truth, Freud already made this general claim in chapter 4 of *BPP*, where the patient's "wish" is implicitly facilitated by the positive transference. As he says, while traumatic dreams arise "in obedience to the compulsion to repeat . . . that compulsion is supported by the wish (which is encouraged by 'suggestion') to conjure up what has been forgotten and repressed" (1920a: 32).[34]

Why does Freud qualify in 1923 that it is the *positive*, and not the negative, transference that gives "assistance" to the compulsion to repeat? Freud provides an ingenious answer in "Remarks," where he discusses (as he does more generally in *BPP*) the charge that analytic patients who are in love with their analyst often produce dreams that conform to the analyst's expectations. If the "patient's compliance toward the analyst" is not avoidable, neither is it problematic for Freud:

> In fact, in many dreams which recall what has been forgotten and repressed, it is impossible to discover any other unconscious wish [than the positive transference] to which the formation of the dream can be attributed. So that if anyone wishes to maintain that most of the dreams that can be made use of in

analysis are obliging dreams and owe their origin to suggestion, nothing can be said against that opinion from the point of view of analytic theory. (1923b: 117)

Freud is strangely forthcoming about such compliance in analysis: dreams and memories are revealed during psychoanalysis because the patient has fallen in love with the analyst. "Obliging dreams" are a gift to the analyst who is singularly able to put it to work for the benefit of both parties. Freud, no doubt with Charcot in mind, does not bother to consider the possibility—indeed, the overwhelming probability—that these memories (and their appearance in dreams) are really *false* memories created by his bad technique. For as always Freud is not concerned with this possibility, and he conveniently returns to another point beyond sociality—in this case, to another discussion of *Beyond the Pleasure Principle*.

That Freud returns to the abstract *BPP* in this technical and clinical context is quite simply because a little love is able to distill a piece of death, a foolproof method against which "nothing can be said." The love exhibited in the so-called "positive" transference is, after all, just another name for the patient's *primary masochism*—his or her death drive. Remember that, for Freud, one is trapped by the unhappy choice of killing (or hating) others or of killing (or hating) one's self—sadism or masochism. The positive transference is, therefore, the best place to find the death drive at work, for the patient in love with an analyst only demonstrates on the social stage his or her own self-effacement. That is, the patient's "love" of the Other expresses a latent, metapsychologically determined hostility toward the self that Freud is able to openly analyze in terms of his psychoanalytic therapy—a therapy, as he says, against which *nothing can be said*. Freud thereby brings all criticism to a halt and, like the best dissimulator, does so even as he keeps as close as possible to the truth.

Just as Freud sends the reader of *BPP* to a footnote that refers to another essay, this other essay ("Remarks") sends the reader away one more time: namely, to a book of "crude stuff meant for the masses" (Freud and Andreas-Salomé 1966: 48), namely, the last of the *Introductory Lectures* of 1916–17, "Analytic Therapy." For his send-off in "Remarks" Freud dispenses with actual proof for his extravagant claims, merely contending that "I need only add a reference to what I have said in my *Introductory Lectures*, where I have dealt with the relation between transference and suggestion and shown how little the trustworthiness of our results is affected by a recognition of the operation of suggestion in our sense" (1923b: 117).[35] In effect, Freud forces the conscientious reader to follow the trail of his argument to a text written *before* the new dualism of 1920 had even been introduced.

In this lecture, which Strachey notes "contains Freud's fullest account of the theory of the therapeutic effects of psycho-analysis" (1916–17, 16: 448, n. 1), Freud tries to distinguish psychoanalysis from suggestion and its close associate, hypnosis. Suggestion is not only therapeutically unreliable, he writes, but it is boring to practice: "It was hackwork and not a scientific activity, and it recalled magic, incantations and hocus-pocus" (449). As usual, though, Freud partly rescinds this criticism, stating, "We psychoanalysts may claim to be its [hypnosis's] legitimate heirs and we do not forget how much encouragement and theoretical clarification we owe to it" (462). This recognition does not mean, of course, that Freud is careless about or uninterested in the difference between analytic dream-work and hypnotic "hackwork." On the contrary, it means that he is more compelled than ever to exaggerate and distort their relative merits. For example, Freud mentions that "under favourable conditions we [psychoanalysts] achieve successes which are second to none of the finest in the field of internal medicine" (458), whereas "hypnotic treatment leaves the patient inert and unchanged, and for that reason, too, equally unable to resist any fresh occasion for falling ill" (451). Freud's wild optimism here about psychoanalysis is not merely uncharacteristic and foolhardy, but is quite deceptive. Indeed, he comes very close in this lecture to lying about the efficacy of psychoanalysis.[36] In this respect it is nothing short of a scandal that Freud was unwilling to accept responsibility for the poor results of analytic therapy, which he innocently blames on "unfavourable external conditions" (458). Conveniently, sociality is now of the "greatest," although qualified, importance to Freud. He writes:

> The external resistances which arise from the patient's circumstances, from his environment, are of small theoretical interest but of the greatest practical importance. Psychoanalytic treatment may be compared with a surgical operation.... Ask yourself now how many of these operations would turn out successfully if they had to take place in the presence of all the members of the patient's family, who would stick their noses into the field of the operation and exclaim aloud at every incision. In psychoanalytic treatments the intervention of relatives is a positive danger. (459)

"There was obviously a prejudice against psychoanalysis" (461–62), Freud thus contends toward the end of his lecture.

This optimistic picture about the possibilities of analytic therapy is bluntly denied by Freud in other places, for instance, in his *New Introductory Lectures* (see 1933a: 136–57) and in his "Analysis Terminable and Interminable" (see 1937). But Freud had good reasons for putting the best face on the questionable results of analytic therapy, not the least of which has to do with the threat—a threat he makes sure to weave into his narrative—that some of his medical colleagues were intending to publish a "collection of the failures and damaging results of analysis" (1916–17: 458).[37] If we keep these enemies in mind, Freud's political savvy in this lecture seems considerable. Analysis is, he now counters, still a young science and, in any case, it is *as efficacious as surgery*. This is an extremely loaded statement, which to modern ears is bound to sound arrogant and ridiculous. But this, I think, is not at all what Freud was saying in 1916–17. On the contrary, surgery at the turn of the century was barely more successful, or less scandalous, than psychoanalysis. Freud in other words was not simply brushing psychoanalysis up against a hard medical science to his own advantage, but was brushing surgery up against psychoanalysis *to their disadvantage*. If so, his famous equation of psychoanalysis and surgery amounts to a counterthreat: If you expose the scandal of analysis, I will expose the even greater scandal of surgery.[38]

It is, then, perhaps no accident that Freud's medical colleagues failed to publish a collection of botched analytic cases. Freud's checkmate seems to have brought about a temporary stalemate between psychoanalysis and its immediate enemies in medicine.

TO BE OR NOT TO BE METAPSYCHOLOGICAL

> Freud himself, so it has been said, is the only man who has been able to impress his own neurosis on the world, and remould humanity in his own image.
> —Hans Eysenck, *Decline and Fall of the Freudian Empire*[39]

As argued above, the taming of metapsychology to the aims of psychoanalysis is reflected in and reinforced by Freud's tricky approach to transference in BPP. If suggestion and the positive transference help the patient and analyst re-cover some old experiences, instinctual or mimetic, then something else is still needed to bring this emotionally charged scene to a reasonable close. How does psychoanalysis end? Freud introduces such closure in BPP with his discussion of the "aloofness" that a patient should ultimately feel toward the constructions and suggestions of the analysis. As Freud says, the analyst

> must get him [the patient] to re-experience some portion of his forgotten life, but must see to it, on the other hand, that the patient retains some degree of aloofness, which will enable him, in spite of everything, to recognize that *what appears to be reality is in fact only a reflection* of a forgotten past. If this can be successfully achieved, the patient's sense of conviction is won, together with the therapeutic success that is dependent on it. (1920a: 19; my emphasis)

The vicissitudes of transference are revealed to the aloof patient "only as a reflection" of instinct; more exactly, such reflections are a puppet show on the office wall, a piece of theater in a cave of dissimulation. With aloofness as his measure, Freud comes close to saying that the termination of analysis coincides with a recognition, not so much of the reality of the reproductions within the cave called transference, *but of the procedure of psychoanalysis itself.* In short, the patient's love for the analyst, the emotional tie, should give way to an educational appreciation of the therapeutic enterprise in general.

In his lecture on "Analytic Therapy," Freud briefly considers the difference between cure and education, patient and pupil. Having just claimed, à la Charcot, that "it is impossible to make suggestions to a patient" that do not somehow hook up with his or her own neurosis, he writes:

> The doctor has no difficulty, of course, in making him [the patient] a supporter of some particular theory and in thus making him share some possible error of his own. In this respect the patient is behaving like anyone else—like a pupil—but this only affects his intelligence, not his illness. After all, his conflicts will only be successfully solved and his resistances overcome if the anticipatory ideas he is given [as "assistance"] tally with what is real in him. Whatever in the doctor's conjecture is inaccurate drops out in the course of the analysis; it has to be withdrawn and replaced by something more correct. (1916–17, 16: 452)[40]

In this passage Freud proposes two kinds of suggestive assistance, one for pupils and another for patients. Those patients in love with their analyst are easily made into pupils, a member of an intellectual group—for instance, an analytic society. These patients may, for this reason, "share some possible error" with the therapist, since their education is always a matter of right or wrong hypotheses. But again, when a patient is truly a patient and not a pupil—in a word, when the patient is *sick*—then a degree of aloofness is the final piece in the puzzle of the cure. Freud insists that this formula for the cure is not effected by the analyst's suggestion, but according to how well the analyst is able to guess the patient's "real" motives for illness.

It is certainly peculiar that Freud reserves for the *patient* the kind of "aloofness" that one would normally expect of a *pupil*. As he says, it is the patient who finds some objectivity about his or her experience of analysis, whereas the pupil is more or less consigned to repeating the master. The difference between pupil and patient, didactic and therapeutic analysis, is similarly alluded to in *BPP*, where it is a matter of distinguishing between a repetition that is active (and thus social or psychoanalytic) and a repetition that is passive (and thus asocial or metapsychologic). Because Freud is obsessed with the suggestive Others outside the psychic apparatus, he is naturally "much more impressed" by instances of a passive relation to repetition, where one is seemingly pursued by a daemonic force from within. Freud gives the example, among some others, of "the lover each of whose love affairs with a woman passes through the same phases and reaches the same conclusion" (1920a: 22). Yet Freud never proposes that the daemonic force from within is inoperative in "active" or socially determined instances of repetition compulsion. Once again, he only claims that it is infinitely more difficult to isolate the instinctual-daemonic from the social-mimetic. It is helpful to recall this blurring of the lines of society and instinct when Freud begins to list some examples of a repetition compulsion that seem blatantly autobiographical. They are also concerned with the relation between teacher and pupil:

> We have come across people all of whose human relationships have the same outcome: such as the benefactor who is abandoned in anger after a time by each of his *protégés*, however much they may otherwise differ from one another, and who thus seems doomed to taste all the bitterness of ingratitude; or the man whose friendships all end in the betrayal by his friend; or the man who time after time in the course of his life raises someone else into a position of great private or public authority and then, after a certain interval, himself upsets that authority and replaces him by a new one. (22)

Freud certainly seems to be discussing his own troubles within the psychoanalytic movement. But, if so, he is remarkably forthright about his own responsibility for the political turmoil in which he found himself embroiled by 1920 (with Stekel, Adler, and Jung) and which would be repeated yet again in years following the publication of *BPP* (with Rank and Ferenczi). Metapsychoanalytically speaking, Freud seems to admit that his role in this repetitious history of the same is symptomatic of a death drive.

Still, the heavy hand of Freud's clinical technique tends to make the Other—patient or pupil—into the true sinner, since the place of the analyst remains basically unimpeachable. Placed outside or beyond or before or even deep within the very sociality that contaminates the patient's discourse, the analyst is described by Freud as a sort of ideal medium who communes with the dead spirits, otherwise called instincts, who are the truest guides of our actions. Freud's patients, pupils, and everyone else in the external world occupy the space of the Others, the mass; in effect, they are the demons of Descartes's hyperbolic doubt, always tempting one into error and dissimulation. The Freudian analyst, on the other hand, does not occupy the space of doubt, but of absolute certainty; the analyst is Descartes's God, the only real guarantor of our existence. In this way Freud, as suggested already, reserves for himself the only position outside the structure of mind that he devised: the impossible position of the super-man-child of absolute narcissism. As such, Freud imagines himself less a part of the mass of energy outside the psychic apparatus, than a hitherto unknown and godlike "subject" beyond this entire machine of force and counterforce, energy and growth.

And it is upon this basis that we can finally understand why suggestion is always an appropriate means to a psychoanalytic end. For it is always *Freud's* suggestion, and not that of some Other caught up in the inauthentic, mimetically charged social world. Or, failing the hocus-pocus of the master himself, it is the suggestion of a legitimate heir and descendant.

Indeed, psychoanalysis is nothing more than the seemingly endless repetition of Freud's divine right in the everyday miracle of his disciples. Or again, his pupils remain his proof by—or as—repetition—the concrete, objective, transferred, and transmissible "reality" of Freud's subjective science (Dufresne 1997a). It follows that this religious monstrosity is as good an example of the death drive as any and, more importantly, that any truly *deep* understanding of psychoanalytic theory lies in the apparent superficiality of its politics. For what is reflected in the theory is only written large in the psychoanalytic movement—a movement that seeks to remake the Others in its own image, that is, to negate the effects of the external world, those effects that are subject to inheritance, in the creation of a unified body of adherents. The detour of this movement is precisely the limit of psychoanalytic theory, which is bound to die of its own causes once the appropriation of all resistance is complete.

At the end of the day, everyone plays a secondary role to the absolute narcissist that Freud imagined in his metapsychology and reserved for himself as the undisputed father of psychoanalysis. Psychoanalysis was his idea, after all, his psychic apparatus projected on to the world of all Others. And so we are all mere fodder for analysis, impersonal forces which make the narcissistic fantasy grow this way and that. I have tried to show that the modifications of psychoanalytic theory are part and parcel of Freud's defensive strategy to protect himself from those critics who said he had suggested his findings. To this end metapsychology became the delicate inner space of psychoanalysis, a theater or cave from which everything began and will return again and against which nothing truly critical can be said. The psychoanalytic movement and its literature is the length or time of a detour traveling away from this inevitable end, and thus a collective expression of a will to live, or perhaps a fear of death, *Todesangst*.

What has not killed psychoanalysis has, therefore, only made it stronger—but also, to complicate this picture, more and more obtuse, callused, fossilized. To preserve itself psychoanalysis became an institution, and then a fashion—an elaborate window-dressing devised to cover over the fact that Freud never had any clothes on. For better and for worse, we are the threads that form the patterns on this now tattered cloth.

*Afterword: How to Be a Freudian;
or, The Economics of Not Thinking*

> With all great deceivers there is a noteworthy occurrence to which they owe their power. In the actual act of deception . . . they are overcome by belief in themselves: it is this which then speaks so miraculously and compellingly to those who surround them. The founders of religions are distinguished from these great deceivers by the fact that they never emerge from this state of self-deception. . . . Self-deception has to exist if a grand effect is to be produced. For men believe in the truth of that which is plainly strongly believed.
> —Friedrich Nietzsche, *Human, All Too Human*

From a narrativist or hermeneutic perspective, psychoanalysis is neither simply true nor simply false. It is a theory that helps us to understand ourselves and the world, or at least a Freudian-inspired film or book, and is to that extent self-justified. However, whether or not one buys such circularity, interpretation should not preclude the possibility of, if not the responsibility for, weighing the merits of the theory against itself (at the very least), and of judging its effects. In principle even the most efficacious form of psychotherapy is open to critique, which means that it is open to the possibility of a beyond—to begin with, the beyond called criticism.

The unfortunate truth is that psychoanalysis is not efficacious and is not open to critique. Narcissistically closed within and upon itself, the brute fact of psychoanalysis—the fact that Freud was born, produced some works, began an institution—remains its only possible justification. Incredibly, this set of fairly unremarkable circumstances has been enough for generations of gullible patients and academics. What can explain this exceptional, in some ways unprecedented, blindness? Without pretending to know the whole answer, which is something of a mystery, I can think of four partial answers: (1)

Because Freud and his followers have systematically fudged the historical record, thereby creating the illusion that an outside reality (e.g., consciousness, objectivity) really is consonant with the inside of analytic constructions (e.g., the unconscious, subjectivity). To this end, the institutional apparatus has repeatedly issued its own audits that the unaware and naive have accepted, and still accept, on good faith. (2) Because advocates of psychoanalysis insist that criticism from "outside" is illegitimate, that only the converted, in an early rehearsal of identity politics, are privy to the truths of psychoanalysis. In its most outrageous and vicious form, this means that critics are portrayed, literally, as ayatollahs, Nazis, anti-Semites, fascists, rightwing fanatics, in short, as people totally lacking moral or intellectual integrity.[1] (3) Because speaking for *or* against psychoanalysis, as every reader of analytic literature knows, is already to speak the language of transference and/or resistance. Given such intellectual blackmail on the "inside," there appears to be no option but to accept Freudian assertions as inescapable. Silence (fearful or otherwise) in the face of this situation becomes the ultimate proof that one has become sublimely ensconced within the analytic order of "reality." (4) Finally, and similarly, because we are supposedly trapped within the famous circle of representation, popularized by French intellectuals, where one speaks "always already" from within language and its logic. As a result, we seem committed to the manipulations of psychoanalysis, and much else, on pain of the nagging question: psychoanalysis is a fantastic lie and an absurd science, sure, but as opposed to what, the Truth? This is typically followed by looks of pity, and possibly a condescending chuckle or two.

The blindness of the literature on psychoanalysis is currently ensured, in fact celebrated, by advocates of the lattermost explanation, which is based on the philosophy of representation, a philosophy that has, no doubt unwittingly, become the perfect analog to a totalizing theory of psychoanalysis (see Borch-Jacobsen 1997). No matter that Freud created his theory of human behavior without regard for the debilitating philosophy of representation, even though he foreshadowed that game with his own hall of mirrors (see explanation 3, above). It is certainly an irony that Freud's refusal to play that game has resulted in an institution that we, sophisticated to the point of an all-knowing silence, are unwilling or unable to challenge on the basis of this philosophy. Such is the unquestionable truth, some hermeneuts will say, of Freud's delusion, which, as such, is beyond judgment—so far beyond, in fact, that historical investigations into the veracity and viability of his claims are quite simply beside the point or, worse yet, silly and inherently positivistic. But this is the (let's be honest) *laughable* ahistoricism of much poststructuralist thought, which shares precisely this defect with structuralism. At the risk of spoiling the party, it is obviously not true that we are automatically barred in advance from weighing Freud's so-called "discoveries" against his *own* goals and pretensions and, moreover, of viewing them against the backdrop of history. There is no good reason why we cannot judge Freud and find him wanting, both spiritually and scientifically. After all, when you take into account the history of Freud's work—carefully separating the basic truths he repeated (e.g., human beings are tormented by civilization) from the lies, tautologies, and patchwork theories—then the whole economy of psychoanalysis tumbles down around our feet. To reply, rather lamely, that the historically informed conclusion is naive or dogmatic or positivistic is to get the actual state of affairs totally ass-backward (see Dufresne 1998a).

Given the devastating critiques of Freud and psychoanalysis now available[2]—for example, from Sulloway (1979), Crews (1993), Borch-Jacobsen (1996b), Swales (1997), and Cioffi (1998)—Freud's continuing popularity must be seen as a function of ignorance, naivete, religiosity, and the politics of the psychoanalytic movement (or of a mixture therein); which is to say that it is a function of the transmissibility of holy doctrine from generation to generation, and from analyst to patient. Or, once again, it is a function of suggestion written large—repeated compulsively until habit is mistaken for law, and law for nature. Uninformed belief in the bad habit called psychoanalysis has long determined the *apparent* efficacy of its therapy, the legitimacy of its history, and the viability of its theories. But, as always, let's not mince words: psychoanalysis does not work, has not worked, and could never work, even though psychoanalysts have yet to stop working. From inside the movement few have read the obituaries, and those that have cannot believe the news.

Structured, it almost seems, by a deadly theory of conservation—as exemplified so beautifully by the humorless repetition of book after book on psychoanalysis, each a grim parody of the last—the psychoanalytic edifice has already crumbled to pieces. In the meantime, intellectuals, patients, and intellectual patients continue to seek shelter amidst the dangerous ruins. This is obviously a grave mistake. Psychoanalysis is dead, and burial and obituary get the last word at the end of the psychoanalytic century.

Notes

Chapter 1: Twilight of the Idols

1. Weizsaecker 1957: 71.
2. As the inimitable Karl Kraus once put it: "If mankind, with all its repulsive faults, is an organism, then the psychoanalyst is its excrement. Psychoanalysis is an occupation in whose very name 'psycho' and 'anus' are united" (quoted in Szasz 1976: 115).
3. Confronted with the same translation problems with Freud that others in France previously found with Martin Heidegger, new words are being invented to more faithfully approximate the German originals—a fetishistic practice that many argue muddies the water more often than not.
4. This sentiment seems to resonate with something Freud once said to Joseph Wortis. Wortis remarks that he is not overly interested in self-examination, to which Freud states: "You have made everything you said up to now so clear it has not interested me either" (in Wortis 1954: 26). Freud's comment is also a response to Wortis's "honesty," which, while essential for analysis (as a fundamental rule), must ultimately be distorted for Freud to begin his work. For Freud, true psychoanalysis begins with the patient's deception, the attempt to hide (or repress) a darker truth. That is, Freudian psychoanalysis proceeds upon the presumption of dissimulation, that the patient is an (unconscious) liar.
5. It is notable in this regard that Abraham A. Brill delivered a psychoanalytic paper on Abraham Lincoln in June 1931. For an account of Abe v. Abe, see Jacob L. Moreno's interesting monograph *The Psychodrama of Sigmund Freud*.

6. Essentially, Lacan thought as little of these analysts as Freud thought of dissident analysts during his own lifetime. Freud once wrote to Jung that Adler's ego "behaves as the ego always behaves, like the clown in the circus who keeps grimacing to assure the audience that he has planned everything that is going on. The poor fool!" (Freud and Jung 1974: 404).

7. The end of this string ["Moi-la-Cause-freudienne"] is a pointed reference to Jacques-Alain Miller's controversial movement of that name, the "Freudian Cause," and not just to the general phenomena of Freudianism. In an unpublished interview of 1994, conducted by e-mail, Borch-Jacobsen recounts some mimetic aspects of the followers' " 'transference onto the theory' " of the founding analyst (see Roustang 1982). His enlightened assessment, with which I am in agreement (see Dufresne 1997a), is worth citing:

> Lacanians would repeat Lacan's latest pronouncements like parrots, they would dress like him, emulate his way of sighing in the middle of a sentence, smoke the same cigars as him, and so forth. This may sound anecdotal, but in reality it raised a fundamental problem. Indeed, the goal of a Lacanian analysis is to free your desire from its "imaginary"—that is to say, its identificatory—alienation in some specular "alter ego." In his essay, "Situation de la psychoanalyse et formation du psychoanalyste en 1956," Lacan had even criticized sharply the psychoanalytic institution for being based on such an identificatory solidarity, proposing instead that they be founded in a purely "symbolic" pact with the "dead father" (i.e., Freud's text). So how could you account for the fact that his own school was plagued by exactly these same mimetic mechanisms, very often to the point of caricature? Didn't this point to the inability of analysis to dissolve the transference in its identificatory components? And didn't this in turn raise some tough questions about "desire" and "the subject," and their alleged difference from "imaginary" identification?

8. Similar sentiments are expressed by David James Fisher, who recalls meeting in Paris in 1987 one of Lacan's former patients, now an analyst. Annoyed by the follower's "messianic enthusiasm," Fisher reminded him of Lacan's critique of the "subject supposed to know": "Without hesitation, the Lacanian replied to me with yet another epistemological question: 'What happens if your analyst *truly* knows?' " (1994: 377).

Chapter 2: The Heterogeneous Beyond

1. See Freud's correspondence to Ferenczi (Freud and Ferenczi 1996: 341).

2. The scientist in Jones never liked the theory of the death drive, and told Freud as much. However, that did not stop him from investing his own thought with metapsychological layers of meaning—including his book on figure skating, which is just as humorless as it is wild psychoanalysis (see Dufresne and Genosko 1995: 127–28). There Jones actually maps "*the interplay of two systems of bodily twist*" onto the "two great systems . . . called the primary and secondary systems" (1931: 49–50). The book appeared, incidentally, in *two* editions, the second (1952) being enlarged and revised.

3. Kurt Eissler, for example, argues that Freud was inspired by Schiller in the formation of the death-drive theory (1965: 156).

4. Readers may be interested to know that Spielrein was Jean Piaget's analyst.

5. For example, as he states of psychoanalysis and Adler's deviations: "The two theories form an interesting pair of opposites: in the latter not a trace of a castration complex, in the former nothing else than its consequences" (1925d: 253–54, n. 4).

6. It seems likely that Freud used the words *Trieb* and *Instinkt* uncritically and perhaps interchangeably (see Rycroft 1972); at the very least, he never bothered to reserve a special word for a nonbiological, metaphorical force (i.e., "drive"), such as the French claim. On the contrary, the French preoccupation with this issue is characteristically ideological and ahistorical, a desperate attempt to save Freud from his essential biologism (as I will argue later in this book). However, for a contrary view see Jean Laplanche (1992: 274–76).

7. As Ellenberger notes: "The classical pair of opposites were *Eros-Neikos* (Love-Strife), and *Bios-Thanatos* (Life-Death), but not *Eros-Thanatos*" (1970: 515). The usual reference to the life and death drives ignores the difference between *Eros* and *Bios*.

8. Nietzsche 1986: 15–16.

9. This is contrary to Sulloway's claim, which he lifts directly from Jones, who had in turn accepted Freud's questionable view on the matter (1979: 394).

10. For the best treatment of the Tausk affair, see Roustang (1982); for generally related work on transference and suggestibility, see Roustang (1983).

11. Armed with this rather odd perspective, Sandor Rado would theorize that Karl Abraham "killed himself to avoid" an impending struggle with Freud (quoted in Roazen and Swerdloff, 1995: 90). Certainly a recurrent theme in the literature is the overvaluation of Freud's Godlike powers over life and death; a theme that indicates the intensity of relations that defined the disciple's lamentable position within the transference relation.

12. For this reason, though, a critic like Fromm viewed the death drive, not entirely convincingly, as a mixed blessing: it may have been bad biology, but it was for that very reason proof that Freud had finally turned away from his old mechanistic philosophy (see Burston 1991: 196–99).

13. But as Bakan admits, there is one aspect of Freud's psychoanalysis that deviates importantly from this tradition. "The ability of the Jew to withstand opposition," Bakan writes, "has historically been based in the Jewish community rather than in individual heroes. In instances in which individual Jews have stood alone in the face of opposition or in the willingness to accept martyrdom, they have done so with a sense that they were defending a tradition, rather than as 'solitary opposition' for the sake of a radical innovation" (1958: 43). As I will argue later, Freud's theory is individualistic to the point of narcissism.

14. Jacques Derrida makes the interesting observation that Freud claimed to have harbored death wishes, as a child, against his own younger brother. And this younger brother did in fact die. The situation thus repeats itself with Ernst and Heinz—although Freud identified himself more fully with the younger child (1980: 334–36).

15. Just about the only in-depth discussion of this subject, at least as it relates to

Freud's life, is found in Sharon Romm's helpful work. There she outlines the history of the genital-based theory of rejuvenation: in 1869, French physiologist Charles Édourd Brown-Séquard proposed and tested the injection of a semen-juice extract from dog testicles; this was followed by the actual transplant of monkey testicles to older men by Serge Voronoff, chief surgeon at the Russian hospital in Paris, and then by Eugen Steinach. Steinach, a professor of physiology at the University of Vienna, created a sensation in the popular press of the time. It is probably no coincidence that Steinach's collaborator was Freud's own radiologist, Guido Holzknecht. Apparently Freud found special encouragement from Federn, whose interest had been piqued by Rudolph von Urban, an internist with an interest in psychoanalysis. But the operation was performed by Victor Gregor Blum, urologist to the Viennese elite (Romm 1983: 73–85). Although Freud later denied that his vasectomy had been very rejuvenating (Jones 1957: 98–99), he did paint a rosy picture for the procedure in his essay of 1920, "The Psychogenesis of a Case of Homosexuality in a Woman" (see 1920b: 171–72). In that essay he considers Steinach's claim that the procedure could (and did) "cure" homosexuality, an idea that interested Freud very much.

16. It does seem that Reich connected his later "discovery" of "orgone energy"—supposedly a physical manifestation of libido—with the life drives that Freud described, and even imagined that this "blue" life energy could counter the effects of a cancer-causing death drive. (Freud himself never thought that libidinal energy was measurable [see Freud 1921: 90].) To some extent, then, it seems that Reich devoted his bizarre life-researches to curing Freud from cancer. As Reich once remarked: "[Freud] was very beautiful at that Congress (Berlin 1923), as he always was when he spoke. Then it hit him just here in the mouth. And that was where my interest in cancer began. I began cancer studies in 1926–1927" (1952: 74).

17. See Dufresne (1997a), wherein I explore the line between a naive objectivist history and deconstruction. For a lighter treatment of history and fiction, see my "L'histoire de la psychanalyse—ragot, fiction, ou histoire de l'histoire de la psychanalyse?" (1996a), as well as the commentary by Argentinean psychoanalyst Roberto Harari (1996), "La 'verdadera' carta de Freud a Lacan."

18. Ferenczi 1926a: 377.

19. Ferenczi 1924: 4.

20. Only five of the twelve were ever published. Apparently Freud had second thoughts and destroyed the remainder.

21. The names for which were dropped in the 1950's in favor of "anxiety" and "depression" (Shorter 1985: 144).

22. Probably the first discussions of the constancy principle are found in the *Sketches for the 'Preliminary Communication' of 1893*, written between June 1892 and the year's end (Freud 1892: 145–54).

23. As Freud and Bullitt write: "The libido must be stored somewhere. We conceive that it 'charges' certain areas and parts of our psychic apparatus, as an electric current charges a storage battery or accumulator; that, like a charge of electricity, it is subject to quantitative alterations; that, dwelling without discharge, it shows ten-

sion in proportion to the quantity of the charge and seeks outlet; further, that it is continually fed and renewed by physical generators" (Freud and Bullitt 1966: 37).

24. A debate on masturbation, in which Wilhelm Stekel argued against Freud that it was harmless, is recorded in the *Minutes of the Vienna Psychoanalytic Society* during 1911 and 1912 (see Nunberg and Federn 1962–75).

25. Cannon was a distinguished Harvard physiologist and experimenter. His book, *The Wisdom of the Body*, details the physiological view of stability (of the blood stream and of the respiratory system), which he also links in his epilogue to the "body politic" (1932: 305–324). His impeccable scientific credentials made it easy for analysts of that time to import the notion of "homeostasis" into their dubious works on the death drive. Nowadays, Cannon's name is rarely recalled in a literature that still, on occasion, invokes his idea.

26. Jung's remarks about Indian spirituality resonate slightly against the grain of both Freud or Fechner's belief in the constancy of Buddhism. According to Jung, "The Indian feels himself to be outside good and evil, and seeks to realize this state by meditation or yoga. My objection is that, given such an attitude, neither good nor evil takes on any real outline, and this produces a certain stasis" (1961: 276). For a different (as in peculiar) approach to nirvana and Buddhism, see Hartmann's *The Philosophy of the Unconscious* (1931: iii, 90–91) and Schopenhauer's *The World as Will and Representation* (1844: 508–509).

27. Yabe writes: "This reasoning pleased Freud tremendously. Since he had been attacked for this theory, and had modified it somewhat, he was happy to feel that he had suddenly acquired many colleagues who would agree with him. He called out to his daughter in the next room: 'Anna, Anna!' " (in Freud 1992: 70). We can thank Michael Molnar for compiling and editing Freud's sparse diary entries between 1929 and 1939, upon which this information is based. Molnar informs us: "Yabe was a psychologist to the government railways of Japan and had been sent to Europe for three months to investigate psychoanalysis" (Molnar 1992: 276, n. 1). After a brief analysis, Freud and his colleagues happily accepted Yabe as a certified analyst. One can reasonably assume that Yabe, like so many others, became interested in psychoanalysis via the theory of traumatic neurosis made popular in the wake of the great rail disasters in nineteenth-century America. This may also explain Yabe and his government's interest in *BPP*, in which such traumas are discussed. On the origins of traumatic neurosis, "railway spine," and so on, see Schivelbusch's (1979) comprehensive book.

28. The theory of recapitulation was shared by many of Freud's contemporaries, but not the theory of acquired characteristics, which fell out of fashion when Mendelian genetics was rediscovered in 1900 (see Gould 1987: 18). Pressured by Ernest Jones to drop parts of his Lamarckian conclusions in *Moses and Monotheism*, Freud responded by adding the following lines: "My position, no doubt, is made more difficult by the present attitude of biological science, which refuses to hear of the inheritance of acquired characteristics by succeeding generations. I must, however, in all modesty confess that nevertheless I cannot do without this factor in biological evolution" (1939: 100; cf. Jones 1957: 313).

29. "Thou owest God a death," from Shakespeare's *Henry IV*. As the editors in-

dicate, Freud also wrote his adapted phrase in a letter to Fliess in 1899, where he also attributed them to Shakespeare. No one, to my knowledge, has connected the modified line to Schopenhauer, who deserves more scholarship in this and other connections.

30. See Freud 1940: 207; taken from *Faust*, part 1, scene 1.

31. In his review of *A Phylogenetic Fantasy*, Gould provides a masterful commentary—with one exception. He is too eager to paint Ferenczi as the wild thinker, and Freud as the innocent victim of incorrect hypotheses; a great thinker allowed to fail greatly. For example: "Freud, eschewing Ferenczi's overblown, if colorful, inferences about an earlier past, begins with the glacial epoch" (14). But Freud began with Ferenczi's Ice Ages only because it was, as I note, "The Coming of Man"—that is, the beginning of psychology. Such a focus doesn't mean that Freud eschewed anything. On the contrary, it just means that Freud uncritically adopted Ferenczi's bizarre framework as his own, using it to "scientific" ends that are hardly less overblown or colorful.

32. In fact, the Hungarian title of Ferenczi's work is *Katasztrofák*, or *Catastrophe*. Not incidentally, it was Ferenczi's push to a time before life, literally before birth, that saved him from Rank's fate—at least temporarily. With *The Trauma of Birth*, also of 1924, about which Ferenczi and Freud were initially enthusiastic, Rank laid the ground for what was among the earliest full-blown pre-Oedipal, mother-centered theories; in Rank's case, a theory grounded upon the catastrophe of being born. Eventually Rank came to loggerheads with Abraham, Jones, and finally with Ferenczi and Freud. However, Ferenczi's theory derives from the same metapsychological impulse as Rank, which is far more true to Freud than the less adventurous theories of Abraham and Jones; and this despite Jones's (1955: 160) ridiculous claims to the contrary. As Marthe Robert writes of Ferenczi: "The eternal wish to return to the mother's womb no longer sprang, as with Rank, from the memory of intrauterine ecstasy which is lost and repressed by every man born, but from nostalgia for the initial ocean from which all species issued. The human mother was merely the symbol or late substitute of Thalassa, the original sea and matrix of the world" (1964: 349). From Freud's perspective, Ferenczi's catastrophe theory was better than Rank's precisely because it proposed an etiology free from life concerns, including (perhaps most especially) the mother-child relation, a relation Freud idealized as free from ambivalence and of no special concern to a father-centered, Oedipal analysis. But it should be said that Rank, as Robert Kramer points out, was just as interested in such ultimate, unthinkable questions of existence: "Rank peered underneath biological bedrock to confront the ontological, or, more precisely, the *pre*ontological, mystery of *Dasein* [Being] itself: the awesome difference—the ineffable difference—between nonexistence and existence" (1997: 232). Freud would surely have embraced Rank's more philosophically oriented birth theory, which after all was based on hints in his own work (see Freud 1900, 5: 400–401; 1910b: 173; 1916–17, 16: 396–97, 407), if not for the heretical implications it held for the mother-child bond. Freud's relationship with both Rank and Ferenzci would decline precisely to the extent that the mother-

child bond became increasingly more central to their clinical work. For a well-informed discussion of Rank, see Kramer's valuable essays (1996; 1997).

33. However, Ferenczi takes this point back in a later footnote (1924: 78, n. 1).

34. Note that if life is traumatic it is because conception itself is always already split between the "component parts" of the male and female. Thus Ferenczi wonders: perhaps all subsequent psychic splitting (e.g., the so-called split personality) is written into the very fabric of our genes (1932: 81).

35. It may be worth mentioning that Ferenczi does not just follow Freud's *BPP* in *Thalassa*, but also his speculations on mass psychology that were published in 1921. Like Freud, Ferenczi claims that once-upon-a-time unicellular organisms united into groups—an adaptive response to a catastrophe that was effected along dialectical lines according to which the individual cells (to make this properly Hegelian) fought each other in a struggle to the death without, however, actually dying. This origin of life is repeated in the struggle for supremacy between the sexes, in which true adaptation is always on the side of the woman (i.e., the slave [cf. 103–104]).

36. Apparently Freud also linked the dangers of the active technique to some folly from Ferenczi's past, writing: "According to my recollection a tendency to sexual play with patients was not completely alien to you in preanalytic times, so that the new technique could well be linked to an old [i.e., immature] error" (in Ferenczi 1932: 3–4, n. 3). Jones had similar troubles with female patients (three times), and left this part of Freud's letter to Ferenczi out of his biography.

37. Karl Menninger (1938; 1942) is another example, although I will not discuss his work here.

38. As Kleinian psychoanalysis is distinguished from Freudian psychoanalysis on account of their different theories of fantasy, it has become customary to telegraph the distinction by preserving Klein's British spelling of this word from the American spelling. Hence, "phantasy" refers to Klein's intricate revision of the term as it normally operates.

39. Janet Sayers claims that Klein began her analysis in 1912, "or shortly thereafter" (1991: 210).

40. Some years later Melitta became an analyst herself, and also a staunch critic of her mother.

41. A similar situation exists with Freud's "Papers on Technique," which were only published between 1911 and 1915, that is, years after he declared the therapeutic value of psychoanalysis. Freud was just as reluctant to make public the fact that he had dropped the "seduction theory" in 1897, waiting until 1905 to correct the record—a very long time indeed.

42. True, Freud himself has a fairly good record in his dealings with women analysts. He did encourage women to make careers of analysis, unlike some of his less enlightened colleagues. In fact, he was increasingly surrounded by women in his later years. On the other hand, Freud's record may owe more to his feelings of superiority over women, who may have seemed less threatening and rebellious than his male colleagues (e.g., Jung, Stekel, Adler, Rank, and even Ferenczi). Moreover,

Freud thought that women analysts had necessarily renounced some of their feminine characteristics.

43. However, Klein had a history of depression, having spent two and a half months in a fashionable Swiss sanatorium in 1909. Klein was stuck in an unhappy marriage, and in 1909 was apprehensive about the possibility of being pregnant (see Grosskurth 1986: 56–57).

44. It is interesting that both centers had one rich supporter in their ranks: Freud, a brewer, gave money to help establish the Hungarian Society, among other ventures, while Max Eitingon gave money to establish a psychoanalytic clinic in Berlin.

45. Hug-Hellmuth was an early competitor of Klein's in the area of child analysis and was associated with Abraham's Society when Klein arrived; she experimented with play therapy before Klein systematized its use. Unlike Klein, her clinical experience was limited to children aged six or seven.

46. Abraham 1923: 90.

47. According to Esther Menaker, by the 1930's "everyone used the play technique, including Anna Freud. Once I came into her office for my session and she had a chest with dolls all along the shelf. She said a little child was coming for a session" (from an unpublished interview with Menaker, October 13, 1997, in New York).

48. "I find it a little odd," Jones quite rightly wrote of Klein's clinical application of the death drive, "that I should be criticizing her for a too faithful adherence to Freud's views, and odder still that certain Viennese analysts see in it a divergence from his views" (1975: 340). Jones said as much to Freud during a period of heated correspondence in 1927 (see Freud and Jones 1993: 579, 617–25). For his part, Freud took Jones's attitude as an affront to his daughter Anna and to himself.

49. As Pontalis suggests, Klein "thought she would be able to participate in the 'birth' of an unconscious and, as it were, to mother it" (1981b: 103).

50. See also Ferenczi's essay "The Problem of Acceptance of Unpleasant Ideas—Advances in Knowledge of the Sense of Reality" (1926: 366). In this essay Ferenczi suggests that the stages of introjection, the transition stage, and projection roughly correspond to what Freud outlined in *Totem and Taboo* as "a succession of magical, religious, and scientific stages" (373).

51. Incredibly, there are still people who believe this and related nonsense. See, for example, the recent work of Otto Weininger, called *Being and Not Being: Clinical Applications of the Death Instinct* (1996).

52. Despite her suggestion, in 1955, that she referred to this patient as "Fritz" in her earliest published papers (see 1975: 122), Klein referred to him by name in the original German edition. Klein didn't hide the identity of her patient until later versions of her essays. As she states in a letter to Ferenczi (December 14, 1920): "I would like to change my son Erich to little Fritz, the son of relations of mine, whose mother had been faithfully following my instructions and whom I had often the opportunity to see informally. . . . I think the disguise will be perfect" (in Grosskurth 1986: 91). That she felt obliged to disguise the identity of her early patients is nothing new in the history of psychoanalysis. Freud did it all the time, invoking patient

confidentiality whenever he needed to dissimulate an embarrassing piece of information. But Klein, in fact, must have felt (at least at first) that she had nothing to hide: her analytic colleagues knew she was analyzing her own children and, moreover, were inclined to do the same sort of thing themselves. Abraham, for example, published a case study of his seven-year-old daughter (Grosskurth 1986: 96). This particular abuse has often been repeated in the history of psychoanalysis, most sensationally when Freud analyzed his own daughter Anna—an open secret until the 1960's.

53. Apparently her estranged husband, Arthur Klein, thought as much, and at one point in the mid-twenties attempted (and failed) to gain custody of Erich-Fritz (see Grosskurth 1986: 110).

54. Ferenczi (1924: 72).

55. As Deleuze and Guattari say, such transcendence is conditioned by the fact that the death drive "has neither a model nor an experience" upon which to ground it (1972: 332).

56. See Nietzsche (1886: 122).

57. Lenin makes a few explicit remarks about this "disorder" (see 1970: 23, 25, 56, 86), which he applies to his deviant comrades less as a psychiatric category than as a bit of spicy polemic. For instance, the closing line of the pamphlet reads: "There is every reason to hope for a rapid and complete recovery of the international communist movement from the infantile disorder of 'Left-wing' communism" (86). Given this tactic, it may be stretching it to connect Freud and Lenin very closely; if anything, it just shows the extent to which Freud was in the air by that time (ca. 1920), and also that Lenin was willing to adopt such loaded language in his pamphlet.

58. Of course, the hopes for social change were high well before the 1930's. As Friedrich Engels says in his *Anti-Dühring* of 1877, "The possibility of securing for every member of society, through social production, an existence which is not only fully sufficient from a material standpoint and becoming richer from day to day, but also guarantees to them the complete unrestricted development and exercise of their physical and mental faculties—this possibility now exists for the first time, but it *does exist*" (1877: 304; his emphasis).

59. A pseudonym for Reuben Osbert (Jones 1957: 517, n. 29).

60. Reich claims that it was the "exaggerations and generalizations" in Theodor Reik's book *Compulsion to Confess and Need for Punishment* that first made him realize the problems with Freud's death-drive theory (see Reich 1952: 211–12; cf. Reich, 1927–33: 232).

61. Reich's skepticism about the liberatory aspects of Freud's later doctrine was echoed by Joseph Wortis, a former patient of Freud's and a self-described socialist, when I interviewed him in early 1994. At that time he explicitly tied an instinct-driven, individualistic psychoanalysis to the questionable ideology of capitalism (see Dufresne 1996b: 600).

62. Reich felt that both Marx and Freud were pioneers in their respective fields: "Both claimed that social life was governed by factors independent of conscious

human will. For Marx, it was the economic conditions and processes. For Freud, it was psychic, instinctive forces. Both sciences had been built on as yet undiscovered biosocial and biological laws" (in Higgins 1994: xiv).

63. Malinowski was on friendly terms with Reich on the basis of their work and correspondence and met him for the first time in London, 1933 (see Sharaf 1983: 197). As the first anthropologist to take Freudian psychoanalysis seriously, significant portions of Malinowski's *Sex and Repression* are devoted to a discussion of Freud's work. While this particular work was important for Reich, he may have found some passages in Malinowski's *The Sexual Life of Savages* just as interesting. Here I am not thinking so much of the passages where Malinowski refers to psychoanalysis in passing, but of his discussion of sexuality generally, and of *"ipipisi momona"*—orgasm—specifically. Reich must have agreed with the Trobriand Islanders who, Malinowski tells us, "are certain that white men do not know how to carry out intercourse effectively. As a matter of fact, it is one of the special accomplishments of native cook-boys and servants . . . to imitate the copulatory methods of their masters. . . . In this the brevity and lack of vigour of the European performances were caricatured. Indeed, to the native idea, the white man achieves orgasm far too quickly" (1929: 338). And hence, one is inclined to think, they fell neurotic.

Reich may have found some consolation in the preface to Malinowski written by the famed sexologist Havelock Ellis. Ellis refers to "the genius of Freud" and comments upon Freud's relevance to Malinowski's work: "To these developments [in psychoanalysis] Dr. Malinowski is fully alive. He was even prepared at one time to be much more nearly a Freudian than we can now describe him. To-day he is neither Freudian nor anti-Freudian; he recognizes the fertilizing value of Freud's ideas, and he is prepared to utilize them whenever they seem useful" (Malinowski 1929: xi). This was more or less Reich's own attitude toward Freud throughout his life.

64. Apparently Mailer even built for himself an orgone accumulator to capture and concentrate orgone energy (Torrey 1992: 261).

65. By this time, Freud was already cool with Reich; when he received the dedicated manuscript for Reich's first major work, *The Function of the Orgasm*, in May 1926, he apparently responded, "So thick?" (Higgins 1994: xii). This book was later heavily revised by Reich in 1942; the early book, sans additions, appeared in English as *Genitality* in 1980.

66. Interestingly enough, Reich's colleague Richard Sterba has suggested that Reich's orgasm theory was biographical first and paradigmatic later. Reich once told Sterba that "if he did not have an orgasm for two days, he felt physically unwell and saw 'black before his eyes' " (1982: 87; cf. Burston 1991: 235, n. 3).

67. It is interesting, in this connection, that Freud himself always recommended abstinence during analysis as a way of heightening the dream content and thus the value of psychoanalysis. This recommendation was similarly repeated by Freud's followers. As Herman Nunberg once exclaimed to an analytic understudy, "*Coitieren oder analysieren!*"—"Either sexual intercourse or analysis!" (in Menaker 1989: 77).

68. This new dualism might owe something to the disagreement that Reich had

with Albert Einstein over orgone research; that is, perhaps Reich identified himself with the good orgone just as he projected the deadly orgone onto Einstein.

69. Through Malinowski, but also in Fromm's case through the Swiss anthropological theorist Johann Jacob Bachofen (see Jay 1973: 94–96).

70. This leads one commentator, adopting the Freudian stance, to wonder if the differences that eventually appeared amongst the small group of Freudian-Marxists can be understood in terms of "sibling rivalry" (Burston 1991: 226–27).

71. Whereas the physician, Marcuse writes in *One-Dimensional Man*, is compelled "to restore the patient's health, to make him capable of functioning normally in the world ... the philosopher is not a physician; his job is not to cure individuals but to comprehend the world in which they live—to understand it in terms of what it has done to man, and what it can do to man" (1964: 183).

72. It is strange that French historian Elisabeth Roudinesco gets this fundamental point backwards (1990: 482); she also ties Marcuse more closely to Reich than is actually the case. These misstatements are either blunders, or an attempt to emphasize the impression that Marcuse and Lacan were very different in their relative positions as prophets in the 1960's; by association, that is, Roudinesco's Marcuse was just as crazy as Reich.

73. According to one commentator, Marcuse lifted this phrase from Alfred North Whitehead's *Science and the Modern World*—of all places (Geoghegan 1981: 63).

74. Despite the apparent sophistication of their thinking, theorists often fall prey to the most naive beliefs. Max Horkheimer, for example, was in analysis with Karl Landauer in 1928 for "an inability to lecture without a prepared text" (Jay 1973: 87–88)—an absurd use of therapy made less so by the analytic penchant for dignifying latent motivations with deeper, hidden, serious ones. Horkheimer was apparently cured of this grave disorder. Of course, Freud to this day continues to find his most uncritical, if blind, support from those outside institutional psychoanalysis.

75. The question of Heidegger and dialectics creates another problem, but one that exceeds the scope of this examination; suffice to note that Marcuse praised Heidegger's work on Hegel in his "habilitation" thesis *Hegels Ontologie und die Grundlegung einer Theorie der Geschichtlichkeit*, published in 1932 (see Robinson 1969: 192).

76. During this time of antiauthoritarian activity, Horkheimer rejected his old critical-theory views and even defended the pope's assessment of birth-control pills (Slater 1977: 116).

77. Hegel 1807: 111.

78. Kojève 1939: 10.

79. In later years, it is true, Ricoeur would tone down his critique of Lacan's linguistic approach to Freud. In fact, he praised this approach, stating that "these attempts at reformulation have given us not only original but also liberating work, especially with regard to the prejudices that even Freud remained trapped in concerning the function of language" (1978: 305). In this article, "Image and Language in Psychoanalysis," Ricoeur takes a major step toward Lacan's linguistic

conception of Freud, but—of course—reserves a space for his own originality by advocating the more authentic place of the *image* in psychoanalytic discourse.

80. Those interested in the deconstruction of Freud are, in fact, better served by Weber and Gasché, who echo some of Derrida's ideas but, I think, with greater success. In this respect, my treatment of Derrida is not meant to be representative of the entire "field"—assuming for the moment that such a thing exists. Just the same, I try to draw some conclusions and underline a problematic that is not restricted to Derrida's work alone.

81. Derrida 1967: 220.

82. Derrida returns haphazardly to the themes of the "prosthetic" (extended) psyche and the death drive in *Archive Fever: A Freudian Impression* (1995)—a slight book that, in my opinion, is a cautionary tale about the excesses of self-referentiality. Interested readers might consult my critical review (1997b).

83. For more on *différance*, see Derrida's essay of that name (1968), and also his various remarks in *Positions* (1972b).

84. Derrida actually refers to this new field as "*psychoanalytic graphology*" (1967: 231; his emphasis), naively pointing readers in the direction of Melanie Klein. "Klein's entire thematic," he exudes, speaking of good and bad objects and so on, "could doubtlessly begin to illuminate, if followed prudently [sic!], the entire problem of the archi-trace."

85. For a detailed examination of Derrida's theory of writing, I recommend Johnson's book, *System and Writing in the Philosophy of Jacques Derrida* (1993).

86. Nietzsche 1887: 168. Nietzsche also writes: "What if pleasure and displeasure were so tied together that whomever wanted to have as much of one must also have as much of the other?" (85). Consider also Schopenhauer in this context: "The truth is that the two [life and death] belong to each other inseparably, since they constitute a deviation from the right path, and a return to this is as difficult as it is desirable" (1844: 579).

87. Because of its meandering style, *The Post Card* is far more than an analysis of Freud, the reading of which is caught up in a network of others and of other thematics. As Christopher Norris puts it, the book "takes up a great variety of philosophic themes, among them the relationship of Plato to Socrates, the Heideggerian questioning of metaphysics, the status of truth-claims in the discourse of Freudian psychoanalysis, and the way that all these topics return to haunt the seemingly detached, almost clinical idiom of Oxford linguistic philosophy" (1992: 176–77). Without advocating Oxford philosophy, I am not sold on this diversity, which is fun but also reckless—or fun because it is reckless. As already suggested, I have restricted my reading of Derrida to Freud and *BPP*.

88. For another appearance of the "crypt" in Derrida's work, see his essay "Fors: The Anglish Words of Nicholas Abraham and Maria Torok" (1977). A warning, though, since this is one of his least accessible, almost unreadable, efforts. There are perhaps three areas in the essay which resonate with my discussion of Derrida's Freud: the "logic" of the proper name; the role of fiction in psychoanalysis; and the self-involvement of Freud in his text, in this case that of the Wolf Man. Similar but

more accessible discussions can be found in *The Ear of the Other* (1985), which examines Nietzsche's legacy.

89. It is here that Derrida reads Freud's *da* against Heidegger's *Da-sein*, making the proper death coincide with the discourse of authenticity (1980: 359–60). For Derrida, like some others in the French tradition, Freud and Heidegger correspond, without, however, having ever corresponded.

90. The sometimes extreme self-indulgence of Derrida's work has been an inspiration, or license, for Derridians and non-Derridians alike. Gregory Ulmer's (1989) theory of "mystory" is the logical, if absurd, culmination of Derrida's self-involved writing. But so is John O'Neill's (1992) "Deconstructing Fort/Derrida," which is distinguished by being the best example of the worst of this genre (if that is the right word).

91. Derrida's violent appropriation of the other to the deconstructive cause, to the papa, is repeated in his recent discussions of Foucault and Lacan. In each case the appropriation came after their deaths in the early 1980's. Given Derrida's difficult relations with Foucault and Lacan while they were alive, this seems a bit opportunistic, not to mention distasteful. Of course, if Derrida is not Freud, neither is he Foucault or Lacan.

Chapter 3: *The Other* Beyond

1. Freud 1933a: 110.
2. Freud writes that the "fact" of constancy, of a "Nirvana principle," "is one of our strongest reasons for believing in the existence of death instincts" (1920a: 56).
3. Freud clarifies this view in a letter to Jones in early 1935, stating that because the death drive is "intent on destroying its own living mass . . . it is therefore assumed that the direction outwards [i.e., growth] originates from Eros" (Freud and Jones 1993: 741). As he put it in *The Ego and The Id*, "The clamour of life proceeds for the most part from Eros. And from the struggle against Eros!" (1923a: 46).
4. As noted earlier, the connection between sleep and death is more explicitly laid out by Ferenczi in *Thalassa* (1924: 73–80). See also Nunberg (1955: 212).
5. The child's primary narcissism is an "assumption" that Freud makes here, but one he takes over from his examination of the mental lives of "savages." As he says, primary narcissism "is less easy to grasp by direct observation than to confirm by inference from elsewhere" (1914b: 90). To this end he turns to his adult patients for (obviously questionable) inferential evidence.
6. Like the sexual instinct, she tends to "watch over" the "elementary organism" and "provide them with a safe shelter while they are defenceless against the stimuli of the external world" (1920a: 40).
7. Freud 1941: 300.
8. As Freud writes in *The Interpretation of Dreams*, "The unconscious is the true psychical reality; *in its innermost nature it is as much unknown to us as the reality of the external world, and it is as incompletely presented by the data of consciousness as is the external world by the communications of our sense organs*" (1900, 5: 613; his emphasis).

9. It seems to me that the psychic apparatus not only conjures up the militaristic image of the walled city—for instance, the inner city of Vienna that defends itself, grows, and finally outgrows its walls; the walls that in turn become the *Ringstrasse*, a street upon which Freud walked every day—but also the more mundane image of the living tree. Freud mentions trees once in *BPP*, noting that they can live an extraordinary long time. The "impression," he writes, "that there is a fixed average duration of life . . . is countered when we consider that certain large animals and certain gigantic arboreal growths reach a very advanced age and one which cannot at present be computed" (1920a: 45). Not unlike the ancient cities buried underfoot, the tree holds a number of secrets about the past that may have piqued Freud's archaeological interests. It is possible, then, that Freud proceeded by analogy to model and measure his "pre-psychoanalytic" theories of 1895 on tree physiology and what was later to become the field of dendrochronology, the study of *dendron* over *chronos*, trees over time—a field of invaluable importance for modern archaeology, where growth rings provide researchers with a picture of the past. The possible connections are tantalizing. First, the crust that protects the organism from the external world functions like the bark that protects the tree from the elements. Second, the past health and maturity of the psyche, like the tree, can be assessed by a certain kind of interpretation.

Many have observed the presence of tree rings throughout history, but it was not really until the seventeenth and eighteenth century that growth rings were recognized as an annual calendar written in real time. Leonardo da Vinci recognized this fact, as did Montaigne, but their advances went unnoticed for years. It is likely that Freud, who loved to walk in the woods and pick mushrooms, understood that tree rings record a hidden past. It is even possible that Freud's archaeological contacts discussed this idea with him, even though it was mostly unknown until the 1920's and later. If so, trees may have provided Freud a model for understanding the repressed memories of individual patients: like geological layers in the earth, the passing seasons leave marks within the vegetative and psychic organism as layers piled one on top of the other. The rings of a tree, like trauma, are literally the *internal* representations of a past encounter with the external world. If the psychic apparatus is thus arborescent, an important feature of Freud's theory of memory thereby becomes more sensible: his idea that the effects of the original trauma are often unknown until much later. For as energy from the external world bombards the psychic apparatus over a period of years, causing defense and then growth, the outermost layers of growth are only slowly absorbed into the organism. In other words, what was once written on the surface of the organism eventually becomes the very stuff of the interior: in one case, wood, in the other, memories. In the meantime, the traumas are slowly covered over with fresh growth and hidden beneath the surface crust/bark; time heals all wounds. However, by wielding the proper tool—the lumberjack's ax, the surgeon's knife, the archaeologist's shovel, or the psychoanalyst's words—the researcher is able to conduct an investigation, sometimes an autopsy, on the organism.

It should be noted that dendrochronology, unlike psychoanalysis, has born out its earliest scientific hopes. According to Michael G. L. Baillie, tree-ring dating is today a "revolution" and the fulfilment of "the chronological holy grail" (1995: 12–13).

10. Descartes's dualism of mind and body, thought and extension, is loosely traced in Freud's own dualism of the death and life drives. In addition, like Descartes's follower A. Geulincx, Freud more or less devised two separate though parallel worlds of mind and body—the movements of which I am unpacking here and in the pages that follow.

11. As far as I can tell, this point has gone virtually unnoticed in the literature, with perhaps one exception. In his *Critical Dictionary of Psychoanalysis*, Charles Rycroft makes passing comment of "unwarrantable deductions from the fact that organisms are poisoned by their own excreta" (1972: xiv).

12. Moreover, bowel complaints were all the rage in Paris by the 1890's (Shorter 1985: 116–17), a fact that may have caught Freud's attention in 1885 while he studied with Charcot at the Salpêtrière.

13. These theories may even have played a part in Freud's own racial prejudices about Eastern Jews, since constipated patients were sometimes said to acquire a "dirty color"—precisely the kind of description that permitted medical doctors to assert, according to Sander Gilman (1997), that the dark skin color of the Jew reflected a degeneration of the race and a concurrent disposition to hysteria, syphilis, and so on.

14. Freud seems to have avoided the problem of constipation in his own life and in the lives of his patients. During toilet training, Little Hans, for example, was constipated, a fact that Freud neglects but which goes a long way toward explaining the boy's obsession with "Lumf," or feces. Also, constipation may have played a role in Freud's analysis of the Wolf Man, in particular impacting upon the Wolf Man's unresolved transference problem with Freud. (I owe this last speculation to a personal communication with Mikkel Borch-Jacobsen.) But possibly the most direct evidence of Freud's avoidance of the psychological problem of constipation appears in Smiley Blanton's *Diary*. Closing his entry for September 4, 1929, Blanton writes: "When I spoke again of my colits, Freud said perhaps it was caused by the heat. *Not once has he suggested that it was due to resistance*" (1971: 29; his emphasis).

15. According to Max Schur, Freud's personal physician between 1928 and 1939, "This 'cure,' which consisted of drinking considerable amounts of mildly laxative, warm Karlsbad water pumped directly from natural springs, was at the time a standard prescription for a variety of gastrointestinal and biliary symptoms. Karlsbad also had beautiful woods, good hotels, and excellent food—comforts provided by all European spas in those decades" (1972: 255).

16. Shorter notes that it was mostly women who exhibited these symptoms at the turn of the century, although as one London physician in 1923 states: "An abdominal man, on the other hand, is by comparison a rare bird, and when caught has a way of turning out to be a Jew—or a doctor" (1985: 117). Freud may have agreed with this sentiment and produced the appropriate symptoms.

17. See Freud 1921: 102.

18. This was not a meeting of the Vienna Psychoanalytical Society, which Freud stopped attending after his first operation for cancer in 1923. Instead, it was a gathering of a few select members of the Society, in this case (and in two previous instances) organized by Paul Federn (Freud 1992: 50).

19. It is perhaps no accident that Freud cites this precise ode (in Latin) in a letter of May 27, 1920, to Max Eitingon during a time in which he was "correcting and completing" *Beyond the Pleasure Principle* (in Schur 1972: 331). In the letter the Latin appears as "Fractus si illabatur orbis impavidum, ferient ruinae." Sterba cites the proper English translation of the ode: "Yea, if the globe should fall, he'll stand / fearless amidst the crash" (1982: 115). Schur also provides an English translation, which reads: "If the sky should fall in pieces, the ruins will not daunt it" (1972: 331, n. 10). Schur provides, in addition, Horace's original Latin, which is in fact the version Sterba gives. It is likely, then, that Sterba worked backward from this correct Latin passage to the mistranslated version Freud offered; he does not offer the German translation of the Latin. Because Sterba often gets small details wrong in this book, I am inclined to think that the version Freud gives to Eitingon in writing was also the one he gave to Sterba and his guests orally.

20. "Whatever is done from love," as Nietzsche states, "always occurs beyond good and evil" (1886: 90).

21. These sentiments are, however, also present in Schopenhauer, who as suggested provides a list of similar statements throughout the ages (1844: 585–588). But Nietzsche's version is as good as any, especially since it was the most current version at that time. Incidentally, it is worth noting that Rank used this citation from Nietzsche as the epigraph for *The Trauma of Birth* (Kramer 1996: 7). Rank's skepticism about analytic therapy was merely a reflection of Freud's own therapeutic pessimism: both knew that analysis had become interminable and that patients were being sacrificed to the grail of "research." But Rank, just like Ferenczi, sought to alter that theory and therapy accordingly, making it more humane and hopeful; but it was here that they betrayed Freud's dark philosophy of resignation and fell afoul of his sycophantic followers.

22. As Freud puts it in a letter of April 21, 1918, "This has been a troubled time, marked by a growing resentment against the whole outer world, which was no doubt intensified by the necessity of being kind and tolerant every day to ten human beings [patients] who had gone off the rails" (Freud and Andreas-Salomé 1966: 77).

23. Esther Menaker, who was analyzed by Anna Freud in the early 1930's, is decidedly critical of what she calls Freud's "destructive" practice. During an interview in 1997, she stated flatly, and in my opinion correctly, "Psychoanalysis denigrates the individual's self by putting him or her in a submissive, narcissistic position. . . . At best it is suited to those few people who live a submissive life; a life which psychoanalysis is only too happy to reinforce" (from an unpublished interview with Menaker, October 13, 1997, in New York).

24. If psychoanalysis is merely a detour on the way to better things, it at least has the merit of making sociality—in reality, therapy—a positively *unheimlich* experience: "that class of the frightening which leads back to what is known of old and long fa-

miliar" (Freud 1919b: 220). A careful reading of even the first chapter of "The 'Uncanny' " (*Das Unheimliche*), an essay that foreshadows *Beyond the Pleasure Principle*, reveals that the uncanny return "to what is known and old" is always already a return to the crypt.

After reviewing various interpretations across cultures, Freud uncovers in this first chapter a basic ambivalence at the heart of the word *uncanny*. As a result he is able to conclude that "What is *heimlich* thus comes to be *unheimlich*" (224). But if the canny can become strange and uncanny, Freud defies this essential ambivalence—which in principle should work both ways—and makes of the latter a mere part of the former: "*unheimlich* is in some way or other a subspecies of *heimlich*" (226). This is a strange but inevitable conclusion given Freud's views about constancy and pleasure. For the canny is obviously the "old and familiar" *instinct*—so old that it has become natural, biological, inheritable—that characterizes death and nonexistence. Life, on the other hand, is a source of increased tension and unpleasure that is bound (or, more literally, is unbound) to promote new, uncanny, and frightening experiences. Metapsychology, then, is the realm of the canny, a homey place beyond the pleasure principle that naturally exceeds existence and its analysis, while psychoanalysis is a piece of sociality that is at once a falling away from the canny and a desperate attempt to reinstate it among the living as the compulsive repetition of the transference neurosis.

25. Freud and Andreas-Salomé 1966: 154.

26. McDougall 1936: 2.

27. Freud only retrospectively claimed that his patients believed in stories of seduction. In his original papers of 1896, the so-called "memories" of seduction were recorded as mere *visualizations* introduced by Freud himself. For more details on this important point, see Frank Cioffi's recent work, *Freud and the Question of Pseudoscience* (1998). I thank Frederick Crews for bringing this fact to my attention.

28. In later life Ernst had no memory of this game (in Freud 1992: 61), which isn't unusual. But to analysts this fact would no doubt signify the normal postanalytic "amnesia" that Freud, for example, found with Little Hans (Freud 1909: 148–49).

29. Freud not incidentally informs the reader that Ernst's mother literally disappeared just a few years later when she died (from influenza). As Freud states in a footnote, "Now that she was really 'gone' ('o-o-o'), the little boy showed no signs of grief" (1920a: 16). The mother drops out of the picture just as easily as the "o" in the transition from "o-o-o-o" (*fort*) to "o-o-o." The German word *ort* means, interestingly enough, "place"; the transition, then, is from "gone" to "place." What place? *Beyond*.

30. Freud 1933a: 106.

31. It is worth noting that this essay predates, first, the instances of war neuroses that impelled Freud to reconsider the (possibly "daemonic") role of repetition in psychic life as well as, second, Freud's observation of repetition as evidenced in children's play. For the war did not officially begin until 1914—hence physicians were not yet interested in the phenomenon of war neuroses—and Freud's vacation in

Hamburg (where he observed Ernst) did not take place until September 1915. This paper on technique, nonetheless, returns as a supporting reference in chapter 3 of *BPP*—I say "supporting" because it is placed conveniently *after* his preliminary discussion of war trauma and child's play. Analytic technique is thereby put to work for the sake of metapsychology, that is, for the sake of proof. This is, however, a sleight of hand, since repetition of one's social relations from the past (i.e., the theory of transference) is not reducible to this other, instinctual, repetition.

32. In any case, such memories—assuming there are any—are obviously not repressed and, therefore, not of much interest to Freud.

33. Strachey tells us that Freud delivered this essay, one on telepathy, and another on neurotic mechanisms, to some colleagues "during a walking-tour in the Hartz mountains in September, 1921," although he did not complete the writing of "Remarks" until the following July (in Freud 1923b: 108).

34. Freud added the parenthetical clause in 1923, which makes his allusion to suggestion more obvious. The original clause of 1920 was far less direct about the role of suggestion and simply read, according to Strachey's note, "the wish which is not unconscious" (1920a: 32, n. 2).

35. This is a bit confusing, though, since Freud did not update this old work with new references and footnotes, as he did with his favorite works, such as *The Interpretation of Dreams* and *Beyond the Pleasure Principle*. More to the point, *The Introductory Lectures* do not take into consideration the new dualism and the death-drive theory that he introduced in 1920. Perhaps, then, Freud (like his critics) was not very aware of the connection between his treatment of hypnosis, group psychology, and the death drive—but I doubt it.

36. Remember, psychoanalysis was based on the very failures that Freud originally attributed to the seduction theory, failures that were recast as "evidence" of infantile sexuality and fantasy. His later, properly psychoanalytic case studies fare no better, as he published only *failures*. Not surprisingly, Freud became increasingly pessimistic about the efficacy of psychoanalytic treatment, concluding at the end of his life that treatment was "interminable" (Freud 1937). For a brilliant discussion of these and similarly stunning facts, see Frank Cioffi's *Freud and the Question of Pseudoscience* (1998).

37. For example, Poul Bjerre writes: "At the assembly of German Neurologists in October, 1910, physicians belonging to sanatoria were obliged to officially give out a declaration that they had nothing to do with psychoanalysis, and [Emil] Raimann suggested that neurologists should agree among themselves upon the publication of every case in which it could possibly be suspected that psychoanalytical treatment had done the patient harm" (1920: 84). At some point Freud successfully petitioned Julius von Wagner-Jauregg to get Raimann, a pupil, to stop his public criticisms of psychoanalysis (see Ellenberger 1970: 470).

38. Here Freud may have been thinking about Fliess's botched operation on Emma's nose, although he may more generally have been thinking about the untold number of cases of surgical mutilation that were passed off as a treatment for hyste-

ria and other mental illnesses, and for which psychanalysis was obviously a less dangerous treatment (see Bonomi 1997).

39. Eysenck 1985: 19.

40. For a noted discussion of the "Tally Argument," see Adolf Grünbaum (1984: 140–48); I thank Frederick Crews for reminding me of this fact. A convincing critique of the tally argument is made by Frank Cioffi (1998: 252–63).

Afterword: How to Be a Freudian

1. These words, among others, were used in early 1996 to describe the petitioners of the Library of Congress Freud exhibit, which was temporarily postponed from fall 1996 to October 1998. As one of the original petitioners, I can attest to the spin campaign waged against us, especially in North America and France. Although we demanded simply that a wide spectrum of informed opinion be represented at the exhibit, an exhibit, after all, being funded and presented at a *public* institution, we were portrayed in the media by analysts and their sponsors as "censors." This was a total fabrication, of course, one perpetrated by people who knew as much. Elisabeth Roudinesco, for example, was responsible for much of the motivated misrepresentation in France, where she gathered 180 signatures for a counterpetition against us. In turn, Borch-Jacobsen was outrageously accused in the French media of being a "negationist"—a loaded word normally reserved for Holocaust deniers. For an overview of the fiasco, see Dufresne (1998b). The primary documents involved in this international affair, over three hundred pages worth and climbing, have been deposited by Peter Swales in the Library of Congress. The petitioners of the exhibit, a heterogeneous group of over forty scholars and analysts, included the following people: Swales, Borch-Jacobsen, Frederick Crews, Robert Holt, Daniel Burston, Morris Eagle, Phyllis Grosskurth, Frank Cioffi, Malcolm Macmillan, Frank Sulloway, John Kerr, Adolf Grünbaum, Oliver Sacks, and Freud's own granddaughter, Sophie Freud.

2. An excellent reader of revisionist work on psychoanalysis has been compiled by Crews, called *Unauthorized Freud: Doubters Confront a Legend* (1998).

Bibliography

Abraham, Karl (1920). "The Cultural Significance of Psychoanalysis." In *Clinical Papers and Essays on Psycho-Analysis*, 116–36. London: The Hogarth Press and the Institute of Psycho-Analysis, 1955.
———. (1923). "Psycho-Analytical Views on Some Characteristics of Early Infantile Thinking." In *Clinical Papers and Essays on Psycho-Analysis*, 86–90. London: The Hogarth Press and the Institute of Psycho-Analysis, 1955.
———. (1924). "A Short Study of the Development of the Libido, Viewed in the Light of Mental Disorders." In *Selected Papers of Karl Abraham*, trans. Douglas Bryan and Alix Strachey, 418–501. New York: Brunner/Mazel, 1979.
Adorno, Theodor (1951). *Minima Moralia: Reflections from Damaged Life*. Trans. E. F. N. Jephcott. New York: Verso, 1991.
Alexander, Franz G., and Sheldon T. Selesnick (1966). *The History of Psychiatry: An Evaluation of Psychiatric Thought and Practice from Prehistoric Times to the Present*. New York: Harper and Row.
Appignanesi, Lisa, and John Forrester (1992). *Freud's Women*. London: Weidenfeld and Nicolson.
Baillie, Michael G. L. (1995). *A Slice Through Time: Dendrochronology and Precision Dating*. London: Batsford.
Bakan, David (1958). *Freud and the Jewish Mystical Tradition*. Princeton, N.J.: D. Van Nostrand.
———. (1966). *The Duality of Human Existence: Isolation and Communion in Western Man*. Boston: Beacon.
Bartlett, Francis (1939). "The Limitations of Freud." *Science and Society* 3: 64–105.

Baudrillard, Jean (1988). *America.* Trans. Chris Turner. New York: Verso.
Becker, Ernest (1973). *The Denial of Death.* New York: Free Press.
Bernfeld, Siegfried, and Sergei Feitelberg (1931). "The Principle of Entropy and the Death Instinct." *The International Journal of Psycho-Analysis* 12: 61–81.
Bettelheim, Bruno (1990). *"Freud's Vienna" and Other Essays.* New York: Knopf.
Bjerre, Poul (1920). *The History of Psychanalysis* [sic]. Rev. ed. Trans. Elizabeth N. Barrow. Boston: Richard G. Badger.
Blanton, Smiley (1971). *Diary of My Analysis with Sigmund Freud.* New York: Hawthorn.
Bloom, Harold (1987). *Ruin the Sacred Truths: Poetry and Belief from the Bible to the Present.* Cambridge: Harvard University Press.
Blumenberg, Hans (1985). *Work on Myth.* Trans. R. M. Wallace. Cambridge: MIT Press.
Bonomi, Carlo (1997). "Freud and the Discovery of Infantile Sexuality: A Reassessment." In *Freud Under Analysis: History, Theory, Practice,* ed. Todd Dufresne, 35–57. Northvale, N.J.: Jason Aronson.
Boothby, Richard (1991). *Death and Desire: Psychoanalytic Theory in Lacan's Return to Freud.* New York: Routledge.
Borch-Jacobsen, Mikkel (1988). *The Freudian Subject.* Trans. Catherine Porter. Stanford, Calif.: Stanford University Press.
——. (1991). *Lacan: The Absolute Master.* Trans. Douglas Brick. Stanford, Calif.: Stanford University Press.
——. (1993). *The Emotional Tie: Psychoanalysis, Mimesis, and Affect.* Trans. Douglas Brick et al. Stanford, Calif.: Stanford University Press.
——. (1994) Interview by Todd Dufresne. Spring (over the course of a few months).
——. (1996a). "Neurotica: Freud and the Seduction Theory." *October* 76: 15–43.
——. (1996b). *Remembering Anna O.: A Century of Mystification.* New York: Routledge.
——. (1997). "*Basta Così!*: Mikkel Borch-Jacobsen on Psychoanalysis and Philosophy." In *Returns of the "French Freud": Freud, Lacan, and Beyond,* ed. Todd Dufresne, 207–227. New York: Routledge.
Bottomore, Tom (1984). *The Frankfurt School.* New York: Tavistock.
Bougnoux, Daniel (1997). "Lacan, Sure—and Then What?" In *Returns of the "French Freud": Freud, Lacan, and Beyond,* ed. Todd Dufresne, 91–106. New York: Routledge.
Brenner, Charles (1973). *An Elementary Textbook of Psychoanalysis.* New York: International Universities Press.
Bronfen, Elizabeth (1989). "The Lady Vanishes: Sophie Freud and *Beyond the Pleasure Principle.*" *The South Atlantic Quarterly* 88, no. 4: 961–91.
Brown, Norman O. (1959). *Life Against Death: The Psychoanalytical Meaning of History.* London: Routledge.
Burston, Daniel (1991). *The Legacy of Erich Fromm.* Cambridge: Harvard University Press.

Butler, Clark (1976). "Hegel and Freud: A Comparison." *Philosophy and Phenomenological Research* 36: 506–522.
Cannon, W. B. (1932). *The Wisdom of the Body.* Rev. ed. New York: Norton, 1939.
Caputo, John (1989). "Mysticism and Transgression: Derrida and Meister Eckhart." In *Derrida and Deconstruction*, ed. Hugh Silverman, 24–39. New York: Routledge.
Chasseguet-Smirgel, Janine, and Bela Grunberger (1986). *Freud or Reich? Psychoanalysis and Illusion.* Trans. Claire Pajaczkowaska. New Haven, Conn.: Yale University Press.
Chessick, Richard (1989). "The Death Instinct and the Future of Humans." *American Journal of Psychotherapy* 43: 546–61.
Choisy, Maryse (1963). *Sigmund Freud: A New Appraisal.* New York: Philosophical Library.
Cioffi, Frank (1998). *Freud and the Question of Pseudoscience.* Chicago: Open Court.
Clark, Ronald (1980). *Freud: The Man and the Cause.* New York: Granada.
Clifford, James (1992). "Travelling Culture." In *Cultural Studies*, ed. Lawrence Grossberg et al., 96–112. New York: Routledge.
Copleston, Frederick (1965). *A History of Philosophy: Modern Philosophy.* Vol. 7, pt. 2. New York: Garden City.
Costigan, G (1965). *Sigmund Freud: A Short Biography.* New York: Macmillan.
Crabtree, Adam (1985). *Multiple Man: Explorations in Possession and Multiple Personality.* Toronto: Collins.
Crews, Frederick (1993). "The Unknown Freud." *New York Review of Books.* 18 November, 58–66. Also published in Crews et al., *The Memory Wars: Freud's Legacy in Dispute* (New York: New York Review of Books, 1995).
———. (1998). *Unauthorized Freud: Doubters Confront a Legend.* New York: Viking.
Deleuze, Gilles (1991). "Coldness and Cruelty." In *Masochism*, 9–138. New York: Zone.
Deleuze, Gilles, and Felix Guattari (1972). *Anti-Oedipus: Capitalism and Schizophrenia.* Trans. Robert Hurley et al. Minneapolis: University of Minnesota, 1990.
de M'Uzan, M. (1977). *De l'art à la mort.* Paris: Gallimard.
Derrida, Jacques (1967a). "Freud and the Scene of Writing." In *Writing and Difference*, trans. Alan Bass, 196–231. Chicago: University of Chicago Press, 1978.
———. (1967b). *Of Grammatology.* Trans. Gayatri Spivak. Baltimore: Johns Hopkins University Press, 1976.
———. (1967c). "Structure, Sign, and Play in the Discourse of the Human Sciences." In *Writing and Difference*, trans. Alan Bass, 278–93. Chicago: University of Chicago Press, 1978.
———. (1968). "Différance." In *Speech and Phenomena and Other Essays on Husserl's Theory of Signs*, trans. David Allison, 129–60. Evanston, Ill.: Northwestern University Press, 1973.
———. (1972a). *Dissemination.* Trans. Barbara Johnson. Chicago: University of Chicago Press, 1981.

———. (1972b). *Positions*. Trans. Alan Bass. Chicago: University of Chicago Press, 1981.
———. (1974). *Glas*. Trans. John P. Leavey and Richard Rand. Lincoln: University of Nebraska Press, 1986.
———. (1977). "Fors: The Anglish Words of Nicholas Abraham and Maria Torok." Trans. Barbara Johnson. In *The Wolf Man's Magic Word: A Cryptonymy*, xi–xlviii. Minneapolis: University of Minnesota Press, 1986.
———. (1980). "To Speculate—On Freud." In *The Post Card: From Socrates to Freud and Beyond*, trans. Alan Bass, 257–409. Chicago: University of Chicago Press, 1987.
———. (1985). "Otobiographies: The Teaching of Nietzsche and the Politics of the Proper Name." In *The Ear of the Other*, trans. Peggy Kamuf, 1–38. Baltimore: Johns Hopkins University Press.
———. (1991). " 'Eating Well,' or the Calculation of the Subject: An Interview with Jacques Derrida." In *Who Comes After the Subject*, ed. Eduardo Cadava et. al., 96–119. New York: Routledge.
———. (1995). *Archive Fever: A Freudian Impression*. Trans. Eric Prenowitz. Chicago: University of Chicago Press, 1996.
———. (1995–96). "For the Love of Lacan." *Journal of European Psychoanalysis*, no. 2 (Fall–Winter): 63–90.
Dickstein, Morris (1977). *Gates of Eden: American Culture in the Sixties*. New York: Penguin.
Doolittle, Hilda [H.D.] (1974). *Tribute to Freud*. New York: New Directions.
Dorer, Maria (1932). *Historische Grundlagen der Psychoanalyse*. Leipzig: Felix Meiner.
Dufresne, Todd (1996a). "L'histoire de la psychanalyse—ragot, fiction, ou histoire de l'histoire de la psychanalyse?" *Scansions: Actualités de l'interrogation freudienne* 6/7 (December): 5.
———. (1996b). "An Interview with Joseph Wortis [1994]." *Psychoanalytic Review* 83, no. 4 (August): 589–610. First published as "Joseph Wortis: Notorischer Anti-Psychoanalytiker und Freud-Analysand," *Werkblatt* 34 (1995): 90–118.
———. (1997a). "Freud and His Followers, or How Psychoanalysis Brings Out the Worst in Everyone." In *Returns of the "French Freud": Freud, Lacan, and Beyond*, ed. Todd Dufresne, 117–31. New York: Routledge.
———. (1997b). "Intellectual Haute Couture." Review of *Archive Fever*, by Jacques Derrida. *Boston Book Review* 4, no. 1 (January/February), 36–37.
———. (1998a). "Analysing Freud: An Interview with Mikkel Borch-Jacobsen." *CAN* 1 (July): 9–12. (Also forthcoming as "Retour à Delboeuf." *Ethnopsy*, no. 1.)
———. (1998b). "Freud in the Library of Congress: A Critic Speaks." *CAN* 1 (September): 9–12.
Dufresne, Todd, and Gary Genosko (1995). "Jones on Ice: Psychoanalysis and Figure Skating." *The International Journal of Psycho-Analysis* 76, pt. 1: 123–33.
Eastman, Max (1962). *Great Companions: Critical Memoirs of Some Famous Friends*. New York: Collier.
Eissler, Kurt R. (1965). *Medical Orthodoxy and the Future of Psychoanalysis*. New York: International Universities Press.

Ekstein, Rudolph (1949). "A Biographical Comment on Freud's Dual Instinct Theory." *American Imago* 6, no. 3: 211–16.
Ellenberger, Henri F. (1956). "Fechner and Freud." In *Beyond the Unconscious: Essays of Henri F. Ellenberger in the History of Psychiatry*, ed. Mark S. Micale, 89–103. Princeton, N.J.: Princeton University Press, 1993.
———. (1970). *The Discovery of the Unconscious: The History and Evolution of Dynamic Psychiatry*. New York: Basic.
Engels, Friedrich (1877). *Herr Eugen Dühring's Revolution in Science*. New York: International, 1939.
Erikson, Erik H. (1950). *Childhood and Society*. New York: Norton.
Eysenck, Hans (1985). *Decline and Fall of the Freudian Empire*. New York: Viking.
Falzeder, Ernst (1996). "Whose Freud Is It? Some Reflections on Editing Freud's Correspondence. *International Forum of Psychoanalysis* 5.
Fancher, Raymond E. (1973). *Psychoanalytic Psychology: The Development of Freud's Thought*. New York: Norton.
Fechner, Gustav Theodor (1873). *Einige Ideen zur Schöpfungs und Entwickelungsgeschichte der Organismen* (Some Ideas on the History of Creation and Development of Organisms). Leipzig: Breitkopf und Härtel.
Ferenczi, Sandor (1913a). "A Little Chanticleer." In *Sex in Psycho-Analysis*, 204–213. New York: Dover, 1956.
———. (1913b). "Stages in the Development of the Sense of Reality." In *Sex in Psycho-Analysis*, trans. Ernest Jones and Caroline Newton, 181–203. New York: Dover, 1956.
———. (1924). *Thalassa: A Theory of Genitality*. Trans. Henry A. Bunker. New York: Norton, 1968.
———. (1926a). "The Problem of Acceptance of Unpleasant Ideas—Advances in Knowledge of the Sense of Reality." In *Theory and Technique of Psycho-Analysis*, comp. John Rickman, trans. Jane Isabel Suttie et al., 366–79. New York: Basic, 1952.
———. (1926b). "To Sigmund Freud on His Seventieth Birthday." In *Final Contributions to the Problems and Methods of Psycho-Analysis*, ed. Michael Balint, 11–17. London: The Hogarth Press and the Institute of Psycho-Analysis.
———. (1929). "The Unwelcome Child and the Death Instinct." In *Final Contributions to the Problems and Methods of Psycho-Analysis*, ed. Michael Balint, 102–107. London: The Hogarth Press and the Institute of Psycho-Analysis, 1955.
———. (1932). *The Clinical Diary of Sandor Ferenczi*. Ed. Judith Dupont. Trans. Michael Balint and Nicola Zarday Jackson. Cambridge: Harvard University Press, 1995.
Fish, Stanley (1988). "Withholding the Missing Portion: Psychoanalysis and Rhetoric." In *The Trial(s) of Psychoanalysis*, ed. Françoise Meltzer, 183–209. Chicago: University of Chicago Press, 1988.
Fisher, David James (1994). Review of *Jacques Lacan & Co. Psychoanalytic Books* 5, no. 3: 365–78.

Flugel, J. C. (1955). *Studies in Feeling and Desire*. London: Gerald Duckworth.
Forrester, John (1990). *The Seductions of Psychoanalysis: Freud, Lacan, Derrida*. Cambridge: Cambridge University Press.
———. (1996). Personal communication to Todd Dufresne, 11 July.
Freud, Anna (1926). "Introduction to the Technique of the Analysis of Children." In *The Psycho-Analytical Treatment of Children*, trans. Nancy Procter-Gregg, 1–52. New York: International Universities Press, 1965.
Freud, Sigmund (1892). "Sketches for the 'Preliminary Communication' of 1893." In *The Standard Edition of the Complete Psychological Works of Sigmund Freud* [*SE*], trans. James Strachey, 1: 145–54. 24 vols. London: Hogarth, 1953–74.
———. (1895a). *Project for a Scientific Psychology*. In *SE*, 1: 281–397.
———. (1895b). *Studies on Hysteria*. Vol. 2 of *SE*.
———. (1900). *The Interpretation of Dreams*. Vols. 4–5 of *SE*.
———. (1901a). "On Dreams." In *SE*, 5: 629–86.
———. (1901b). *The Psychopathology of Everyday Life*. Vol. 6 of *SE*.
———. (1905a). *Jokes and Their Relation to the Unconscious*. Vol. 8 of *SE*.
———. (1905b). *Three Essays on the Theory of Sexuality*. In *SE*, 7: 123–243.
———. (1906). "My Views on the Part Played by Sexuality in the Aetiology of the Neuroses." In *SE*, 7: 269–79.
———. (1907). "The Sexual Enlightenment of Children." In *SE*, 9: 129–39.
———. (1908a). "Creative Writers and Day-Dreaming." In *SE*, 9: 141–53.
———. (1908b). "On the Sexual Theories of Children." In *SE*, 9: 205–226.
———. (1909). "Analysis of a Phobia in a Five-Year-Old Boy [Little Hans]." In *SE*, 10: 1–149.
———. (1910a). "Leonardo da Vinci and a Memory of His Childhood." In *SE*, 11: 57–137.
———. (1910b). "A Special Type of Choice of Object Made by Men." In *SE*, 11: 163–75.
———. (1911). "Psycho-Analytic Notes on an Autobiographical Account of a Case of Paranoia." In *SE*, 12: 3–79.
———. (1913a). "The Claims of Psycho-Analysis to Scientific Interest." In *SE*, 13: 163–90.
———. (1913b). *Totem and Taboo*. In *SE*, 13: 1–161.
———. (1914a). "On the History of the Psycho-Analytic Movement." In *SE*, 14: 3–66.
———. (1914b). "On Narcissism: An Introduction." In *SE*, 14: 67–102.
———. (1914c). "Remembering, Repeating and Working Through." In *SE*, 12: 145–56.
———. (1915a). "Instincts and Their Vicissitudes." In *SE*, 14: 111–40.
———. (1915b). "Thoughts for the Times on War and Death." In *SE*, 14: 273–300, plus appendix.
———. (1916). "On Transience." In *SE*, 14: 303–307.
———. (1916–17). *Introductory Lectures on Psycho-Analysis*. Vols. 15–16 of *SE*.

———. (1917a) "A Metapsychological Supplement to the Theory of Dreams." In *SE*, 14: 216–35.
———. (1917b). [1915]. "Mourning and Melancholia." In *SE*, 14: 237–58.
———. (1918) [1914]. "From the History of an Infantile Neurosis." In *SE*, 17: 1–133.
———. (1919a). "Lines of Advance in Psycho-Analytic Therapy." In *SE*, 17: 157–68.
———. (1919b). "The 'Uncanny.'" In *SE*, 17: 217–56.
———. (1920a). *Beyond the Pleasure Principle.* In *SE*, 18: 1–64.
———. (1920b). "The Psychogenesis of a Case of Homosexuality in a Woman." In *SE*, 18: 145–72.
———. (1921). *Group Psychology and the Analysis of the Ego.* In *SE*, 18: 65–143.
———. (1923a). *The Ego and the Id.* In *SE*, 19: 1–66.
———. (1923b) [1922]. "Remarks on the Theory and Practice of Dream-Interpretation." In *SE*, 19: 107–121.
———. (1924a). Letter to Fritz Wittels, December 1923. In *SE*, 19: 286–88.
———. (1924b). "The Economic Problem of Masochism." In *SE*, 19: 155–70.
———. (1925a). "An Autobiographical Study." *SE*, 20: 3–74.
———. (1925b). "Negation." In *SE*, 19: 233–39.
———. (1925c). "A Note upon the 'Mystic Writing Pad.'" In *SE*, 19: 225–32.
———. (1925d). "Some Psychical Consequences of the Anatomical Distinction Between the Sexes." In *SE*, 19: 241–58.
———. (1926). "Inhibitions, Symptoms, and Anxiety." In *SE*, 20: 75–174.
———. (1927). "The Future of an Illusion." In *SE*, 21: 1–56.
———. (1930). *Civilization and Its Discontents.* In *SE*, 21: 57–145.
———. (1931). "Female Sexuality." In *SE*, 21: 221–43.
———. (1933a). *New Introductory Lectures on Psycho-Analysis.* In *SE*, 22: 1–182.
———. (1933b). "Sandor Ferenczi." In *SE*, 22: 225–29.
———. (1937). "Analysis Terminable and Interminable." In *SE*, 23: 209–253.
———. (1939). *Moses and Monotheism: Three Essays.* In *SE*, 23: 3–137.
———. (1940). "An Outline of Psycho-Analysis." In *SE*, 23: 139–207.
———. (1941). "Findings, Ideas, Problems." In *SE*, 23: 299–300.
———. (1960). *Letters of Sigmund Freud.* Ed. Ernst Freud. Trans. Tania and James Stern. New York: Basic.
———. (1987). *A Phylogenetic Fantasy: Overview of the Transference Neurosis.* Ed. Ilse Grubrich-Simitis. Trans. Axel Hoffer and Peter T. Hoffer. Cambridge, Mass.: Belknap.
———. (1992). *The Diary of Sigmund Freud, 1929–1939: A Record of the Final Decade.* Trans., annot., intro. by Michael Molnar. New York: Scribner's.
Freud, Sigmund, and Karl Abraham (1965). *A Psychoanalytic Dialogue: The Letters of Sigmund Freud and Karl Abraham, 1907–1926.* Ed. Hilda C. Abraham and Ernst L. Freud. New York: Basic.
Freud, Sigmund, and Lou Andreas-Salomé (1966). *Sigmund Freud and Lou Andreas-Salomé: Letters.* Ed. Ernst Pfeiffer. Trans. William and Elaine Robson-Scott. London: Hogarth, 1972.

Freud, Sigmund, and William C. Bullitt (1966). *Thomas Woodrow Wilson: A Psychological Study*. Boston: Houghton Mifflin.
Freud, Sigmund, and Sandor Ferenczi (1993). *The Correspondence of Sigmund Freud and Sandor Ferenczi*. Vol. 1, *1908–1914*. Ed. Eva Brabant et al. Trans. Peter Hoffer. Cambridge, Mass.: Belknap.
———. (1996). *The Correspondence of Sigmund Freud and Sandor Ferenczi*. Vol. 2, *1914–1919*. Ed. Ernst Falzeder and Eva Brabant. Trans. Peter Hoffer. Cambridge, Mass.: Belknap.
Freud, Sigmund, and Wilhelm Fliess (1985). *The Complete Letters of Sigmund Freud to Wilhelm Fliess, 1887–1904*. Ed. and trans. Jeffrey M. Masson. Cambridge: Harvard University Press.
Freud, Sigmund, and Ernest Jones (1993). *The Complete Correspondence of Sigmund Freud and Ernest Jones, 1909–1939*. Ed. R. Andrew Paskauskas. Cambridge, Mass.: Belknap.
Freud, Sigmund, and Carl Jung (1974). *The Freud/Jung Letters: The Correspondence Between Sigmund Freud and C. G. Jung*. Ed. William McGuire. Trans. Ralph Manheim and R. F. C. Hull. Cambridge: Harvard University Press.
Freud, Sigmund, and Arnold Zweig (1970). *The Letters of Sigmund Freud and Arnold Zweig*. Ed. Ernst Freud. Trans. Professor and Mrs. Robson-Scott. London: Hogarth.
Fromm, Erich (1931). *The Dogma of Christ and Other Essays on Religion, Psychology, and Culture*. New York: Holt, Rinehart, and Winston, 1963.
———. (1941). *Escape from Freedom*. New York: Rinehart.
———. (1955). "The Human Implications of Instinctivist 'Radicalism' [A Reply to Herbert Marcuse]." *Dissent* 2, no. 4 (Autumn): 342–49.
———. (1959). *Sigmund Freud's Mission: An Analysis of His Personality and Influence*. New York: Grove.
———. (1970). "The Method and Function of an Analytic Social Psychology: Notes on Psychoanalysis and Historical Materialism." In *The Crisis of Psychoanalysis: Essays on Freud, Marx, and Social Psychology*, 110–34. New York: Holt, Rinehart, and Winston.
———. (1973). *The Anatomy of Destructiveness*. New York: Holt, Rinehart, and Winston.
———. (1981). *"On Disobedience" and Other Essays*. New York: Seabury.
Gamwell, Lynn (1989). "The Origins of Freud's Antiquities Collection." In *Sigmund Freud and Art: His Personal Collection of Antiquities*, ed. Lynn Gamwell and Richard Wells, 21–32. New York: Harry N. Abrams.
Gasché, Rodolphe (1974). "The Witch Metapsychology." In *Returns of the "French Freud": Freud, Lacan, and Beyond*, ed. Todd Dufresne, 169–207. New York: Routledge, 1997.
———. (1986). *The Tain of the Mirror: Derrida and the Philosophy of Reflection*. Cambridge: Harvard University Press.
Gay, Peter (1988). *Freud: A Life for Our Times*. New York: Norton.
Geoghegan, Vincent (1981). *Reason and Eros: The Social Theory of Herbert Marcuse*. London: Pluto.

Gilman, Sander (1997). "Freud's Dora." In *Freud Under Analysis: History, Theory, Practice*, ed. Todd Dufresne, 3–21. Northvale, N.J.: Jason Aronson.

Goodman, Paul (1945). "The Political Meaning of Some Recent Revisions of Freud." *Politics* 2: 197–203.

——. (1960). *Growing Up Absurd: Problems of Youth in Organized Society*. New York: Vintage.

Gould, Stephen Jay (1977). *Ontogeny and Phylogeny*. Cambridge, Mass.: Belknap.

——. (1987). "Freud's Phylogenetic Fantasy." *Natural History* 96, no. 12 (December), 10–19.

Gray, Paul (1993). "The Assault on Freud." *Time*, 29 November, 47–50.

Greenberg, Jay R., and Stephen A. Mitchell (1983). *Object Relations in Psychoanalytic Theory*. Cambridge: Harvard University Press.

Grosskurth, Phyllis (1986). *Melanie Klein: Her World and Her Work*. Toronto: McClelland and Stewart.

——. (1991). *The Secret Ring: Freud's Inner Circle and the Politics of Psychoanalysis*. Reading, Mass.: Addison-Wesley.

Grossman, Carl, and Sylvia Grossman (1965). *The Wild Analyst: The Life and Work of George Groddeck*. New York: George Braziller.

Grubrich-Simitis, Ilse (1987). "Metapsychology and Metabiology." In Sigmund Freud, *A Phylogenetic Fantasy: Overview of the Transference Neurosis*, ed. Ilse Grubrich-Simitis, trans. Axel Hoffer and Peter T. Hoffer, 73–107. Cambridge, Mass.: Belknap.

Grünbaum, Adolf (1984). *The Foundations of Psychoanalysis: A Philosophical Critique*. Berkeley: University of California Press.

Hale, Nathan G. (1995). *The Rise and Crisis of Psychoanalysis in the United States: Freud and the Americans, 1917–1985*. Oxford: Oxford University Press.

Harari, Roberto (1996). "La 'verdadera' carta de Freud a Lacan." *Las disipaciónes de lo inconsciente*. Buenos Aires: Amorrortu editores.

Hartmann, Eduard von (1869). *The Philosophy of the Unconscious: Speculative Results According to the Inductive Method of Physical Science*. Trans. William Chatterton Coupland. New York: Harcourt, Brace, 1931.

Hauser, Andrée (1961). "The Doctrine of Adler." In *Problems in Psycho-Analysis*, 69–87. London: Burns and Oates.

Hegel, Georg W. F. (1807). *Phenomenology of Spirit*. Trans. A.V. Miller. Oxford: Oxford University Press, 1977.

Heimann, Paula, and Susan Isaacs (1991). "Regression." In *The Freud-Klein Controversies, 1941–45*, ed. Pearl King and Riccardo Steiner. New York: Routledge.

Higgins, Mary Boyd (1994). "Reich's Development, 1922–1934." In Wilhelm Reich, *Beyond Psychology: Letters and Journals*. New York: Farrar, Straus and Giroux.

Idhe, Don (1974). Introduction to *Conflict and Interpretation: Essays in Hermeneutics*, ed. Don Idhe. Evanston, Ill.: Northwestern University Press.

Jay, Martin (1973). *The Dialectical Imagination: A History of the Frankfurt School and the Institute of Social Research, 1923–1950*. Boston: Little, Brown.

———. (1993). *Force Fields: Between Intellectual History and Cultural Debate*. New York: Routledge.
Jekels, Ludwig (1941). "Psycho-Analysis and Dialectic." *The Psychoanalytic Review* 28: 228–53.
Johnson, Christopher (1993). *System and Writing in the Philosophy of Jacques Derrida*. Cambridge: Cambridge University Press.
Johnston, Thomas (1965). *Freud and Political Thought*. New York: Citadel.
Jones, Ernest (1931). *The Elements of Figure Skating*. London: Methuen.
———. (1953). *The Life and Works of Sigmund Freud*. Vol. 1, *The Formative Years and the Great Discoveries: 1856–1900*. New York: Basic.
———. (1955). *The Life and Works of Sigmund Freud*. Vol. 2, *The Years of Maturity: 1901–1919*. New York: Basic.
———. (1957). *The Life and Works of Sigmund Freud*. Vol. 3, *The Last Phase: 1919–1939*. New York: Basic.
———. (1975). "Introductory Notes." In *"Envy and Gratitude" and Other Works*, by Melanie Klein, 337–41. London: Delacourte.
Jung, Carl (1961). *Memories, Dreams, Reflections*. Ed. Aniela Jaffé. Trans. Richard and Clara Winston. New York: Vintage, 1989.
Kerr, John (1993). *A Most Dangerous Method: The Story of Jung, Freud, and Sabina Spielrein*. New York: Vintage.
Klein, Melanie (1921). "The Development of a Child." In *"Love, Guilt, and Reparation" and Other Works*, 1–53. London: The Hogarth Press and the Institute of Psycho-Analysis, 1981.
———. (1923). "The Role of the School in the Libidinal Development of the Child." In *"Love, Guilt, and Reparation" and Other Works*, 59–76. London: The Hogarth Press and the Institute of Psycho-Analysis, 1981.
———. (1926). "The Psychological Foundations of Child Analysis." In *The Psycho-Analysis of Children*, trans. Alix Strachey, 3–15. London: The Hogarth Press and the Institute of Psycho-Analysis, 1980.
———. (1932). *The Psycho-Analysis of Children*. Trans. Alix Strachey. London: The Hogarth Press and the Institute of Psycho-Analysis, 1980.
———. (1936). "Weaning." In *"Love, Guilt, and Reparation" and Other Works*, 290–305. London: The Hogarth Press and the Institute of Psycho-Analysis, 1981.
———. (1946). "Notes on Some Schizoid Mechanisms." In *"Envy and Gratitude" and Other Works*, 1–24. London: Delacourte, 1975.
———. (1952). "The Origins of Transference." In *"Envy and Gratitude" and Other Works*, 48–56. London: Delacourte, 1975.
———. (1955). "The Psycho-Analytic Play Technique: Its History and Significance." In *"Envy and Gratitude" and Other Works*, 122–40. London: Delacourte, 1975.
———. (1957). "Envy and Gratitude." In *"Envy and Gratitude" and Other Works*, 176–235. London: Delacourte, 1975.
———. (1958). "On the Development of Mental Functioning." In *"Envy and Gratitude" and Other Works*, 236–46. London: Delacourte, 1975.

———. (1981). *"Love, Guilt, and Reparation" and Other Works, 1921–1945.* Intro. R. E. Money-Kryle. London: The Hogarth Press and the Institute of Psycho-Analysis.
Kojève, Alexandre (1939). "In Place of an Introduction." In *Introduction to the Reading of Hegel*, comp. Raymond Queneau, ed. Allan Bloom, trans. James H. Nichols, Jr., 3–30. Ithaca, N.Y.: Cornell University Press, 1980.
Kramer, Robert (1996). "Insights and Blindness: Visions of Rank." Introduction to *A Psychology of Difference: The American Lectures*, by Otto Rank. Princeton, N.J.: Princeton University Press.
———. (1997). "Otto Rank and 'The Cause.' " In *Freud Under Analysis: History, Theory, Practice*, ed. Todd Dufresne, 221–47. Northvale, N.J.: Jason Aronson.
Lacan, Jacques (1953). "Some Reflections on the Ego." *International Journal of Psycho-Analysis* 34, pt. 1: 11–17.
———. (1953–54). *The Seminar of Jacques Lacan. Book I: Freud's Papers on Technique, 1953–1954.* Ed. Jacques-Alain Miller. Trans. John Forrester. Cambridge: Cambridge University Press, 1988.
———. (1954–55). *The Seminar of Jacques Lacan, Book II: The Ego in Freud's Theory and in the Technique of Psychoanalysis, 1954–1955.* Ed. Jacques-Alain Miller. Trans. Sylvana Tomaselli. New York: Norton, 1991.
———. (1966). *Écrits: A Selection.* Trans. Alan Sheridan. New York: Norton, 1977.
———. (1968). "Introduction de Scilicet." *Scilicet*, no. 1, Paris: Seuil.
———. (1978). *The Four Fundamental Concepts of Psychoanalysis.* Trans. Alan Sheridan. New York: Norton.
Laplanche, Jean (1970). *Life and Death in Psychoanalysis.* Trans. Jeffrey Mehlman. Baltimore: Johns Hopkins University Press, 1976.
———. (1989). *New Foundations for Psychoanalysis.* Trans. David Macey. Oxford: Basil Blackwell.
———. (1992). "La pulsion de mort dans la théorie de la pulsion sexuelle." In *La révolution copernicienne inachevée, travaux 1967–1992*, 273–86. Paris: Aubier.
Laplanche, Jean, and Jean-Bertrand Pontalis (1973). *The Language of Psycho-Analysis.* Trans. D. Nicholson-Smith. New York: Norton.
Lauzun, Gerard (1963). *Sigmund Freud: The Man and His Theories.* Trans. Patrick Evans. London: Souvenir.
Lenin, Vladimir (1970). *"Left-wing" Communism, an Infantile Disorder.* Moscow: Progress Publishers.
MacIntyre, Alasdair (1970). *Marcuse.* London: Fontana.
Mahony, Patrick J. (1987). *Freud as a Writer.* Exp. ed. New Haven, Conn.: Yale University Press.
Malinowski, Bronislaw (1927). *Sex and Repression in Savage Society.* New York: Harcourt, Brace.
———. (1929). *The Sexual Life of Savages in North-Western Melanesia.* New York: Harcourt, Brace.
Mann, Edward W. (1973). *Orgone, Reich, and Eros: Wilhelm Reich's Theory of Life Energy.* New York: Simon and Schuster.

Mannoni, Octave (1968). *Freud.* Trans. Renaud Bruce. New York: Random House, 1971.
Marcuse, Herbert (1955a). *Eros and Civilization: A Philosophical Inquiry into Freud.* 2d ed. Boston: Beacon, 1966.
———. (1955b). "The Social Implications of Freudian 'Revisionism.' " *Dissent* 2, no. 3 (Summer): 221–40.
———. (1956). "A Reply to Erich Fromm." *Dissent* 3, no. 1 (Winter): 79–83.
———. (1957). "Theory and Therapy in Freud." *Nation,* 28 September, 200–201.
———. (1964). *One-Dimensional Man: Studies in the Ideology of Advanced Industrial Society.* Boston: Beacon.
———. (1970). *Five Lectures: Psychoanalysis, Politics, and Utopia.* Trans. Jeremy J. Shapiro and Shierry M. Weber. Boston: Beacon.
Masson, Jeffrey (1984). *The Assault on Truth: Freud's Suppression of the Seduction Theory.* New York: HarperCollins.
McDougall, William (1936). *Psycho-Analysis and Social Psychology.* London: Methuen.
Menaker, Esther (1989). *Appointment in Vienna.* New York: St. Martin's.
———. (1997). Interview with Todd Dufresne, October 13.
Menninger, Karl (1938). *Man Against Himself.* New York: Harcourt, Brace, 1966.
———. (1942). *Love Against Hate.* New York: Harcourt, Brace.
Molnar, Michael (1992). Introduction to *The Diary of Sigmund Freud, 1929–1939: A Record of the Final Decade,* trans. and annot. Michael Molnar. New York: Scribner's.
Moreno, Jacob L. (1967). *The Psychodrama of Sigmund Freud.* New York: Beacon House.
Morgan, Thomas B. (1963). "How Hieronymous Bosch (XVth Century) and Norman O. Brown (XXth) Would Change the World." *Esquire,* March, 100–135.
Natenberg, Maurice (1955). *The Case History of Sigmund Freud: A Psycho-Biography.* Chicago: Regent House.
Nietzsche, Friedrich (1872). *The Birth of Tragedy and The Genealogy of Morals.* Trans. Francis Golffing. New York: Doubleday, 1956.
———. (1886). *Beyond Good and Evil.* Trans. Walter Kaufmann. New York: Vintage, 1989.
———. (1887). *The Gay Science.* Trans. Walter Kaufmann. New York: Vintage, 1974.
———. (1954). *The Portable Nietzsche.* Ed. and trans. Walter Kaufmann. New York: Penguin.
———. (1986). *A Nietzsche Reader.* Sel. and trans. R. J. Hollingdale. New York: Penguin.
Norris, Christopher (1982). *Deconstruction: Theory and Practice.* London: Methuen.
———. (1987). *Derrida.* London: Fontana.
———. (1992). "Deconstruction, Postmodernism, and Philosophy: Habermas on Derrida." In *Derrida: A Critical Reader,* ed. David Wood, 167–192. Oxford: Basil Blackwell.
Nunberg, Herman (1955). *Principles of Psychoanalysis: Their Application to the Neuroses.* New York: International Universities Press.
Nunberg, Herman, and Paul Federn, eds. (1962–75). *Minutes of the Vienna*

Psychoanalytic Society. 4 vols. Trans. M. Nunberg in collaboration with Harold Collins. New York: International Universities Press.
O'Neill, John (1992). "Deconstructing Fort/Derrida: The Convention of Clarity." In *Critical Conventions: Interpretation in the Literary Arts and Sciences*. Norman: University of Oklahoma Press.
Osborn, Reuben (1937). *Freud and Marx: A Dialectical Study*. London: Victor Gollancz.
Peck, Martin (1930). *The Meaning of Psychoanalysis*. New York: Sun Dial Press.
Polka, Brayton (1989). "*Beyond the Pleasure Principle*: A Speculative Essay on Freud." *American Journal of Psychoanalysis* 49, no. 4: 297–309.
Pontalis, Jean-Bertrand (1981a). "On Death-Work." In *Frontiers in Psychoanalysis: Between the Dream and Psychic Pain*, intro. M. Masud and R. Khan, trans. Catherine Cullen and Philip Cullen, 184–93. London: The Hogarth Press and the Institute of Psycho-Analysis.
———. (1981b). "Between Knowledge and Fantasy." In *Frontiers in Psychoanalysis*, 95–103. London: The Hogarth Press and the Institute of Psycho-Analysis.
Rank, Otto (1924). *The Trauma of Birth*. New York: Dover, 1994.
———. (1925). *The Double: A Psychoanalytic Study*. Trans. Harry Tucker. Chapel Hill: University of North Carolina Press, 1971.
———. (1926a). "The Genesis of the Guilt-Feeling." In *A Psychology of Difference: The American Lectures*, sel., ed., and intro. Robert Kramer, 131–39. Princeton, N.J.: Princeton University Press.
———. (1926b). "The Genesis of the Object Relation." In *A Psychology of Difference*, 140–50. Princeton, N.J.: Princeton University Press.
Rawcliffe, D. H. (1952). *The Psychology of the Occult*. London: Derricke Ridgway.
Reich, Ilse Ollendorff (1969). *Wilhelm Reich: A Personal Biography*. New York: St. Martin's Press.
Reich, Wilhelm (1927). *Genitality in the Theory and Therapy of the Neurosis*. Trans. Philip Schmitz. New York: Farrar, Straus, and Giroux, 1980.
———. (1927–33). *Character Analysis*. Trans. Vincent R. Carfagno. New York: Farrar, Straus, and Giroux, 1972.
———. (1931). *The Invasion of Compulsory Sex Morality*. New York: Farrar, Straus, and Giroux, 1971.
———. (1952). *Reich Speaks of Freud*. New York: Farrar, Straus, and Giroux, 1967.
———. (1956). "Re-emergence of the Death Instinct as 'DOR' Energy." *Orgonomic Medicine* 2: 2–11.
———. (1970). *The Mass Psychology of Fascism*. Trans. Vincent R. Carfagno. New York: Farrar, Straus, and Giroux.
Ricoeur, Paul (1965). *Freud and Philosophy: An Essay on Interpretation*. Trans. Denis Savage. New Haven, Conn.: Yale University Press, 1970.
———. (1974a). "Consciousness and the Unconscious." In *Conflict and Interpretation: Essays in Hermeneutics*, ed. Don Ihde, 99–120. Evanston, Ill.: Northwestern University Press.

———. (1974b). "A Philosophical Interpretation of Freud." In *Conflict and Interpretation*, 160–76. Evanston, Ill.: Northwestern University Press.

———. (1978). "Image and Language in Psychoanalysis." In *Psychoanalysis and Language*, ed. Joseph H. Smith, 293–324. New Haven, Conn.: Yale University Press.

Rieff, Philip (1959). *Freud: The Mind of the Moralist*. New York: Garden City, 1961.

———. (1968). *The Triumph of the Therapeutic: Uses of Faith After Freud*. New York: Harper and Row.

Roazen, Paul (1969). *Brother Animal: The Story of Freud and Tausk*. New York: Knopf.

———. (1975). *Freud and His Followers*. New York: Meridian, 1976.

———. (1985). *Helene Deutsch: A Psychoanalyst's Life*. New York: Doubleday.

———. (1992). "The Historiography of Psychoanalysis." In *Psychoanalysis in Its Cultural Context*, ed. Edward Timms and Ritchie Robertson. Edinburgh: Edinburgh University Press.

———. (1995). *How Freud Worked: First-Hand Accounts of Patients*. Northvale, N.J.: Jason Aronson.

———. (1997). "Nietzsche, Freud, and the History of Psychoanalysis." In *Returns of the "French Freud": Freud, Lacan, and Beyond*, ed. Todd Dufresne, 11–23. New York: Routledge.

Roazen, Paul, and Bluma Swerdloff (1995). *Sandor Rado and the Psychoanalytic Movement*. Northvale, N.J.: Jason Aronson.

Robert, Marthe (1964). *The Psychoanalytic Revolution: Sigmund Freud's Life and Achievement*. Trans. Kenneth Morgan. New York: Harcourt, Brace, 1966.

Robinson, Paul A. (1969). *The Freudian Left*. New York: Harper and Row.

Romm, Sharon (1983). *The Unwelcome Intruder: Freud's Struggle with Cancer*. New York: Praeger.

Roudinesco, Elisabeth (1990). *Lacan & Co.: A History of Psychoanalysis in France, 1925–1985*. Trans. Jeffrey Mehlman. Chicago: University of Chicago Press.

Roustang, François (1982). *Dire Mastery: Discipleship from Freud to Lacan*. Trans. Ned Lukacher. Baltimore: Johns Hopkins University Press.

———. (1983). *Psychoanalysis Never Lets Go*. Trans. Ned Lukacher. Baltimore: Johns Hopkins Press.

———. (1990). *The Lacanian Delusion*. Trans. Greg Sims. Oxford: Oxford University Press.

Rycroft, Charles (1972). Introduction to *A Critical Dictionary of Psychoanalysis*. Harmondsworth, England: Penguin.

Sachs, Hans (1945). *Freud: Master and Friend*. London: Imago.

Sartre, Jean-Paul (1938). *Nausea*. Trans. Lloyd Alexander. New York: New Directions, 1964.

Sayers, Janet (1991). *Mothering Psychoanalysis*. London: Hamish Hamilton.

Scagnelli, Paul (1994). *Deadly Dr. Freud*. Durham, N.C.: Pinewood.

Schivelbusch, Wolfgang (1979). *The Railroad Journey: Trains and Travels in the Nineteenth Century*. New York: Urizen.

Schneiderman, Stuart (1983). *Jacques Lacan: The Death of an Intellectual Hero*. Cambridge: Harvard University Press.

Schopenhauer, Arthur (1819). *The World As Will and Representation.* Vol. 1. Trans. E. F. J. Payne. New York: Dover, 1966.
———. (1844). *The World As Will and Representation.* Vol. 2. Trans. E. F. J. Payne, New York: Dover, 1966.
———. (n.d.). *Studies in Pessimism.* New York: Boni and Liveright.
Schur, Max (1972). *Freud: Living and Dying.* New York: International Universities Press.
Sharaf, Myron (1983). *Fury on Earth: A Biography of Wilhelm Reich.* New York: St. Martin's Press.
Shepherd, William C. (1976). *Symbolical Consciousness: A Commentary on Love's Body.* Missoula, Mont.: Scholar's Press.
Shorter, Edward (1985). *Bedside Manners: The Troubled History of Doctors and Patients.* New York: Simon and Schuster.
———. (1994). *From the Mind into the Body: The Cultural Origins of Psychosomatic Symptoms.* New York: Free Press.
———. (1996). "Lundbeck Lecture Series in the History of Psychiatry." Clarke Institute of Psychiatry, Toronto, October 10–November 28. See his *A History of Psychiatry: From the Era of the Asylum to the Age of Prozac* (New York: John Wiley, 1996).
Slater, Phil (1977). *Origin and Significance of the Frankfurt School: A Marxist Perspective.* London: Routledge and Kegan Paul.
Spenser, Herbert (1855). *Principles of Psychology.* London: Williams and Norgate.
Stekel, Wilhelm (1950). *The Autobiography of Wilhelm Stekel: The Life Story of a Pioneer Psychoanalyst.* Ed. Emil A. Gutheil. New York: Liveright.
Sterba, Richard F. (1949). "The Cosmological Aspect of Freud's Theory of Instincts." *American Imago* 6, no. 3: 157–61.
———. (1982). *Reminiscences of a Viennese Psychoanalyst.* Detroit: Wayne State University Press.
Stevenson, Robert Louis (1886). *The Strange Case of Dr. Jekyll and Mr. Hyde.* New York: Random House, 1945.
Strachey, John (1937). Introduction to *Freud and Marx*, by Reuben Osborn. London: Victor Gollancz.
Sulloway, Frank J. (1979). *Freud, Biologist of the Mind: Beyond the Psychoanalytic Legend.* New York: Basic.
Sussman, Henry (1990). "Psychoanalysis Modern and Postmodern." In *Psychoanalysis and . . .*, ed. Richard Feldstein and Henry Sussman, 129–50. New York: Routledge.
Swales, Peter (1997). "Freud, Filthy Lucre, and Undue Influence." *Review of Existential Psychology and Psychiatry* 23, nos. 1, 2, and 3: 115–41. (Special issue; *Festschrift* for Thomas Szasz.)
Szasz, Thomas (1976). *Karl Kraus and the Soul Doctors: A Pioneer Critic and His Criticism of Psychiatry and Psychoanalysis.* Baton Rouge: Louisiana State University Press.
Thornton, E. M. (1983). *Freud and Cocaine: The Freudian Fallacy.* London: Blond and Briggs.

Torrey, E. Fuller (1992). *Freudian Fraud: The Malignant Effect of Freud's Theory on American Thought and Culture*. New York: HarperCollins.

Trilling, Lionel (1987). Introduction to *The Life and Works of Sigmund Freud*, by Ernest Jones. New York: Basic.

Turkle, Sherry (1992). *Psychoanalytic Politics: Jacques Lacan and Freud's French Revolution*. 2d ed. New York: Guilford.

Ulmer, Gregory (1985). *Applied Grammatology: Post(e)-Pedagogy from Jacques Derrida to Joseph Beuys*. Baltimore: Johns Hopkins University Press.

———. (1989). *Teletheory: Grammatology in the Age of Video*. New York: Routledge.

Updike, John (1996). "Elusive Evil." *New Yorker*, 22 July, 62–70.

Wallon, Henri (1931). "Comment se développe chez l'enfant la notion du corps propre." *Journal de psychologie* (n.v.): 705–48.

Weber, Samuel (1982). *The Legend of Freud*. Minneapolis: University of Minnesota Press.

———. (1988). "The Debts of Deconstruction, and Other Related Assumptions." In *Taking Chances: Derrida, Psychoanalysis, and Literature*, ed. Joseph H. Smith and William Kerrigan, 33–65. Baltimore: Johns Hopkins University Press.

Webster, Richard (1995). *Why Freud Was Wrong: Sin, Science, and Psychoanalysis*. New York: Basic.

Weininger, Otto (1996). *Being and Not Being: Clinical Applications of the Death Instinct*. London: Karnac.

Weiss, Edoardo (1970). *Sigmund Freud as a Consultant: Recollections of a Pioneer in Psychoanalysis*. New Brunswick, N.J.: Transaction Publishers, 1991.

Weizsaecker, Viktor von (1957). "Reminiscences of Freud and Jung." In *Freud and the Twentieth Century*, ed. Benjamin Nelson, 59–75. New York: Meridian.

Whitebook, Joel (1995). *Perversion and Utopia: A Study in Psychoanalysis and Critical Theory*. Cambridge: MIT Press.

Wittels, Fritz (1924). *Sigmund Freud: His Personality, His Teachings, and His School*. London: Allen and Unwin.

———. (1931). *Freud and His Time*. New York: Grosset and Dunlap.

Wortis, Joseph (1954). *Fragments of an Analysis with Freud*. Northvale, N.J.: Jason Aronson, 1984.

Young, Christopher, and Andrew Brook (1994). "Schopenhauer and Freud." *International Journal of Psychoanalysis* 75: 101–118.

Zilboorg, Gregory (1959). Introduction to *Beyond the Pleasure Principle*, by Sigmund Freud. New York: Bantam.

Index

In this index an "f" after a number indicates a separate reference on the next page, and an "ff" indicates separate references on the next two pages. A continuous discussion over two or more pages is indicated by a span of page numbers, e.g., "57 – 59." *Passim* is used for a cluster of references in close but not consecutive sequence.

Abraham, Karl, 34, 55, 66, 69–75
Abreaction, 86, 99, 170, 175. *See also* Transference
Absolute narcissism. *See* Narcissism
Adler, Alfred, 8, 20f, 28, 86, 90, 141, 181
Adler, Friedrich, 42
Adler, Victor, 42
Adorno, Theodor, 12, 103–109 *passim*
Alexander, Franz, 66, 69, 103
Alienation, 10, 90, 115, 120f
Andreas-Salomé, Lou, 31, 33, 48, 86, 164, 172
Appignanesi, Lisa, 22
Aristophanes, 84
Aristotle, 81, 92, 153
Audry, Colette, 120

Bakan, David, 27, 35ff
Balint, Michael, 66
Bartlett, Francis, 94

Baudrillard, Jean, 8
Becker, Ernest, 16
Bernfeld, Siegfried, 91
Bernheim, Hippolyte, 167
Bettelheim, Bruno, 17f, 29
Bibring, Edward, 32
Binswanger, Ludwig, 31
Bjerre, Poul, 204n37
Blanton, Smiley, 7, 12, 40, 201n14
Bleuler, Eugen, 165
Bloom, Allan, 111
Bloom, Harold, 35
Blumenberg, Hans, 33f
Bonaparte, Princess Marie, 16, 19, 50
Borch-Jacobsen, Mikkel, 2, 5, 11, 115, 120, 166ff, 186, 188n7
Breaching (causing trauma), 130, 133f, 148f
Brenner, Charles, 24
Brentano, Franz, 81

INDEX

Breuer, Josef, 50
Bronfen, Elizabeth, 30
Brooks, Peter, 143
Brown, Norman O., 8, 111f
Buckle, Henry Thomas, 81
Bullitt, William C., 7, 73, 149
Burroughs, William, 98
Burston, Daniel, 35
Butler, Clark, 90
Byron, Lord, 83

Cancer, 29–38 passim, 190n16, 202n18
Cannon, Walter B., 52, 191n25
Capitalism, 96–110 passim, 195n61
Catastrophe, Ferenczi's theory of, 59, 61
Charcot, Jean-Martin, 167, 177, 180
Chasseguet-Smirgel, Janine, 98
Child analysis, 65–79 passim, 149ff, 168–71, 194–95n52. See also Klein, Melanie
Choisy, Maryse, 39
Cioffi, Frank, 186
Clark, Ronald, 16, 99
Clarke, J. Mitchell, 165
Clausius, Rudolph, 52
Clifford, James, 5
Communism, 98, 106
Compulsion to repeat. See Repetition
Constancy, principle of, 50–53, 57, 95, 118, 147
Copelston, Frederick, 89
Costigan, Giovanni, 33, 37
Crabtree, Adam, 18
Crews, Frederick, 2, 186

Darwin, Charles, 20, 55, 61
Death drive, *ubique*:
reception of, xiii, 8, 14–17, 23–27, 44, 65f, 79f, 143; Freud's ambivalence toward, 15–20 passim; and doubling, 18f, 30f, 60, 115, 122; as "Thanatos," 18, 21, 24, 36, 75, 125, 189n7; originators of, 20ff, 62, 82ff; as negative therapy reaction, 34; "cure" for, 38, 64f, 94f, 98, 156f, 190n15, 201n15; as nirvana, 52, 89, 191n26, 199n2; as thalassal (womb) regression, 57–62, 66, 76, 78, 192n32; and "bio-analysis", 60, 63, 65; and destructive impulse, 69–77 passim, 107; and dialectics, 80, 84, 88–94, 104–112 passim, 119–24 passim; and theory of writing, 130–35; and performativity, 137ff; and constipation 157f, 201n11–n14; and trees, 200n9
—antecedents: cultural, 17, 29, 39; literary, 18f; scientific, 19f, 22, 47–62 passim
—interpretations: subjective, 27–43 passim, 158; psychological, 39–43; scientific, 43, 48–64; clinical 65f, 70–79; Freudo-Marxist, 94–111; Lacanian, 113–22; hermeneutic, 122–27; deconstructive, 129–44; group psychological, 145–65
Death wish, 19, 21, 39f, 42, 189n14
Defense. See Protective shield
Deleuze, Gilles, 23, 80, 87, 98
Derrida, Jacques, 10, 23, 83f, 124, 127–44, 169, 198n87
Derrida, Marguerite, 136
Descartes, René, 10, 154f, 181
Desire, 116, 120–26 passim, 188n7
Destruction, 16, 20–24 passim, 33, 72–77 passim, 124f, 161f
Deutsch, Felix, 32f
Deutsch, Helene, 68f
Dialectic, master/slave, 11, 98, 116, 120, 126f, 193n35
Dickstein, Morris, 112
Doolittle, Hilda (H.D.), 29
Dorer, Maria, 52
Dostoevsky, Fyodor, 8
Dreams, 39, 45f, 59, 70, 148, 153, 172, 175–78 passim
Dufresne, Todd, ixff

Eastman, Max, 7
Eeden, Fredrik van, 28
Ego psychology, 5, 9, 107, 112–17 passim, 121
Eissler, Kurt, 37
Eitingon, Max, 16, 29, 30
Ekstein, Rudolf, 36
Ellenberger, Henri, 19f, 52f
Ellis, Havelock, 196n63
Engels, Friedrich, 91

Entrophy, 52f
Erikson, Erik H., 8
Existentialism, 11, 20, 90, 116, 152, 158, 164f
Exner, Sigmund, 54
External world, existence of, 72–76, 149–55 passim, 163, 181f, 199n8. See also Growth, theory of
Eysenck, Hans, 179

False memory. See Memory
Fancher, Raymond, 46
Fechner, Gustav Theodor, 52ff, 82, 147
Federn, Paul, 12, 24, 32, 38, 86
Fenichel, Otto, 96
Ferdinand, Franz, 42
Ferenczi, Sandor, 16, 21, 28, 43, 47f, 55, 57–69, 72–79 passim, 103, 145, 147f, 155, 160, 181, 192n32, 193n35
Feuerbach, Ludwig, 81
Fish, Stanley, 143
Fliess, Wilhelm, 21, 39ff, 47f, 50, 58, 136
Flugel, J. C., 49, 52
Forrester, John, 22
Fort/da game, 45f, 168f
Frazer, Sir James, 97
Freud, Anna, 70f
Freud, Emmanuel, 42
Freud, Ernst, 28
Freud, John, 42
Freud, Martha, 38, 158
Freud, Martin, 28
Freud, Sigmund, ubique
Freud, Sophie. See Halberstadt, Sophie
Freund, Anton von, 29f, 37, 66, 74
Fromm, Erich, 29, 90, 92, 101–104, 106–109 passim, 113

Gamwell, Lynn, 39
Gasché, Rodolphe, 83, 129
Gay, Peter, 7, 29
Ginsberg, Allen, 98
Glover, Edward, 69
Goethe, Johann Wolfgang von, 15, 83
Goodman, Paul, 103, 111f
Gould, Stephen Jay, 55, 58, 192n31
Graf, Herbert, 67

Graf, Max, 67
Greenberg, Jay, 77
Groddeck, Georg, 37, 103
Grosskurth, Phyliss, 66, 68
Growth, theory of, ix, 56f, 147, 153f, 166, 168, 182, 199n3
Grubrich-Simitis, Ilse, 28, 48
Grunberger, Bela, 98
Guattari, Felix, 23, 87, 98
Guilt, 25, 34f, 45, 72, 75f, 125, 146, 158, 161, 172

Haeckel, Ernst, 54f, 60, 143
Halberstadt, Ernst, 45, 137f, 168ff, 171
Halberstadt, Heinz Rudolf, 35f
Halberstadt, Sophie, 29ff, 36, 46, 168
Happiness, the possibility for, 89, 103, 105, 159–64 passim, 172
Hartmann, Eduard von, 88f, 97
Hate, 64, 79, 160
Hegel, Georg Wilhelm Friedrich, 5, 8, 10, 80, 84, 87f, 90, 92, 98, 104, 109–116 passim, 120–28 passim
Heidegger, Martin, 5, 87, 110, 116, 124, 126f, 130, 143
Helholtz, Hermann von, 52
Hermeneutics, 110, 118, 122f, 126, 130, 144, 184f
Hertz, Neil, 143
Hitler, Adolf, 17
Hitschmann, Eduard, 84
Hobbes, Thomas, 20
Hoffmann, E. T. A., 18
Homeostasis, 191n25. See also Constancy, principle of
Honegger, Johann, 32
Horace, 159
Horkheimer, Max, 101, 103, 107, 109, 197n74
Horney, Karen, 103
Hug-Hellmuth, Hermine von, 69, 194n45
Human nature, 27f, 36, 77, 79, 112
Hume, David, 81
Husserl, Edmund, 127
Hypnosis, 60, 146, 152, 167, 178, 204n35
Hyppolite, Jean, 80

Ihde, Don, 124
Inheritance of acquired characteristics, x, 43, 54–65 passim, 143, 149, 153–56 passim, 163, 166. See also Lamarck, Jean-Baptiste
Instinct, self-preservation, 23, 44
Introjection, 66, 72f, 79, 149, 194n50

Jackson, John Hughlings, 54
Jay, Martin, 107
Johnson, Christopher, 132f
Johnston, Thomas, 91, 93
Jokl, Robert, 36
Jones, Ernest, 6, 14, 16, 20, 24, 26, 30, 38, 40f, 50–55 passim, 71, 74, 78–82 passim, 86, 145, 158, 169, 188n2
Jones, Gwenith, 78
Jones, Katherine, 78
Jones, Mervyn, 78
Jung, Carl Gustav, 6, 21ff, 28, 40f, 47, 66, 141, 153, 181

Kahane, Max, 32
Kant, Immanuel, 80, 152
Kardiner, Abram, 103
Kelvin, Lord, 52
Kerr, John, 19, 22
Klein, Erich, 78, 194n52
Klein, Melanie, 24, 65–79
Klein, Melitta, 67
Kojève, Alexandre, 5, 10, 115f, 119–22, 126f
Krafft-Ebing, Richard von, 165
Kramer, Robert, 74, 192n32
Kun, Bela, 69

Lacan, Jacques, 3–7, 9–12, 14, 42, 98, 107–30 passim, 134f, 143f, 159
Lamarck, Jean-Baptiste, 54–57, 61f, 64, 143, 163
Landauer, Karl, 32
Language, 112, 116–22 passim, 134, 136, 197n79
Laplanche, Jean, 14, 23
Lauzun, Gerard, 8
Leclaire, Serge, 6
Leibniz, G.W., 88

Lenin, Vladimir, 91, 111, 195n57
Lévi-Strauss, Claude, 5, 130, 133
Life. See Love; Sociality; Trauma
"Little Hans," 20, 67f, 201n14
Lombroso, Cesare, 20
Love, 9, 19, 23, 31, 64, 79, 136, 154–62 passim, 176f, 180, 189n7, 202n20
Low, Barbara, 52
Löwenfeld, Leopold, 165
Lukacher, Ned, 143
Lukács, Georg, 11

MacIntyre, Alasdair, 110f
Magnetism, 19, 54, 99
Mailer, Norman, 98
Malinowski, Bronislaw, 97, 196n63
Mannoni, Octave, 3, 5, 49
Marcuse, Herbert, 23, 90, 92, 103–13 passim, 118
Marx, Karl, 80, 84, 88, 90–94, 96, 101–12 passim, 116, 120, 126ff
Masochism, 25, 32, 46, 60, 79, 95f, 102, 106f, 152, 163, 177
Masson, Jeffrey M., 167
Mastery, drive for, 46, 138, 170
Masturbation, 51, 54
Mayer, Robert, 52
McDougall, William, 16, 166
Memory, 35, 43, 131, 133, 165ff, 175, 177, 188n7, 203n27
Mesmer, Franz Anton, 18, 54, 99
Metchnikoff, Elie, 19f, 22, 157
Meyer, Monroe, 32
Meynert, Theodor, 54
Miller, Jacques-Alain, 4, 188n7
Miller, Judith, 4
Mimesis (or Imitation), 171–75 passim
Mitchell, Stephen J., 77
Moll, Albert, 165f
Morgenstern, Sophie, 32
Mother, 47, 72, 74, 149ff, 159, 168f, 192n32, 199n6

Nachträglichkeit, 74, 134
Narcissism, xff, 18, 29, 36f, 44, 73, 115, 121, 146–65 passim, 172, 182, 184, 199n5, 202n23

INDEX 227

Natenberg, Maurice, 12, 40
Nature Philosophy, 19, 82, 117
Negation, 10, 35, 73, 105, 120, 124f
Neo-Freudianism, 103–113 *passim*
Neurology, 48f, 123, 125, 130f, 133, 147
Neurosis, transference. *See* Transference
Nietzsche, Friedrich, 2, 8, 20–26 *passim*, 80f, 83–88, 109, 126, 130, 136, 139, 161, 163f, 184
Norris, Christopher, 138
Novalis, 19
Nunberg, Herman, 38, 149

Orgasm, 51, 94–99 *passim*, 111, 196n63, 196n66
Osborn, Reuben, 92f

Pappenheim, Bertha, 50
Paul, Jean, 18
Pauly, August, 55
Peck, Martin, 16, 32
Pessimism, Freud's, 8, 28, 35, 58, 87f, 102, 112, 128, 145, 158, 202n21
Pfister, Oskar, 29
Pink, Annie, 99
Planck, Max, 52
Plato, 3, 81, 84, 143
Play, children's, 45f, 70, 106, 114, 125, 169
Pleasure principle, 37, 41, 45f, 50–53, 82, 106, 118f, 121, 137–41, 158, 168, 170–73
Plutarch, 83
Polka, Brayton, 57
Pontalis, Jean-Bertrand, 17, 23, 75
Pre-oedipal dynamics, 47, 60, 70f, 192n32
Primal father, 46, 59, 97, 108, 161–64
Primary narcissism. *See* Narcissism
Priority, intellectual, 21f, 40, 81–85, 138
Projection, 66, 73, 96, 148, 152f, 158, 182, 194n50
Prophylaxis (against neurosis), 74, 98f
Protective shield, ix, 98, 131, 147–54 *passim*, 164, 183
Psychoanalysis: critics of, ix–xiii *passim*, 144, 164f, 182, 185f, 205n1; in America, 2–6 *passim*, 98, 100, 111; in France, 2–6, 46, 80, 98, 111, 122; as radical, 3, 7, 11, 15, 93, 104, 108, 112–15 *passim*, 126, 129; as conservative, 7, 11, 17, 91, 96, 102, 104, 109; as "wild," 7, 41, 71, 188n2; technique of, 9, 63ff, 70f, 113, 116, 165, 172f, 177, 181, 193n36, 193n41, 204n31; and surgery, 178f, 204n38
Psychology, female, 60, 151f, 193n35
Putnam, James Jackson, 17
Puységur, Marquis de, 18

Rado, Sandor, 34, 66, 69
Rank, Otto, 19, 47, 59, 74, 86f, 151, 181, 202n21
Recapitulation, 43, 55–61 *passim*, 108, 143, 191n28. *See also* Haeckel, Ernst
Recognition, 116–22 *passim*, 126f, 155, 180
Reich, Ilse Ollendorff, 99
Reich, Wilhelm, 16, 28, 34, 37f, 90, 94–107 *passim*, 112, 190n16
Reik, Theodor, 69
Relations, object, 65, 69, 74, 76, 79, 95, 102, 149, 160
Repetition, 14, 19, 30, 37, 41, 45f, 53, 70, 80, 119f, 133f, 137–41, 153, 158, 168–73, 175f, 180ff, 186, 203n24, 203n31, 204n31
Representation, 135, 141f, 173, 185
Resignation, 8, 35, 37f, 87, 202n21. *See also* Pessimism, Freud's
Ricoeur, Paul, 122–130 *passim*, 197n79
Rieff, Philip, 97f
Rilkin, Franz, 40
Roazen, Paul, 24, 31–38 *passim*, 86
Robert, Marthe, 65, 192n32
Robinson, Paul, 98, 107f, 110
Roheim, Geza, 66
Romanticism, 9, 18f, 60, 88, 102
Romm, Sharon, 38, 190n15
Rosenthal, Tatiana, 32
Roudinesco, Elisabeth, 5, 11, 122, 127
Rousseau, Jean-Jacques, 130
Roustang, François, 4f

Sachs, Hanns, 33, 69
Sadism, 25, 32, 75, 79, 96, 99, 102, 151f, 171, 177

Said, Edward, 5
Sartre, Jean-Paul, 164
Saussure, Ferdinand de, 5, 130
Scagnelli, Paul, 42
Schelling, Friedrich Wilhelm, 88
Schiller, Friedrich von, 19
Schneiderman, Stuart, 3
Schopenhauer, Arthur, 32, 57, 81–89 passim, 97, 145, 202n21
Schrötter, Karl, 32
Schubert, Gotthilf Heinrich von, 19
Schur, Max, 39, 41, 146
Seduction theory, 74f, 146, 150, 165, 167, 193n41, 203n27, 204n36
Seminar, Lacan's, 3, 5, 122, 126
Sexuality, xiii, 17, 21–25 passim, 34, 44, 51, 59, 71, 82, 95, 98, 104ff, 111, 146, 149, 154, 196n63
Shakespeare, William, 57, 83
Shorter, Edward, 49
Silberer, Herbert, 32
Simmel, Ernst, 69, 91
Sociality, 20, 32, 64f, 152, 158, 162–71 passim, 177f, 202n24
Sokolonicka, Eugenia, 32
Solipsism, 155ff
Spenser, Herbert, 52
Spielrein, Sabina, 20ff, 157
Stability, principle of. See Constancy, principle of
Stage, mirror, 114ff, 121, 127
Steinach, Eugen, 38, 190n15
Stekel, Wilhelm, 20f, 24, 28, 32, 181
Stephen, Karin, 32
Sterba, Richard, 24, 85, 95, 159
Stevenson, Robert Louis, 18
Strachey, Alix, 69
Strachey, James, 9, 146, 178
Strachey, John, 90
Structuralism, 3, 122, 144, 186
Strümpell, Adolf von, 165
Stürgh, Prime Minister, 42
Subject, Cartesian, 9–12, 113ff, 119f, 126f, 137, 154ff, 158, 182, 188n7
Suggestion, xiv, 78, 142–46 passim, 165–82 passim, 186, 189n1; of Suicide, 31–34, 89, 100

Sullivan, Harry Stack, 6, 103
Sulloway, Frank, 44–49 passim, 86, 143, 186
Super-ego. See Guilt
Swales, Peter, 186

Tausk, Victor, 21, 31–34, 100
Thompson, Clara, 103
Thornton, Elizabeth M., 47
Tokarsky, A., 19
Transference, 11, 31, 45, 70f, 136, 138, 155, 173–85 passim, 188n7, 189n10, 203n24, 204n31
Trauma, life as, 61, 148f, 158, 192n32, 193n34, 200n9
Trilling, Lionel, 35
Trotsky, Leon, 92
Trotter, Wilfred, 162
Turkle, Sherry, 2, 8

Uncanny, the, 18, 115, 168, 202–3n24
Updike, John, 17

Vogt, Oskar, 165

Wagner, Richard, 87
Wallon, Henri, 114
War, 9, 17, 28f, 46, 67, 125, 169, 203–4n31
Weber, Samuel, 129
Webster, Richard, 48, 53
Weiss, Edoardo, 17, 24
Weissmann, August, 51, 54
Weizaecker, Viktor von, 1
Whitehead, Alfred North, 3
Wilson, President Woodrow, 7, 149
Winnicott, Donald W., 72, 150
Wittels, Fritz, 29f, 82
"Wolf Man, The," 174, 201n14
Woodruff, L. L., 156f
Work Cited (Freud), Selected:
   Beyond the Pleasure Principle (1920) ubique; *Project for a Scientific Psychology* (1895), xi, 41, 47–50, 54, 117, 130–34, 147, 154, 172; "On Narcissism: An Introduction" (1914), xi, 149f, 160; *New Introductory Lectures in Psycho-Analysis* (1933), xvii, 33, 83, 147, 152, 172, 178;

The Interpretation of Dreams (1900), 9, 12, 41, 117, 155, 174, 199n8, 204n35 "The 'Uncanny' " (1919), 18f, 30, 41, 202–3n24; *Civilization and Its Discontents* (1930), 20, 36, 73, 94, 100, 105, 125, 159, 161; *The Ego and the Id* (1923), 25, 37, 51, 75, 147, 149, 199n3; *Totem and Taboo* (1913), 55, 58, 62, 85, 97, 160; *A Phylogenetic Fantasy: Overview of the Transference Neurosis* (1987), 58, 172, 192n31; *Group Psychology and the Analysis of the Ego* (1921), 145ff, 151f, 158–71 *passim*

Wortis, Joseph, 99, 187n4

Yabe, Yaekichi, 52, 191n27

Zilboorg, Gregory, xii, 14f, 23
Zollner, J. C. F., 52p
Zweig, Arnold, 84f

Library of Congress Cataloging-in-Publication Data

Dufresne Todd, 1966-
    Tales from the Freudian crypt : the death drive in text and context / Todd Dufresne.
        p.   cm.
    Includes bibliographical references and index.
    ISBN 0-8047-3491-7 (alk. paper). — ISBN 0-8047-3885-8 (pbk.: alk. paper)
    1. Death instinct.   2. Psychoanalysis.   3. Freud, Sigmund, 1856–1939.
    I. Title.
BF175.5.D4D84   2000
150.19'52—dc21   99-39776

⊚ This book is printed on acid-free, archival quality paper.

Original printing 2000

Last figure below indicates the year of this printing:
09 08 07 06 05 04 03 02 01 00

Tyepeset in 10.5/12.5 Bembo by BookMatters, Richmond, Calif.

The authorized representative in the EU for product safety and compliance is:
Mare Nostrum Group
B.V Doelen 72
4831 GR Breda
The Netherlands

www.ingramcontent.com/pod-product-compliance
Lightning Source LLC
Chambersburg PA
CBHW030540230426
43665CB00010B/963